PROBLEMS OF THE MODERN ECONOMY

Monopoly Power and Economic Performance

PROBLEMS OF THE MODERN ECONOMY

General Editor: EDMUND S. PHELPS, *Columbia University*

Each volume in this series presents
prominent positions in the debate of
an important issue of economic policy

AGRICULTURAL POLICY IN AN AFFLUENT SOCIETY

THE BATTLE AGAINST UNEMPLOYMENT

CHANGING PATTERNS IN FOREIGN TRADE
AND PAYMENTS

THE CRISIS OF THE REGULATORY COMMISSIONS

DEFENSE, SCIENCE, AND PUBLIC POLICY

THE GOAL OF ECONOMIC GROWTH

INEQUALITY AND POVERTY

LABOR AND THE NATIONAL ECONOMY

MONOPOLY POWER AND ECONOMIC PERFORMANCE

POLLUTION, RESOURCES, AND THE ENVIRONMENT

PRIVATE WANTS AND PUBLIC NEEDS

THE UNITED STATES AND THE DEVELOPING ECONOMIES

Monopoly Power and Economic Performance

THE PROBLEM OF INDUSTRIAL CONCENTRATION

Edited with an introduction by

EDWIN MANSFIELD

UNIVERSITY OF PENNSYLVANIA

THIRD EDITION

NEW YORK

W · W · NORTON & COMPANY · INC ·

Library of Congress Cataloging in Publication Data

Mansfield, Edwin, ed.
  Monopoly power and economic performance.

  Includes bibliographical references.
  1. Big business—United States.   2. Trusts,
Industrial—United States.   I. Title.
HD2785.M357   1974   338.8 0973   73–18027
ISBN 0-393-05448-9
ISBN 0-393-09990-3 (pbk.)

The Case Against Big Business, by George J. Stigler. Reprinted from May 1951 issue of
Fortune by special permission; copyright 1951 by Time Inc.
A Defense of Bigness in Business, by Sumner H. Slichter. Copyright 1957 by *The New
York Times Magazine*. Reprinted by permission of the publishers and the estate of
the author.
Capitalism and the Process of Creative Destruction, from *Capitalism, Socialism and
Democracy* by Joseph A. Schumpeter. Copyright 1942 by Joseph A. Schumpeter. Re-
printed by permission of Harper & Row, Publishers, Inc.
The Economics of Technical Development, from *American Capitalism* by John Kenneth
Galbraith. Published by Houghton Mifflin Company. Reprinted by permission of the
publisher.
The Concentration of Research and Development in Large Firms, from *Technology,
Economic Growth, and Public Policy* by Richard Nelson, Merton Peck, and Edward
Kalachek. Copyright 1967 by the RAND Corporation. Reprinted by permission of the
RAND Corporation and The Brookings Institution.
Monopoly Power, Big Business, and Technological Change from *Microeconomics:
Theory and Applications* by Edwin Mansfield. Reprinted by permission of W. W.
Norton & Company, Inc. Copyright 1970 by W. W. Norton & Company.
Monopoly and the Social Responsibility of Business and Labor, from *Capitalism and
Freedom* by Milton Friedman. Copyright 1962 by the University of Chicago Press.
Reprinted by permission of the University of Chicago Press.
The Social Responsibility of Business and Environmental Pollution, originally printed
as "How Social Responsibility Fits the Game of Business," reprinted from the Decem-
ber 1970 issue of *Fortune* Magazine by special permission; © 1970 Time Inc.
The General Explanation of the Development of Concentration, from *Industrial Organi-
zation* by Joe S. Bain. Copyright by John Wiley & Sons, Inc., Publishers. Reprinted
by permission of the publisher.
Collusion Among Electrical Equipment Manufacturers, originally printed as "Antitrust
and Organization Man" (January 10, 1961) and "The Problems of Price Fixing"
(January 12, 1961) in *The Wall Street Journal*. Copyright 1961 by Dow Jones &
Company, Inc. Reprinted by permission of the publisher.
Substantive Provisions of the Antitrust Laws, from *Public Policies Toward Business* by
Clair Wilcox. Copyright by Richard D. Irwin, Inc. Reprinted by permission of the
publisher.
The Effectiveness of the Antitrust Laws, originally entitled "The Effectiveness of Federal
Antitrust Laws; A Symposium" by Thurman Arnold, Arthur R. Burns, Edward H.
Levi, Edward S. Mason, and George W. Stocking, in the *American Economic Review*,
June 1949. Copyright 1949 by the American Economic Association. Reprinted by
permission.
Standards for Antitrust Policy, by Alfred E. Kahn. From the *Harvard Law Review*,
November 1953. Copyright 1953 by The Harvard Law Review Association. Reprinted
by permission of the publishers.
Comments on Standards for Antitrust Policy, by Edward S. Mason. From *Antitrust Policy:
An Economic and Legal Analysis* by Carl Kaysen and Donald F. Turner. Copyright
1959 by The President and Fellows of Harvard College. Reprinted by permission of
the Harvard University Press.
A New "Worst" in Antitrust, reprinted from the April 1966 issue of *Fortune* Magazine
by special permission; © 1966 Time Inc.
The Antitrust Chief Replies, by Donald Turner. Reprinted from the April 1966 issue of
Fortune Magazine by special permission; © 1966 Time Inc.

Contents

PART THREE: The Antitrust Laws: Provisions,
Effectiveness, and Standards

PART FOUR: Competition: Its Relation to Some
Major Macroeconomic and Social Problems in
the United States

Introduction

ECONOMIC POWER in the United States is distributed very un-evenly, 500 corporations controlling over one half of the total assets in the nonfarm economy. Within particular industries there is also considerable concentration of ownership; e.g., more than 75 percent of autos, sheet glass, light bulbs, aluminum, cigarettes, metal cans, and computers are produced by the four largest firms in each of these industries. These facts are viewed with concern by economists and lawyers like A. A. Berle, who asserts that the 500 largest firms "—each with its own little dominating pyramid within it—represent a concentration of power over economies which makes the medieval feudal system look like a Sunday School party. In sheer economic power this has gone far beyond anything we have yet seen." [1]

Economists have kept a wary eye on the large firm ever since Adam Smith's attack on monopolies.[2] Smith preached and gener-ations of economists since have taught that a monopolist charges a price in excess of the price which would prevail if the product were produced by small competitive producers, no one large enough to affect the price. The result of the monopolization is that consumers have to contract their consumption of the product; resources which would have been used in that industry go else-where to produce other products which are less badly wanted by consumers; and there is less output of the monopolized product and more of other goods than would be produced under a regime of pure competition.

Why should the competitive outcome be desired over that re-sulting from the monopoly? Under pure competition we know that the price of each product equals the cost of producing it, more precisely, the additional (marginal) cost of producing an extra unit. This is exactly what the economist wishes the price of

1. *Economic Power and the Free Society* (Fund for the Republic), p. 14.
2. Of course, hostility toward monopoly did not originate with Smith. For example, the Edict of Zeno in 483 prohibited all monopolies, whether created by imperial decree or by private action.

every good to do: to signal or measure the cost—in terms of the value of other goods which must be foregone—of consuming one more unit of the good.[3] Then and only then will consumers' purchases in the market place take proper account of society's true productive possibilities. Hence, in the traditional view, concentration of economic power, by distorting the allocation of resources, impairs the performance of the economy in satisfying human wants. This is why economists have traditionally viewed the breakdown of competition in many industries as a threat to the efficient operation of the free market mechanism. It is the reason, in addition to the concern over the political and social implications of the concentration of power, why economists have traditionally urged the forceful application of antitrust laws to keep firms from becoming too big.

But this traditional view has many dissenters. The large firms have triumphed over competition because they have advantages over small firms. Are these advantages not advantages to society too? Does not the very size of the giant firm offer many benefits to the economy? Or are the advantages enjoyed by the large firm simply those of getting to be big before other firms do, and its size a burden to the economy, as the traditional view argues? The postwar period has witnessed an enlarging debate over these issues.

MARKET STRUCTURE, RESOURCE ALLOCATION, AND ECONOMIC PROGRESS

In the first essay, George Stigler states that there are two basic criticisms of big business: the giant firms "act monopolistically, and they encourage and justify bigness in labor and government." Contrary to popular opinion, they are not appreciably more efficient than smaller rivals, and he questions whether they are technically more progressive. Since "an industry which does not have a competitive structure will not have competitive behavior," he favors dissolution of giant companies. Sumner Slichter

3. We presume here that the marginal private cost equals the marginal social cost. This need not always be the case, as we shall see in our discussions of matters like environmental pollution.

disagrees, his position being that policies designed to restrict mergers and break up firms exceeding a certain size would weaken rather than strengthen competition. Mergers help "to build stronger enterprises, better able to compete and to hold their own in competition." A policy designed to break up large concerns would be a mistake because bigness is required to carry on the research and development which is vital to technical progress.

As noted previously, a fundamental criticism leveled at monopoly and oligopoly is that they result in a malallocation of economic resources. In the next essay, Joseph Schumpeter asserts that these static inefficiencies are relatively unimportant and that the competition which counts arises from innovation—new technology, new products, new organization. "As soon as we go into details and inquire into the individual items in which progress was most conspicuous, the trail leads not to the doors of those firms that work under conditions of comparatively free competition but precisely to the doors of the large concerns . . ." Agreeing with Schumpeter, J. Kenneth Galbraith explains in more detail why the "modern industry of a few large firms [is] an almost perfect instrument for inducing technical change." First, the costs of research and development are so great that only large firms can now become involved. Second, projects must now be carried out on a large enough scale so that successes and failures can in some sense balance out. Third, for invention to be worthwhile, a firm must have sufficient control over the market to reap the rewards.

Richard Nelson, Merton Peck, and Edward Kalachek are skeptical of the Schumpeter-Galbraith thesis, believing that the evidence suggests "quite a different conclusion than the one equating large firms and technological advances. No single size of firm is an optimum for conceiving and introducing all inventions of an industry." The following article, by the editor of this volume, goes further in examining the relationship between market structure and technological change. The available evidence is more limited than one would like, but what evidence we have does not seem to support the Schumpeter-Galbraith thesis. On the contrary, in my view, "there is little evidence that industrial giants generally are needed to insure rapid technological change and rapid utilization of new techniques."

What are the social responsibilities of the large corporation? If businessmen have social responsibilities other than the maximization of profits, how are they to know what these responsibilities are? Who can rightfully claim to know what is in the public interest? The next paper, by Milton Friedman, is concerned with these questions, as well as with the extent and sources of monopoly power. According to Friedman, "Few trends could so thoroughly undermine the very foundations of our free society as the acceptance by corporate officials of a social responsibility other than to make as much money for their stockholders as possible." The following paper, taken from *Fortune*, describes some of the important social issues that bear on the large corporation today, particular attention being devoted to the pressing problem of environmental pollution. According to this article, businessmen themselves are less convinced than Friedman that their proper role is to pursue profits, and profits alone.

INDUSTRIAL CONCENTRATION, BUSINESS BEHAVIOR, AND THE ROLE OF LARGE AND CONGLOMERATE FIRMS

Economists generally use the term "industrial concentration" to mean the number and size-distribution of firms in an industry or larger segment of the economy. An industry where the bulk of the productive facilities and employment is in the hands of a few firms is "highly concentrated." Using data regarding the proportion of total sales made by the largest four firms, Table 1, taken from Willard Mueller's article, shows the extent of industrial concentration in selected manufacturing industries in 1962.

TABLE 1. *Percent of Total Sales
Made by Four Largest United States Firms
in Each Industry, 1962*

80.8	Motor vehicles	27.3	Primary nonferrous metals
47.3	Aircraft	14.7	Other fabricated metal products
30.3	Other transportation equipment	18.1	Stone, clay, and glass products
34.4	Electrical machinery	5.2	Furniture and fixtures
14.5	Metalworking machinery	21.2	Lumber and wood products
20.6	Other machinery	37.9	Instruments
40.2	Primary iron and steel	16.3	Miscellaneous manufacturing

42.9	Dairy products	31.0	Drugs and medicines
33.6	Bakery products	28.5	Other chemicals
12.5	Other food	50.3	Petroleum refining
22.0	Textile mill products	48.1	Rubber
4.9	Apparel	26.7	Leather
20.7	Paper	41.4	Alcoholic beverages
42.0	Basic industrial chemicals	70.9	Tobacco

In recent years, many economists have expressed their concern over the postwar increase in the percentage of all manufacturing assets held by the largest firms. For example, Mueller points out that the "share of the 100 largest companies increased from 40.2 percent in 1950 to 45.7 in 1962—an increase of 5.5 percentage points, while that of the 200 largest companies increased from 48.9 percent in 1950 to 55 percent in 1962—an increase of 6.1 percentage points." To a large extent, he attributes this increase in overall concentration to an important merger movement in the postwar period. Morris Adelman challenges the significance of Mueller's findings. He suggests that, although there was some increase in overall concentration in the fifties, there has been little or no increase over a period of thirty years, from 1931 to 1960.

Does technical efficiency require the high level of concentration that is shown to exist in many industries? Joe Bain lists the broad determinants of the extent of concentration and argues, like Stigler, that it is not true "that existing degrees of business concentration are adequately explained simply as the result of adjustments to attain maximum efficiency in production and distribution . . . Industries probably tend to be more concentrated than necessary for efficiency—and larger firms bigger than necessary—because of the operation of monopolization, sales promotion, and financial motives, and because of specific entry barriers favoring a few firms in certain industries."

When an industry is highly concentrated, it becomes easier for firms to collude. The next item, an excerpt from the *Wall Street Journal*, is an interesting case study of collusion. In 1961, the electrical equipment producers—General Electric, Westinghouse, Allis Chalmers, and others—pleaded guilty to charges of violation of the antitrust laws. The *Wall Street Journal* subsequently published a series of articles describing the way in which prices were fixed and markets were divided.

The awesome power of the nation's largest firms has led to a widespread debate over their social responsibilities. The paper by Friedman and the one from *Fortune* in the previous section were concerned, at least in part, with this question. The next two items are a major case study in this area. On April 11, 1962, the day after the United States Steel Corporation announced a $6 per ton increase in the price of steel, President Kennedy charged that "a few gigantic corporations have decided to increase prices in ruthless disregard of their public responsibilities." On the following day, Roger Blough, Chairman of the Board of the United States Steel Corporation, replied to this charge, his full statement following Kennedy's herein.

Another topic that has received considerable attention in the last decade is the large conglomerate firm—a firm like Litton Industries or International Telephone and Telegraph that produces many different products and operates in many markets. According to Corwin Edwards, "large conglomerate enterprises possess kinds of power that may involve jeopardy to competition. In some instances, a direct anticompetitive effect is apparent. In other instances, magnitude of resources, internal subsidy, coordinated sales effort, and reciprocity may significantly increase the obstacles to entry by new firms into the affected markets, and may thus significantly diminish competition." Jesse Markham disagrees. In his view, it is "discretionary power over the market unchecked effectively by market forces, and not "conglomerateness," or for that matter "bigness," that makes possible the anticompetitive tactics often erroneously assigned to the large multiproduct firm as such."

Finally, in 1967, John Kenneth Galbraith published *The New Industrial State* in which he argued that "technology; the extensive use of capital; affluent and hence malleable customers; the imperatives of organization; the role of the union; the requirements imposed by public tasks, including arms development and space exploration, have all weakened the authority of the market. At the same time, these developments have both enabled and required firms to substitute planning with its management of markets for a simple response to the market. Bigness and market power, in other words, are but one part of a much larger current of change . . . [The] trend to great size and associated control

[is] immutable, given our desire for economic development, and
. . . the present antitrust efforts to deal with size and market
power [are] a charade." These views, expressed in the article contained in this volume, have been challenged by many economists
on the grounds that no evidence has been mustered to support
them and that, in considerable part, they are wrong. For example,
in the essay following Galbraith's, Walter Adams argues that
"the competitive market need not be condemned to the euthanasia which Galbraith thinks is inexorable, and perhaps even desirable."

THE ANTITRUST LAWS: PROVISIONS, EFFECTIVENESS, AND STANDARDS

The antitrust laws were enacted to help deal with the problems
of collusion and monopolization. Clair Wilcox describes the provisions of these laws and the circumstances leading to their passage.
It is obviously very difficult to tell how effective they have been,
but, judging from the opinions of Thurman Arnold, Arthur
Burns, Edward Levi, and George Stocking, their effectiveness has
been quite limited. Arnold, Levi, and Stocking attribute this to
the lack of necessary public support. Burns, more inclined than
Stigler or Bain to believe that there are considerable economics
of scale, asserts that a choice must often be made between efficiency and competition.

Mason is more optimistic, believing "that the American economy is in fact substantially more 'workably competitive' than it
would have been without the existence of the antitrust acts. This
is due . . . not so much to the contribution that particular judgments have made to the restoring of competition as it is to the
fact that the consideration of whether a particular course of business action may or may not be in violation of the antitrust acts is
a persistent factor affecting business judgment, at least in large
firms."

There has been considerable controversy over the standards
that should be used to determine whether a firm "monopolizes" a
particular industry or market. Various tests, based on market
structure, performance, conduct, and intent, have been proposed.
Alfred Kahn argues that performance tests look "at the wrong
end of the process. The essential task of public policy in a free

enterprise system should be to preserve the framework of a fair field and no favors, letting the results take care of themselves." Kahn also questions the use of a market structure test, based on such factors as the number and size-distribution of buyers and sellers in the market, the ease with which new firms can enter, and the extent of product differentiation. "If monopoly elements inevitably pervade the economy and are in some measure essential to good performance, it would be quixotic to attack monopoly power *per se*." Instead, the "inescapable conclusion is that, from a practical standpoint, the criterion of intent alone 'fills the bill' for a sensible antitrust policy in such cases."

In the next essay, Carl Kaysen argues that concentration measures can play an important role in antitrust policy, and describes the sorts of standards proposed in the well known book he wrote with Donald F. Turner. The following paper by Edward Mason reviews various standards for antitrust policy and comes to quite different conclusions from Kahn. Mason agrees that it would be a mistake to place emphasis on performance tests, since "a proposal to rely on such tests is an invitation to nonenforcement." But he disagrees with Kahn's reliance on intent. "If the rule of 'intent' means merely that the legal significance of action is to be judged largely with reference to the market power of the actor, I have no fault to find with it. . . . But that 'intent to monopolize' inferred exclusively from conduct, either is, or should be, the law I would strongly deny."

In recent years, there has been considerable controversy over the government's antimerger policies. In a direct attack on recent policies, the editors of *Fortune* Magazine have proposed that Congress should amend the antitrust laws to make it clear that "it is not the national policy to prefer any particular size, shape, or number of firms to any other size, shape, or number; and that mergers—horizontal, vertical, or conglomerate—are entirely legal unless they spring from a manifest attempt to restrain trade." In the final article, Donald F. Turner, head of the Antitrust Division of the Department of Justice, replies to the *Fortune* editorial. He says that "no affirmative case has been made out for the proposition which *Fortune* suggests . . . [and] the best economic information and thinking available to us indicates that a strong antimerger policy, at least insofar as horizontal-type mergers are concerned, is almost certainly right."

COMPETITION: ITS RELATION TO SOME MAJOR
MACROECONOMIC AND SOCIAL PROBLEMS
IN THE UNITED STATES

Competition can play an important role in helping to solve some of the nation's most pressing macroeconomic and social problems—the tendency of the American economy to suffer serious inflation at less than full employment, the alleged inefficiencies in defense spending, environmental pollution, and some of the problems of regulated sectors of the economy. It is important that the role of competition in helping to solve these problems be recognized and understood. With regard to the basic problem of inflation at less than full employment, both Abba Lerner and William Fellner attribute this phenomenon to monopoly power held by business and labor. To remedy the situation, they both advocate antimonopoly measures such as stronger enforcement of the antitrust laws. In addition, Lerner favors direct controls over administered prices, but Fellner regards this as "the least desirable alternative." This exchange is particularly interesting in view of the Nixon administration's experiments with peacetime price controls.

Much of the nation's huge defense budget is spent to procure research and development, material, and labor for which contractors are reimbursed. The next article, taken from a report by the Joint Economic Committee of Congress, charges that there has been extensive waste and inefficiency in defense procurement, due in considerable part to the lack of competition among contractors. In the Committee's view, the defense budget could be reduced substantially if more competition—and other methods of cost control—were to be instituted. The next paper, a brief note by the editor of this volume, summarizes the available evidence concerning market structure and racial discrimination. The data are rough and must be interpreted with caution, but they seem to indicate that market power is directly related to discrimination in white-collar employment. The results, although by no means unambiguous, may provide additional ammunition for supporters of competition to fire at monopoly power.

The final two articles are concerned with the important issues of environmental pollution and government regulation. The first article, extending the discussion of environment pollution begun in the first section of the book, describes how the market mechanism fails to produce socially optimal results in this area, and discusses various ways that the government might step in to improve the situation. In particular, this report, by the Council of Economic Advisers, discusses the use of government standards, subsidies for pollution control, effluent fees, and sales of usage rights. The second paper, also by the Council of Economic Advisers, charges that government regulation of railroad freight transportation—one of the nation's basic industries—has resulted in serious inefficiencies and that competition should be fostered and relied on. In the Council's view, "If it appears that the full benefits of competition can not be attained within the framework of the existing regulatory process, substantial deregulation of surface freight transportation may have to be considered."

Discussions of the proper role of competition continue, as do arguments over the benefits to society from the large firm, the social responsibility of big business, the extent of monopoly in the United States, and the proper standards for antitrust policy. The questions at issue are of the utmost importance, since they concern the basic framework within which the nation's economic activity is carried out. They are the fundamental questions of public policy that are touched on by economists interested in the workings of particular industrial markets.

PROBLEMS OF THE MODERN ECONOMY

Monopoly Power and Economic Performance

PART ONE

Market Structure,

Resource Allocation,

and Economic Progress

The Case Against Big Business

GEORGE J. STIGLER

George J. Stigler is Walgreen Professor of American Institutions at the University of Chicago. The following paper first appeared in the May, 1952, issue of Fortune.

WHAT IS BIGNESS?

BIGNESS IN business has two primary meanings. First, bigness may be defined in terms of the company's share of the industry in which it operates: a big company is one that has a big share of the market or industry. By this test Texas Gulf Sulphur is big because it produces more than half the sulfur in America, and Macy's (whose annual sales are much larger) is small because it sells only a very small fraction of the goods sold by New York City retail stores. By this definition, many companies that are small in absolute size are nevertheless big—the only brick company in a region, for example—and many companies that are big in absolute size (Inland Steel, for example) are small. Second, bigness may mean absolute size—the measure of size being assets, sales, or employment as a rule. Then General Motors and U.S. Steel are the prototypes of bigness.

These two meanings overlap because most companies that are big in absolute size are also big in relation to their industries. There are two types of cases, however, in which the two meanings conflict. On the one hand, many companies of small absolute size are dominant in small markets or industries. I shall not discuss them here (although they require attention in a well-rounded antitrust program) for two reasons: they seldom have anywhere near so much power as the companies that are big relative to large markets and industries; and they raise few political problems of the type I shall discuss below. On the other hand, there are a few companies that are big in absolute size but small relative to their markets—I have already given Macy's as an example. These companies are not very important in the total picture, and I shall also put them aside in the following discussion.

For my purposes, then, big businesses will mean businesses that are absolutely large in size and large also relative to the industries in which they operate. They are an impressive list: U.S. Steel, Bethlehem, and Republic in steel; General Electric and Westinghouse in electrical equipment; General Motors, Ford, and Chrysler in automobiles; du Pont, Union Carbide, and Allied Chemical among others in chemicals; Reynolds, Liggett & Myers, and American Tobacco in cigarettes.

What bigness does not mean is perhaps equally important. Bigness has no reference to the size of industries. I for one am tired of the charge that the critics of the steel industry vacillate between finding the output too large and too small: at various times the industry's output has been too small; for fifty years the largest firm has been too large. Concerted action by many small companies often leads to over-capacity in an industry: it is the basic criticism of resale price maintenance, for example, that it encourages the proliferation of small units by fixing excessive retail margins. Industries dominated by one or a few firms—that is, big businesses—seldom err in this direction. Nor does bigness have any direct reference to the methods of production, and opposition to big business is usually compatible with a decent respect for the "economies of large-scale production," on which more later.

The fundamental objection to bigness stems from the fact that big companies have monopolistic power, and this fundamental objection is clearly applicable outside the realm of corporate business. In particular, big unions are open to all the criticisms (and possibly more) that can be levied against big business. I shall not discuss labor unions, but my silence should not be construed as a belief that we should have a less stringent code for unions than for business.

THE INDICTMENT OF BIGNESS

There are two fundamental criticisms to be made of big business: they act monopolistically, and they encourage and justify bigness in labor and government.

First, as to monopoly. When a small number of firms control most or all of the output of an industry, they can individually and collectively profit more by cooperation than by competition. This is fairly evident, since cooperatively they can do everything they can do individually, and other things (such as the charging of non-competitive prices) besides. These few companies, therefore, will usually cooperate.

From this conclusion many reasonable men, including several Supreme Court Justices, will dissent. Does not each brand of cigarettes spend huge sums in advertising to lure us away from some other brand? Do not the big companies—oligopolists, the economists call them—employ salesmen? Do not the big companies introduce constant innovations in their products?

COMPETITION OF A KIND

The answer is that they do compete—but not enough, and not in all the socially desirable ways. Those tobacco companies did not act competitively, but with a view to extermination, against the 10-cent brands in the 1930's, nor have they engaged in price competition in decades (*American Tobacco* vs. *United States, 328 U.S. 781*). The steel companies, with all their salesmen, abandoned cartel pricing via basing-point prices only when this price system was judged a conspiracy in restraint of trade in cement (*Federal Trade Commission* vs. *Cement Institute, 333 U.S. 683*). The plain fact is that big businesses do not engage in continuous price competition.

Nor is price the only area of agreement. Patent licensing has frequently been used to deprive the licensees of any incentive to engage in research; General Electric used such agreements also to limit other companies' output and fix the prices of incandescent lamps (*U.S.* vs. *General Electric, 82 F. Supp. 753*). The hearings of the Bone Committee are adorned with numerous examples of the deliberate deterioration of goods in order to maintain sales.

For example, Standard Oil Development (a subsidiary of the Jersey company) persuaded Socony-Vacuum to give up the sale of a higher-potency commodity (pour-point depressant) whose sale at the same price had been characterized as "merely price cutting."

Very well, big businesses often engage in monopolistic practices. It may still be objected that it has not been shown that all big businesses engage in monopolistic practices, or that they engage in such practices all, or even most of, the time. These things cannot be shown or even fully illustrated in a brief survey,[1] and it is also not possible to summarize the many court decisions and the many academic studies of big business. But it is fair to say that these decisions and studies show that big businesses usually possess monopolistic power, and use it. And that is enough.

For economic policy must be contrived with a view to the typical rather than the exceptional, just as all other policies are contrived. That some drivers can safely proceed at eighty miles an hour is no objection to a maximum-speed law. So it is no objection to an antitrust policy that some unexercised monopoly power is thereby abolished. (Should there be some big businesses that forgo the use of their dominant position, it is difficult to see what advantage accrues from private ownership, for the profit motive is already absent.)

Second, as to bigness in labor and government. Big companies have a large—I would say an utterly disproportionate—effect on public thinking. The great expansion of our labor unions has been due largely to favoring legislation and administration by the federal government. This policy of favoring unions rests fundamentally upon the popular belief that workers individually competing for jobs will be exploited by big-business employers—that U.S. Steel can in separate negotiation (a pretty picture!) overwhelm each of its hundreds of thousands of employees. In good part this is an absurd fear: U.S. Steel must compete with many other industries, and not merely other steel companies, for good workers.

Yet the fear may not be wholly absurd: there may be times and

1. The most comprehensive survey is contained in Clair Wilcox' *Competition and Monopoly in American Industry* (Monograph No. 21 of the Temporary National Economic Committee [TNEC]). Some additional evidence is given in George W. Stocking and Myron W. Watkins' *Cartels in Action* (Twentieth Century Fund, 1946), and in C. Edwards' *Maintaining Competition* (1949).

places where big businesses have "beaten down" wages, although I believe such cases are relatively infrequent. (In any event, the reaction to the fear has been unwise: for every case where big business has held down workers there are surely many cases where big unions have held up employers.) But it cannot be denied that this public attitude underlies our national labor policy, the policy of local governments of condoning violence in labor disputes, etc.

Big business has also made substantial contributions to the growth of big government. The whole agricultural program has been justified as necessary to equalize agriculture's bargaining power with "industry," meaning big business. The federally sponsored milkshed cartels are defended as necessary to deal with the giant dairy companies.

BUSINESS ACROSS THE BOARD

Big business is thus a fundamental excuse for big unions and big government. It is true that the scope and evils of big business are usually enormously exaggerated, especially with reference to labor and agriculture, and that more often than not these evils are merely a soapbox excuse for shoddy policies elsewhere. To this large extent, there is need for extensive education of the public on how small a part of the economy is controlled by big business. But in light of the widespread monopolistic practices—our first criticism of bigness—it is impossible to tell the public that its fears of big business are groundless. We have no right to ask public opinion to veer away from big unions and big government —and toward big business.

EFFICIENCY AND BIG BUSINESS

Are we dependent upon big businesses for efficient methods of production and rapid advances in production methods? If we are, the policy of breaking up big businesses would lower our future standard of living and many people would cast about for other ways than dissolution to meet the problems of bigness.

A company may be efficient because it produces and sells a given amount of product with relatively small amounts of material, capital, and labor, or it may be efficient because it acquires the power to buy its supplies at unusually low prices and sell its products at unusually high prices. Economists refer to these as the social and the private costs of production respectively. Big businesses may be efficient in the social sense, and usually they also possess, because of their monopoly position, private advantages. But the ability of a company to employ its dominant position to coerce unusually low prices from suppliers is not of any social advantage.

It follows that even if big companies had larger profit rates or smaller costs per unit of output than other companies, this would not prove that they were more efficient in socially desirable ways. Actually, big businesses are generally no more and no less efficient than medium-sized businesses even when the gains wrung by monopoly power are included in efficiency. This is the one general finding in comparative cost studies and comparative profitability studies.[2] Indeed, if one reflects upon the persistence of small and medium-sized companies in the industries dominated by big businesses, it is apparent that there can be no great advantages to size. If size were a great advantage, the smaller companies would soon lose the unequal race and disappear.

When we recall that most big businesses have numerous complete plants at various points throughout the country, this finding is not surprising. Why should U.S. Steel be more efficient than Inland Steel, when U.S. Steel is simply a dozen or more Inland Steels strewn about the country? Why should G.M. be appreciably more efficient than say a once-again-independent Buick Motors? A few years ago Peter Drucker reported:

"The divisional manager . . . is in complete charge of production and sales. He hires, fires and promotes; and it is up to him to decide how many men he needs, with what qualifications and in what salary range—except for top executives whose employment is subject to a central-management veto. The divisional manager decides the factory layout, the technical methods and equipment used . . . . He buys his supplies independently from suppliers of his own choice. He determines the distribution of production within the several plants under his jurisdiction, decides which lines to push and decides on the methods of sale and distribution . . . . In everything pertaining to operations he is as much the real head

2. For studies that support this generalization, the reader is referred to J. L. McConnell, "Corporate Earnings by Size of Firm," *Survey of Current Business,* May, 1945; TNEC Monograph No. 13; and *Cost Behavior and Price Policy* (National Bureau of Economic Research, 1943).

as if his division were indeed an independent business." [3]

If big businesses are not more efficient as a rule, how did they get big? The answer is that most giant firms arose out of mergers of many competing firms, and were created to eliminate competition. Standard Oil, General Electric, Westinghouse, U.S. Steel, Bethlehem, the meat packers, Borden, National Dairy, American Can, etc.—the full list of merger-created big businesses is most of the list of big businesses. A few big businesses owe their position to an industrial genius like Ford, and of course future geniuses would be hampered by an effective antitrust law—but less so than by entrenched monopolies or by public regulatory commissions.

We do not know what share of improvements in technology has been contributed by big businesses. Big businesses have made some signal contributions, and so also have small businesses, universities, and private individuals. It can be said that manufacturing industries dominated by big businesses have had no large increases in output per worker on average than other manufacturing industries. This fact is sufficient to undermine the easy identification of economic progress with the laboratories of big businesses, but it does not inform us of the net effect of monopolies on economic progress.

At present, then, no definite effect of big business on economic progress can be established. I personally believe that future study will confirm the traditional belief that big businesses, for all their resources, cannot rival the infinite resource and cold scrutiny of many independent and competing companies. If the real alternative to bigness is government regulation or ownership, as I am about to argue, then the long-run consequences of big business are going to be highly adverse to economic progress.

REMEDIES FOR BIG BUSINESS

Let me restate the main points of the foregoing discussion in a less emphatic—and I think also a less accurate—manner:

1. Big businesses often possess and use monopoly power.

2. Big businesses weaken the political support for a private-enterprise system.

3. Big businesses are not appreciably more efficient or enterprising than medium-size businesses.

3. *Concept of a Corporation*, p. 56.

Few disinterested people will deny these facts—where do they lead?

A considerable section of the big-business community seems to have taken the following position. The proper way to deal with monopolistic practices is to replace the general prohibitions of the Sherman Act by a specific list of prohibited practices, so businessmen may know in advance and avoid committing monopolistic practices. The proper way to deal with the declining political support for private enterprise is to advertise the merits of private enterprise, at the same time claiming many of its achievements for big business. Much of this advertising has taken literally that form, apparently in the belief that one can sell a social system in exactly the same way and with exactly the same copywriters and media that one sells a brand of cigarettes.

GUARD THE SHERMAN ACT

The request for a list of specifically prohibited monopolistic practices will be looked upon by many persons as a surreptitious attack upon the Sherman Act. I am among these cynics: the powerful drive in 1949 to pass a law legalizing basing-point price systems is sufficient evidence that large sectors of big business are wholly unreconciled to the law against conspiracies in restraint of trade. Even when the request for a specific list of prohibitions is made in all sincerity, however, it cannot be granted: No one can write down a full list of all the forms that objectionable monopoly power has taken and may someday take. Moreover, almost all uncertainties over the legality of conduct arise out of the Robinson-Patman Act, not the Sherman Act, and I would welcome the complete repeal of the former act.[4]

We must look elsewhere for the solution of the problems raised by big business, and a satisfactory solution must deal with the facts I listed at the head of this section. Our present policy is not

4. The prohibition against price discrimination was partly designed to cope with a real evil: the use by a large company of its monopoly power to extort preferential terms from suppliers. This exercise of monopoly, however, constitutes a violation of the Sherman Act, and no additional legislation is necessary if this act can be made fully effective. The Robinson-Patman Act and certain other parts of the so-called "antitrust" amendments also have another and objectionable purpose: to supervise and regulate the routine operations of businesses in order to ensure that they will display the symptoms of competitive behavior.

a satisfactory solution. The Sherman Act is admirable in dealing with formal conspiracies of many firms, but—at least with the Supreme Court's present conception of competition and of the proper remedies for demonstrated restraint of trade in oligopolistic industries—it cannot cope effectively with the problem posed by big business. In industries dominated by a few firms there is no need for formal conspiracies, with their trappings of quotas, a price-fixing committee, and the like. The big companies know they must "live with" one another, and the phrase means much the same thing as in the relationships between man and woman. Any competitive action one big company takes will lead to retaliation by the others. An informal code of behavior gradually develops in the industry: Firm X announces the new price, and except in very unusual circumstances Y and Z can be relied upon to follow. So long as there are a few big businesses in an industry, we simply cannot expect more than the tokens of competitive behavior. Antitrust decrees that the big businesses should ignore each other's existence serve no important purpose.[5]

This conclusion, I must emphasize, is not merely that of "economic theorists," although most (academic) economists will subscribe to it. It is also the conclusion our generation is reaching, for our generation is not satisfied with the behavior of big business. More and more, big businesses are being asked to act in "the social interest," and more and more, government is interfering in their routine operation. The steel industry, for example, what with congressional review of prices and presidential coercion of wages, is drifting rapidly into a public-utility status. And the drift will not be stopped by slick advertising.

5. In the National Lead case (*67 Sup. Ct. 1634, 1947*) this company and du Pont were convicted of violating the Sherman Act. The two companies produced about 90 per cent of all titanium, but the Court refused to order divestiture of plants. The Court documented the "vigorous and effective competition between National Lead and du Pont" with the fact that "The general manager of the pigments department of du Pont characterized the competition with Zirconium and Virginia Chemical as 'tough' and that with National Lead as 'plenty tough.'" Economists will always find such testimony an inadequate demonstration of competition. Even more unfortunate was the refusal of the Court to order divestiture of foreign holdings of the Timken Roller Bearing company, which had also been convicted under the Sherman Act (*71 Sup. Ct. 971, 1951*). Here Mr. Justice Reed, the Chief Justice concurring, argues that so "harsh" a remedy as divestiture should be invoked only in extreme cases, perhaps forgetting that inadequate remedies for monopoly are "harsh" treatment of the public interest.

DISSOLUTION THE REMEDY

No such drastic and ominous remedy as the central direction of economic life is necessary to deal with the problems raised by big business. The obvious and economical solution, as I have already amply implied, is to break up the giant companies. This, I would emphasize, is the minimum program, and it is essentially a conservative program. Dissolution of big businesses is a one-for-all measure in each industry (if the recent anti-merger amendment to the Clayton Act is adequately enforced), and no continuing interference in the private operation of business is required or desired. Dissolution involves relatively few companies: one dissolves three or four big steel companies, and leaves the many smaller companies completely alone. Dissolution does not even need to be invoked in a large part of the economy: some of our biggest industries, such as textiles, shoes, and most food industries, will require no antitrust action.

A policy of "trust busting" requires no grant of arbitrary powers to any administrative agency; the policy can be administered by the Antitrust Division acting through the courts. It is sufficient, and it is desirable, that the policy be directed against companies whose possession of monopoly power is demonstrated, and that dissolution be the basic remedy for the concentration of control in an industry that prevents or limits competition. Indeed, the policy requires new legislation only to the extent of convincing the courts that an industry which does not have a competitive structure will not have competitive behavior.

The dissolution of big businesses is only a part of the program necessary to increase the support for a private, competitive enterprise economy, and reverse the drift toward government control. But it is an essential part of this program, and the place for courage and imagination. Those conservatives who cling to the status quo do not realize that the status quo is a state of change, and the changes are coming fast. If these changes were to include the dissolution of a few score of our giant companies, however, we shall have done much to preserve private enterprise and the liberal-individualistic society of which it is an integral part.

In Defense of Bigness in Business

SUMNER H. SLICHTER

Sumner H. Slichter was Lamont University Professor at Harvard University until his death in 1959. This essay appeared in the New York Times Magazine *on August 4, 1957.*

THE 1957 DECISION of the Supreme Court in the du Pont-General Motors case suggests the desirability of a review and an appraisal of American policy toward competition, monopoly, and bigness in business. The decision reveals the strong determination of the court to prevent competition from being weakened and the court's willingness to resort to controversial interpretations of the law in order to implement the public policy of preventing restraints on competition.

But the decision also reminds us that much thinking on the relation of bigness to competition is out of date and unrealistic. Hence, the adaptation of traditional American antitrust policy to the facts of modern industry requires that we take a fresh look at the role of large enterprises in American business—particularly the role of large enterprises as a source of vigorous and dynamic competition.

When one compares the economy of the United States with the economies of other advanced industrial countries, four characteristics stand out conspicuously.

1. The government of the United States endeavors through broad and drastic laws to prevent restraints on competition and to forestall the growth of monopoly. Most other advanced industrial countries either tolerate considerable restraint on competition or even encourage organizations of business men that are designed to control competition.

2. Competition in American industry is far more vigorous and pervasive than in the industries of any other advanced industrial

country. Indeed, the vigor of competition in the United States almost invariably attracted comment from the European productivity teams that visited this country in the years following the war.

3. The United States has many more huge business enterprises than any other country. Several years ago this country had more than 100 corporations (exclusive of purely financial ones) with assets of more than $250 million each. General Motors produces far more cars than the combined British, German and French automobile industries, and the United States Steel Corporation produces more steel than the entire British steel industry.

4. Production in many American industries (especially those requiring large capital investment) is highly concentrated in the hands of a few large concerns. As a general rule, the concentration of production in other industrial countries is far less than here.

These four characteristics of the American economy are not unrelated. It would be wrong to ascribe the widespread and intense competition in American industry *solely* to the strong public policy against restraint of trade, monopolization and interference with competition. Conditions in the United States—the absence of class lines, the abundance of opportunity, the weakness of tradition—have long made life here highly competitive in all its aspects, and competition in business is just one manifestation of this general competitive spirit. But America's unique and firm public policy against restraints on competition has undoubtedly helped greatly to keep industry here strongly competitive.

This strong policy, however, has paradoxically encouraged the development of giant industrial corporations and the concentration of production in many industries among a few large concerns. The growth of enterprises in Europe has been limited by the practice of forming cartels—a practice which governments have tolerated and even encouraged. The cartel or trade association divides markets among its members, limits the growth of the most efficient concerns, and assures the weak, high-cost concern a share of the market.

In the United States, where cartels are illegal, each concern is pretty completely exposed to competition from all other firms, and business goes to the firms that can get it. This means that in many industries production is gradually concentrated in the hands of a few industrial giants, and only a small part of the business is left for small firms.

The trend toward corporate bigness in industry has led many students of anti-monopoly policy to believe that the American policy of encouraging competition and discouraging monopoly is turning out to be a failure and to conclude that steps need to be taken to limit the influences of large enterprises in American industry. Of many proposals that have been made, two principal ones are of particular interest.

One proposal is that new restrictions be placed on mergers. Some have urged that no merger be permitted which cannot be justified by technological reasons. Some have proposed that mergers involving a corporation above a given size be prohibited unless found by the Federal Trade Commission to be in the public interest.

The second proposal deals with the concentration of production in various industries into a few enterprises. It is urged that the government undertake a comprehensive survey of American industry to determine whether enterprises exceed the size required by modern technology and that the government be authorized to break up firms that are unnecessarily large.

Both of these proposals are based on fallacy. They rest upon a mistaken conception of the role of large corporations in American business and particularly upon the relation of large corporations to competition. Each, if put into effect, would weaken rather than strengthen competition. In fact, in order to stimulate competition, existing restrictions on mergers should be relaxed, not tightened, and large enterprises, instead of being threatened with breakup, should be given a clear mandate to grow, provided they use fair means. Let us examine more completely each of these two proposals to restrict the growth of enterprises.

The proposal that new restrictions be placed on mergers arises from the fact that the United States in recent years has been experiencing a great wave of mergers. But recent mergers have not weakened competition. On the contrary, they have indirectly strengthened it because they have enabled managements to build more diversified and better-integrated enterprises—enterprises which are more capable of reaching all parts of the vast domestic market, of adapting themselves to market shifts and changes in technology, of riding out the ups and downs of business, and of supporting technological research and development. Many large firms and firms of moderate size have acquired small firms, but the acquisitions by the very largest firms have not been numerous.

The specific circumstances surrounding each merger are unique, but a case-by-case examination shows how mergers are helping to build stronger enterprises, better able to compete and to hold their own in competition.

Let us consider a few examples. A maker of cans bought a concern manufacturing plastic pipe in order to get a foothold in the plastic pipe business. A maker of railroad freight cars bought companies making electrical equipment, truck trailers and dairy supplies in order to shift from a declining business to expanding businesses. A food manufacturer bought a West Coast manufacturer of salad seasoning in order to give nation-wide distribution to its product. A maker of household ware bought a supplier in order to have a source of pressed wood handles for its appliances.

Unusually competent managements often buy other concerns so that they can spread good administrative methods to less efficiently operated enterprises.

The many advantages produced by mergers show that the proposal that mergers be prohibited unless they can be justified by technological reasons does not make sense. There are good reasons for mergers that have nothing to do with technology.

Moreover, it would be unwise to require government approval of all mergers involving an enterprise above a specified size. That would be substituting the decision of government officials for the decision of businessmen on matters that the businessmen are better able to understand. The public interest is amply protected by the present drastic provision of Section 7 of the Clayton Act.

Indeed, the fact that mergers often make for more vigorous competition by helping managements build stronger and more efficient business enterprises indicates the need for relaxing the present severe restrictions on mergers contained in Section 7 of the Clayton Act. This section prohibits any merger which is likely to lessen competition substantially in *any* line of commerce. The fact that the merger may increase the intensity of competition in *other* lines of commerce makes no difference. As Section 7 now reads, the *total effect* of the merger on competition is irrelevant. If it is likely to lessen competition substantially in any one line of commerce, it is illegal.

Obviously the section, as it now reads, conflicts with the national policy of encouraging competition. It should be rewritten to make the legality of mergers depend upon the *total* effect of competition, thus permitting any merger that has the net effect of increasing competition.

The second proposal—to remake the structure of American industry by breaking up the largest enterprises—rests upon the mistaken view that, where output is concentrated among a few concerns, effective competition does not occur. The error of this view is shown by the vigorous competition in various industries in which most of the output is made by a few firms—in such industries as the automobile, tire, refrigerator, soap, cigarette, paper products, television and many others.

There are two principal reasons why competition tends to be vigorous when production is concentrated among a few large concerns. One is that such enterprises keep close track of their rank in sales and fight hard to move ahead of rivals or to avoid being surpassed by rivals. The second reason, and one that is rapidly gaining in importance, is the fact that competition among large firms is being stimulated by the growth of technological research.

It is only within the last several decades that managements have generally discovered the big returns yielded by technological research. As a result, the outlays by private industry on research and development increased nearly six-fold between 1940 and 1953. In 1957, the total research and development expenditures of private industry, exclusive of the aircraft industry, which is a special case, are running about 71 per cent greater than they were in 1953. By 1960 outlays on research are expected to be 21 per cent above 1957.

No expenditures are more competitive than outlays on research, for the purpose of these expenditures is to improve products, develop new products and cut costs. More than 70 per cent of the outlays on research and development are made by firms with 5,000 or more employees because concerns with large sales can best afford this overhead expense. Hence the rapidly mounting outlays on research indicate both the growing competitiveness of American industry and the increasingly important role large enterprises are playing in making competition more intense.

Incidentally, competition among large firms is superior in quality to competition among small firms and serves consumers more effectively. This is because the greater research by the large firms gives the consumers a wider range of choice over a period of years than competition among a much larger number of small firms that can afford little or no research. In general, the wider the range of choice open to consumers, the more effectively is the welfare of consumers advanced.

In view of the growing importance of large enterprises as a source of competition and the superior quality of this competition, a move to break up large concerns would be a blunder. There is much to be said, however, in favor of incentives for enterprises to split themselves voluntarily, if the managements consider a split desirable. The resulting increase in the number of top managements with independent authority to make policies and to try experiments would be favorable to technological progress—provided the concerns are large enough to support extensive research. A good incentive for voluntary splits would be created by relieving stockholders from liability for the capital gains tax on the appreciation of their holdings from the time they purchased the stock up to the date of the split.

But enforced splitting of enterprises, except as a remedy for flagrant monopolizing of trade by unscrupulous methods, would be another matter. In fact, the present law needs to be clarified in order to encourage a few of the very largest concerns to strive harder for a bigger share of the market. The managements of a few very large and efficient concerns apparently feel that efforts to get more business by cutting prices will be held to be attempts to monopolize. There is need to make clear that efforts to win business by giving consumers the benefits of low costs will not be regarded as monopolistic.

Americans need to understand that a variety of conditions—rapidly changing technology, the growing importance of industrial research, the growing strength of trade unions—tend to increase in many industries the size of the enterprise that is able both to compete and to survive in competition. Hence, we are likely to see a spread of the tendency for production to be concentrated in a few large or fairly large firms.

But this trend, if it occurs, should not disturb us. It will simply represent an adaptation of industry to the conditions of the time.

Capitalism and the Process of Creative Destruction

JOSEPH A. SCHUMPETER

Joseph A. Schumpeter, Professor of Economics at Harvard University until his death in 1950, is one of the leading figures of twentieth-century economics. The following selection is taken from his book Capitalism, Socialism, and Democracy.

PLAUSIBLE CAPITALISM

UNLIKE THE CLASS of feudal lords, the commercial and industrial bourgeoisie rose by business success. Bourgeois society has been cast in a purely economic mold: its foundations, beams and beacons are all made of economic material. The building faces toward the economic side of life. Prizes and penalties are measured in pecuniary terms. Going up and going down means making and losing money. This, of course, nobody can deny. But I wish to add that, within its own frame, that social arrangement is, or at all events was, singularly effective. In part it appeals to, and in part it creates, a schema of motives that is unsurpassed in simplicity and force. The promises of wealth and the threats of destitution that it holds out, it redeems with ruthless promptitude. Wherever the bourgeois way of life asserts itself sufficiently to dim the beacons of other social worlds, these promises are strong enough to attract the large majority of supernormal brains and to identify success with business success. They are not proffered at random; yet there is a sufficiently enticing admixture of chance: the game is not like roulette, it is more like poker. They are addressed to ability, energy and supernormal capacity for work; but if there were a way of measuring either that ability in general or the personal achievement that goes into any particular success, the premiums actually paid out would probably not be found proportional to either. Spectacular prizes much greater than would have been necessary to call forth the particular effort are thrown to a small minority of winners, thus propelling much more efficaciously than a more equal and more "just" distribution would, the activity of that large majority of businessmen who receive in return very modest compensation or nothing or less than nothing, and yet do their utmost because they have the big prizes before their eyes and overrate their chances of doing equally well. Similarly, the threats are addressed to incompetence. But though the incompetent men and the obsolete methods are in fact eliminated, sometimes very promptly, sometimes with a lag, failure also threatens or actually overtakes many an able man, thus whipping up *everyone,* again much more efficaciously than a more equal and more "just" system of penalties would. Finally, both business success and business failure are ideally precise. Neither can be talked away.

The capitalist arrangement, as embodied in the institution of private enterprise, effectively chains the bourgeois stratum to its tasks. But it does more than that. The same apparatus which conditions for performance the individuals and families that at any given time form the bourgeois class, *ipso facto* also selects the individuals and families that are to rise into that class or to drop out of it. This combination of the conditioning and the selective function is not a matter of course. On the contrary, most methods of social selection, unlike the "methods" of biological selection, do not guarantee performance of the selected individual. In most cases the man who rises first *into* the business class and then *within* it is also an able businessman and he is likely to rise exactly as far as his ability goes—simply because in that schema rising to a position and doing well in it generally is or was one and the same thing. This fact, so often obscured by the auto-therapeutic effort of the unsuccessful to deny it, is much more important for an appraisal of capitalist society and its civilization than anything that can be gleaned from the pure theory of the capitalist machine.

But is not all that we might be tempted to infer from "maximum performance of an optimally selected group" invalidated by the further fact that that performance is not geared to social service—production, so we might say, for consumption—but to money-making, that it aims at maximizing profits instead of welfare? Outside of the bourgeois stratum, this has of course always been the popular opinion. Economists have sometimes fought and sometimes espoused it. In doing so they have contributed something that was much more valuable than were the final judgments themselves at which they arrived individually and which in most cases reflect little more than their social location, interests and sympathies or antipathies. They slowly increased our factual knowledge and analytic powers so that the answers to many questions we are able to give today are no doubt much more correct although less simple and sweeping than were those of our predecessors.

To go no further back, the so-called classical economists [1] were practically of one mind. Most of them disliked many things about the social institutions of their epoch and about the way those institutions worked. They fought the landed interest and approved of social reforms—factory legislation in particular—that were not all on the lines of *laissez faire*. But they were quite convinced that within the institutional framework of capitalism, the manufacturer's and the trader's self-interest made for maximum performance in the interest of all. Confronted with the problem we are discussing, they would have had little hesitation in attributing the observed rate of increase in total output to relatively unfettered enterprise and the profit motive—perhaps they would have mentioned "beneficial legislation" as a condition but by this they would have meant the removal of fetters, especially the removal or reduction of protective duties during the nineteenth century.

It is exceedingly difficult, at this hour of the day, to do justice to these views. They were of course the typical views of the English bourgeois class, and bourgeois blinkers are in evidence on almost every page the classical authors wrote. No less in evidence are blinkers of another kind: the classics reasoned in terms of a particular historical situation which they uncritically idealized and from which they uncritically generalized. Most of them, moreover, seem to have argued exclusively in terms of the English interests and problems of their time. This is the reason why, in other lands and at other times, people disliked their economics, frequently to the point of not even caring to understand it. But it

1. The term Classical Economists will be used to designate the leading English economists whose works appeared between 1776 and 1848. Adam Smith, Ricardo, Malthus, Senior and John Stuart Mill are the outstanding names.

will not do to dismiss their teaching on these grounds. A prejudiced man may yet be speaking the truth. Propositions developed from special cases may yet be generally valid. And the enemies and successors of the classics had and have only different but not fewer blinkers and preconceptions; they envisaged and envisage different but not less special cases.

From the standpoint of the economic analyst, the chief merit of the classics consists in their dispelling, along with many other gross errors, the naïve idea that economic activity in capitalist society, because it turns on the profit motive, must by virtue of that fact alone necessarily run counter to the interests of consumers or, to put it differently, that moneymaking necessarily deflects producing from its social goal; or, finally, that private profits, both in themselves and through the distortion of the economic process they induce, are always a net loss to all excepting those who receive them and would therefore constitute a net gain to be reaped by socialization. If we look at the logic of these and similar propositions which no trained economist ever thought of defending, the classical refutation may well seem trivial. But as soon as we look at all the theories and slogans which, consciously or subconsciously, imply them and which are once more served up today, we shall feel more respect for that achievement. Let me add at once that the classical writers also clearly perceived, though they may have exaggerated, the role of saving and accumulation and that they linked saving to the rate of "progress" they observed in a manner that was fundamentally, if only approximately, correct. Above all, there was practical wisdom about their doctrine, a responsible long-run view and a manly tone that contrast favorably with modern hysterics.

But between realizing that hunting for a maximum of profit and striving for maximum productive performance are not necessarily incompatible, to proving that the former will necessarily— or in the immense majority of cases—imply the latter, there is a gulf much wider than the classics thought. And they never succeeded in bridging it. The modern student of their doctrines never ceases to wonder how it was possible for them to be satisfied with their arguments or to mistake these arguments for proofs; in the light of later analysis their *theory* was seen to be a house of cards whatever measure of truth there may have been in their *vision*.

This later analysis we will take in two strides—as much of it, that is, as we need in order to clarify our problem. Historically, the first will carry us into the first decade of this century, the second will cover some of the postwar developments of scientific economics.

The first stride may be associated with two great names revered to this day by numberless disciples—so far at least as the latter do not think it bad form to express reverence for anything or anybody, which many of them obviously do—Alfred Marshall and Knut Wicksell. Their theoretical structure has little in common with that of the classics—though Marshall did his best to hide the fact—but it conserves the classic proposition that in the case of perfect competition the profit interest of the producer tends to maximize production. It even supplied almost satisfactory proof. Only, in the process of being more correctly stated and proved, the proposition lost much of its content—it does emerge from the operation, to be sure, but it emerges emaciated, barely alive. Still it can be shown, within the general assumptions of the Marshall-Wicksell analysis, that firms which cannot by their own individual action exert any influence upon the price of their products or of the factors of production they employ—so that there would be no point in their weeping over the fact that any increase in production tends to decrease the former and to increase the latter—will expand their output until they reach the point at which the additional cost that must be incurred in order to produce another small increment of product (marginal cost) just equals the price they can get for that increment, i.e., that they will produce as much as they can without running into loss. And this can be shown to be as much as it is in general "socially desirable" to produce. In more technical language, in that case prices are, from the standpoint of the individual firm, not variables but parameters; and where this is so, there exists a state of equilibrium in which all outputs are at their maximum and all factors fully employed. This case is usually referred to as perfect competition. Remembering what has been said about the selective process which operates on all firms and their managers, we might in fact conceive a very optimistic idea of the results to be expected from a highly selected group of people forced, within that pattern, by their profit motive to strain every nerve in order to maximize output and to minimize costs. In particular, it might seem at first sight that a system conforming to this pattern would display remarkable absence of some of the major sources of social waste. As a little reflection should show, this is really but another way of stating the content of the preceding sentence.

Let us take the second stride. The Marshall-Wicksell analysis of course did not overlook the many cases that fail to conform to that model. Nor, for that matter, had the classics overlooked them. They recognized cases of "monopoly," and Adam Smith himself carefully noticed the prevalence of devices to restrict competition and all the differences in flexibility of prices resulting therefrom. But they looked upon those cases as exceptions and, moreover, as exceptions that could and would be done away with in time. Something of that sort is true also of Marshall. Although he anticipated later analysis by calling attention to the fact that most firms have special markets of their own in which they set prices instead of merely accepting them, he as well as Wicksell framed his general conclusions on the pattern of perfect competition so as to suggest, much as the classics did, that perfect competition was the rule. Neither Marshall and Wicksell nor the classics saw that perfect competition is the exception and that even if it were the rule there would be much less reason for congratulation than one might think.

If we look more closely at the conditions—not all of them explicitly stated or even clearly seen by Marshall and Wicksell—that must be fulfilled in order to produce perfect competition, we realize immediately that outside of agricultural mass production there cannot be many instances of it. A farmer supplies his cotton or wheat in fact under those conditions: from his standpoint the ruling prices of cotton or wheat are data, though very variable ones, and not being able to influence them by his individual action he simply adapts his output; since all farmers do the same, prices and quantities will in the end be adjusted as the theory of perfect competition requires. But this is not so even with many agricultural products—with ducks, sausages, vegetables and many dairy products for instance. And as regards practically all the finished products and services of industry and trade, it is clear that every grocer, every filling station, every manufacturer of gloves or shaving cream or handsaws has a small and precarious market of his own which he tries—must try—to build up and to keep by price strategy, quality strategy—"product differentiation"—and advertising. Thus we get a completely different pattern which there seems to be no reason to expect to yield the results of perfect competition and which fits much better into the monopolistic schema. In these cases we speak of Monopolistic Competition. Their theory has been one of the major contributions to postwar economics.[2]

There remains a wide field of substantially homogeneous products—mainly industrial raw materials and semi-finished products such as steel ingots, cement, cotton gray goods and the like—in which the conditions for the emergence of monopolistic competition do not seem to prevail. This is so. But in general, similar results follow for that field inasmuch as the greater part of it is covered by largest-scale firms which, either individually or in concert, are able to manipulate prices even without differentiating products—the case of Oligopoly. Again the monopoly schema, suitably adapted, seems to fit this type of behavior much better than does the schema of perfect competition.

As soon as the prevalence of monopolistic competition or of oligopoly or of combinations of the two is recognized, many of the propositions which the Marshall-Wicksell generation of economists used to teach with the utmost confidence become either inapplicable or much more difficult to prove. This holds true, in the first place, of the propositions turning on the fundamental concept of equilibrium, i.e., a determinate state of the economic organism, toward which any given state of it is always gravitating and which displays certain simple properties. In the general case of oligopoly there is in fact no determinate equilibrium at all and the possibility presents itself that there may be an endless sequence of moves and countermoves, an indefinite state of warfare between firms. It is true that there are many special cases in which a state of equilibrium theoretically exists. In the second place, even in these cases not only is it much harder to attain than the equilibrium in perfect competition, and still harder to preserve, but the "beneficial" competition of the classic type seems likely to be replaced by "predatory" or "cutthroat" competition or simply by struggles for control in the financial sphere. These things are so many sources of social waste, and there are many others such as the costs of advertising campaigns, the suppression of new methods of production (buying up of patents in order not to use them) and

2. See, in particular, E. S. Chamberlin, *Theory of Monopolistic Competition*, and Joan Robinson, *The Economics of Imperfect Competition*.

so on. And most important of all: under the conditions envisaged, equilibrium, even if eventually attained by an extremely costly method, no longer guarantees either full employment or maximum output in the sense of the theory of perfect competition. It *may* exist without full employment; it is *bound* to exist, so it seems, at a level of output below that maximum mark, because profit-conserving strategy, impossible in conditions of perfect competition, now not only becomes possible but imposes itself.

THE PROCESS OF CREATIVE DESTRUCTION

The theories of monopolistic and oligopolistic competition and their popular variants may in two ways be made to serve the view that capitalist reality is unfavorable to maximum performance in production. One may hold that it always has been so and that all along output has been expanding in spite of the secular sabotage perpetrated by the managing bourgeoisie. Advocates of this proposition would have to produce evidence to the effect that the observed rate of increase can be accounted for by a sequence of favorable circumstances unconnected with the mechanism of private enterprise and strong enough to overcome the latter's resistance. However, those who espouse this variant at least avoid the trouble about historical fact that the advocates of the alternative proposition have to face. This avers that capitalist reality once tended to favor maximum productive performance, or at all events productive performance so considerable as to constitute a major element in any serious appraisal of the system; but that the later spread of monopolist structures, killing competition, has by now reversed that tendency.

First, this involves the creation of an entirely imaginary golden age of perfect competition that at some time somehow metamorphosed itself into the monopolistic age, whereas it is quite clear that perfect competition has at no time been more of a reality than it is at present. Secondly, it is necessary to point out that the rate of increase in output did not decrease from the nineties from which, I suppose, the prevalence of the largest-size concerns, at least in manufacturing industry, would have to be dated; that there is nothing in the behavior of the time series of total output to suggest a "break in trend"; and, most important of all, that the modern standard of life of the masses evolved during the period of relatively unfettered "big business." If we list the items that enter the modern workman's budget and from 1899 on observe the course of their prices not in terms of money but in terms of the hours of labor that will buy them—i.e., each year's money prices divided by each year's hourly wage rates—we cannot fail to be struck by the rate of the advance which, considering the spectacular improvement in qualities, seems to have been greater and not smaller than it ever was before. If we economists were given less to wishful thinking and more to the observation of facts, doubts would immediately arise as to the realistic virtues of a theory that would have led us to expect a very different result. Nor is this all. As soon as we go into details and inquire into the individual items in which progress was most conspicuous, the trail leads not to the doors of those firms that work under conditions of comparatively free competition but precisely to the doors of the large concerns—which, as in the case of agricultural machinery, also account for much of the progress in the competitive sector—and a shocking suspicion dawns upon us that big business may have had more to do with creating that standard of life than with keeping it down.

The essential point to grasp is that in dealing with capitalism we are dealing with an evolutionary process. It may seem strange that anyone can fail to see so obvious a fact which moreover was long ago emphasized by Karl Marx. Yet that fragmentary analysis which yields the bulk of our propositions about the functioning of modern capitalism persistently neglects it. Let us restate the point and see how it bears upon our problem.

Capitalism, then, is by nature a form or method of economic change and not only never is but never can be stationary. And this evolutionary character of the capitalist process is not merely due to the fact that economic life goes on in a social and natural environment which changes and by its change alters the data of economic action; this fact is important and these changes (wars, revolutions and so on) often condition industrial change, but they are not its prime movers. Nor is this evolutionary character due to a quasi-automatic increase in population and capital or to the vagaries of monetary systems of which exactly the same thing holds true. The fundamental impulse that sets and keeps the capitalist engine in motion comes from the new consumers' goods, the new methods of production or transportation, the new markets, the new forms of industrial organization that capitalist enterprise creates.

The contents of the laborer's budget, say from 1760 to 1940, did not simply grow on unchanging lines but they underwent a process of qualitative change. Similarly, the history of the productive apparatus of a typical farm, from the beginnings of the rationalization of crop rotation, plowing and fattening to the mechanized thing of today—linking up with elevators and railroads—is a history of revolutions. So is the history of the productive apparatus of the iron and steel industry from the charcoal furnace to our own type of furnace, or the history of the apparatus of power production from the overshot water wheel to the modern power plant, or the history of transportation from the mailcoach to the airplane. The opening up of new markets, foreign or domestic, and the organizational development from the craft shop and factory to such concerns as U.S. Steel illustrate the same process of industrial mutation—if I may use that biological term—that incessantly revolutionizes the economic structure *from within*, incessantly destroying the old one, incessantly creating a new one. This process of Creative Destruction is the essential fact about capitalism. It is what capitalism consists in and what every capitalist concern has got to live in. This fact bears upon our problem in two ways.

First, since we are dealing with a process whose every element takes considerable time in revealing its true features and ultimate effects, there is no point in appraising the performance of that process *ex visu* of a given point of time; we must judge its performance over time, as it unfolds through decades or centuries. A system—any system, economic or other—that at *every* given point of time fully utilizes its possibilities to the best advantage may yet in the long run be inferior to a system that does so at *no* given point of time, because the latter's failure to do so may be a condition for the level or speed of long-run performance.

Second, since we are dealing with an organic process, analysis of what happens in any particular part of it—say, in an individual concern or industry—may indeed clarify details of mechanism but is inconclusive beyond that. Every piece of business strategy acquires its true significance only against the background of that process and within the situation created by it. It must be seen in its role in the perennial gale of creative destruction; it cannot be understood irrespective of it or, in fact, on the hypothesis that there is a perennial lull.

But economists who, *ex visu* of a point of time, look for example at the behavior of an oligopolist industry—an industry which consists of a few big firms—and observe the well-known moves and countermoves within it that seem to aim at nothing but high prices and restrictions of output are making precisely that hypothesis. They accept the data of the momentary situation as if there were no past or future to it and think that they have understood what there is to understand if they interpret the behavior of those firms by means of the principle of maximizing profits with reference to those data. The usual theorist's paper and the usual government commission's report practically never try to see that behavior, on the one hand, as a result of a piece of past history and, on the other hand, as an attempt to deal with a situation that is sure to change presently—as an attempt by those firms to keep on their feet, on ground that is slipping away from under them. In other words, the problem that is usually being visualized is how capitalism administers existing structures, whereas the relevant problem is how it creates and destroys them. As long as this is not recognized, the investigator does a meaningless job. As soon as it is recognized, his outlook on capitalist practice and its social results changes considerably.

The first thing to go is the traditional conception of the *modus operandi* of competition. Economists are at long last emerging from the stage in which price competition was all they saw. As soon as quality competition and sales effort are admitted into the sacred precincts of theory, the price variable is ousted from its dominant position. However, it is still competition within a rigid pattern of invariant conditions, methods of production and forms of industrial organization in particular, that practically monopolizes attention. But in capitalist reality as distinguished from its textbook picture, it is not that kind of competition which counts but the competition from the new commodity, the new technology, the new source of supply, the new type of organization (the largest-scale unit of control for instance)—competition which commands a decisive cost or quality advantage and which strikes not at the margins of the profits and the outputs of the existing firms but at their foundations and their very lives. This kind of competition is as much more effective than the other as a bombardment is in comparison with forcing a door, and so much more important that it becomes a matter of comparative indifference whether competition in the ordinary sense functions more or less promptly; the powerful lever that in the long run expands output and brings down prices is in any case made of other stuff.

It is hardly necessary to point out that competition of the kind we now have in mind acts not only when in being but also when it is merely an ever-present threat. It disciplines before it attacks. The businessman feels himself to be in a competitive situation even if he is alone in his field or if, though not alone, he holds a position such that investigating government experts fail to see any effective competition between him and any other firms in the same or a neighboring field and in consequence conclude that his talk, under examination, about his competitive sorrows is all make-believe. In many cases, though not in all, this will in the long run enforce behavior very similar to the perfectly competitive pattern.

Many theorists take the opposite view which is best conveyed by an example. Let us assume that there is a certain number of retailers in a neighborhood who try to improve their relative position by service and "atmosphere" but avoid price competition and stick as to methods to the local tradition—a picture of stagnating routine. As others drift into the trade that quasi-equilibrium is indeed upset, but in a manner that does not benefit their customers. The economic space around each of the shops having been narrowed, their owners will no longer be able to make a living and they will try to mend the case by raising prices in tacit agreement. This will further reduce their sales and so, by successive pyramiding, a situation will evolve in which increasing potential supply will be attended by increasing instead of decreasing prices and by decreasing instead of increasing sales.

Such cases do occur, and it is right and proper to work them out. But as the practical instances usually given show, they are fringe-end cases to be found mainly in the sectors furthest removed from all that is most characteristic of capitalist activity. Moreover, they are transient by nature. In the case of retail trade the competition that matters arises not from additional shops of the same type, but from the department store, the chain store, the mail-order house and the supermarket which are bound to destroy those pyramids sooner or later. Now a theoretical construction which neglects this essential element of the case neglects all that is most typically capitalist about it; even if correct in logic as well as in fact, it is like *Hamlet* without the Danish prince.

MONOPOLISTIC PRACTICES

We have seen that, both as a fact and as a threat, the impact of new things—new technologies for instance—on the existing structure of an industry considerably reduces the long-run scope and importance of practices that aim, through restricting output, at conserving established positions and at maximizing the profits accruing from them. We must now recognize the further fact that restrictive practices of this kind, as far as they are effective, acquire a new significance in the perennial gale of creative destruction, a significance which they would not have in a stationary state or in a state of slow and balanced growth. In either of these cases restrictive strategy would produce no result other than an increase in profits at the expense of buyers except that, in the case of balanced advance, it might still prove to be the easiest and most effective way of collecting the means by which to finance additional investment. But in the process of creative destruction, restrictive practices may do much to steady the ship and to alleviate temporary difficulties.

Practically any investment entails, as a necessary complement of entrepreneurial action, certain safeguarding activities such as insuring or hedging. Long-range investing under rapidly changing conditions, especially under conditions that change or may change at any moment under the impact of new commodities and technologies, is like shooting at a target that is not only indistinct but moving—and moving jerkily at that. Hence it becomes necessary to resort to such protecting devices as patents or temporary secrecy of processes or, in some cases, long-period contracts secured in advance. But these protecting devices which most economists accept as normal elements of rational management are only special cases of a larger class comprising many others which most economists condemn although they do not differ fundamentally from the recognized ones.

If for instance a war risk is insurable, nobody objects to a firm's collecting the cost of the insurance from the buyers of its products. But that risk is no less an element in long-run costs, if there are no facilities for insuring against it, in which case a price strategy aiming at the same end will seem to involve unnecessary restriction and to be productive of excess profits. Similarly, if a patent cannot be secured or would not, if secured, effectively protect, other means may have to be used in order to justify the investment. Among them are a price policy that will make it possible to write off more quickly than would otherwise be rational, or additional investment in order to provide excess capacity to be used only for aggression or defense. Again, if long-period contracts cannot be entered into in advance, other means may have to be devised in order to tie prospective customers to the investing firm.

In analyzing such business strategy *ex visu* of a given point of time, the investigating economist or government agent sees price policies that seem to him predatory and restrictions of output that seem to him synonymous with loss of opportunities to produce. He does not see that restrictions of this type are, in the conditions of the perennial gale, incidents, often unavoidable incidents, of a long-run process of expansion which they protect rather than impede. There is no more of paradox in this than there is in saying that motorcars are traveling faster than they otherwise would *because* they are provided with brakes.

This stands out most clearly in the case of those sectors of the economy which at any time happen to embody the impact of new things and methods on the existing industrial structure. The best way of getting a vivid and realistic idea of industrial strategy is indeed to visualize the behavior of new concerns or industries that introduce new commodities or processes (such as the aluminum industry) or else reorganize a part or the whole of an industry (such as, for instance, the old Standard Oil Company).

As we have seen, such concerns are aggressors by nature and wield the really effective weapon of competition. Their intrusion can only in the rarest of cases fail to improve total output in quantity or quality, both through the new method itself—even if at no time used to full advantage—and through the pressure it exerts on the preexisting firms. But these aggressors are so circumstanced as to require, for purposes of attack and defense, also pieces of armor other than price and quality of their product which, moreover, must be strategically manipulated all along so that at any point of time they seem to be doing nothing but restricting their output and keeping prices high.

On the one hand, largest-scale plans could in many cases not materialize at all if it were not known from the outset that competition will be discouraged by heavy capital requirements or lack of experience, or that means are available to discourage or checkmate it so as to gain the time and space for further developments. Even the conquest of financial control over competing concerns in otherwise unassailable positions or the securing of advantages that run counter to the public's sense of fair play—railroad rebates—move, as far as long-run effects on total output alone are envisaged, into a different light; they *may* be methods for removing obstacles that the institution of private property puts in the path of progress. In a socialist society that time and space would be no less necessary. They would have to be secured by order of the central authority.

On the other hand, enterprise would in most cases be impossible if it were not known from the outset that exceptionally favorable situations are likely to arise which if exploited by price, quality and quantity manipulation will produce profits adequate to tide over exceptionally unfavorable situations provided these are similarly managed. Again this requires strategy that in the short run is often restrictive. In the majority of successful cases this strategy just manages to serve its purpose. In some cases, however, it is so successful as to yield profits far above what is necessary in order to induce the corresponding investment. These cases then provide the baits that lure capital on to untried trails. Their presence explains in part how it is possible for so large a section of the capitalist world to work for nothing: in the midst of the prosperous twenties just about half of the business corporations in the United States were run at a loss, at zero profits, or at profits which, if they had been foreseen, would have been inadequate to call forth the effort and expenditure involved.

Our argument however extends beyond the cases of new concerns, methods and industries. Old concerns and established industries, whether or not directly attacked, still live in the perennial gale. Situations emerge in the process of creative destruction in which many firms may have to perish that nevertheless would be able to live on vigorously and usefully if they could weather a particular storm. Short of such general crises or depressions, sectional situations arise in which the rapid change of data that is characteristic of that process so disorganizes an industry for the time being as to inflict functionless losses and to create avoidable unemployment. Finally, there is certainly no point in trying to conserve obsolescent industries indefinitely; but there is point in trying to avoid their coming down with a crash and in attempting to turn a rout, which may become a center of cumulative depressive effects, into orderly retreat. Correspondingly there is, in the case of industries that have sown their wild oats but are still gaining and not losing ground, such a thing as orderly advance.

All this is of course nothing but the tritest common sense. But it is being overlooked with a persistence so stubborn as sometimes to raise the question of sincerity. And it follows that, within the process of creative destruction, all the realities of which theorists are in the habit of relegating to books and courses on business cycles, there is another side to industrial self-organization than that which these theorists are contemplating. "Restraints of trade" of the cartel type as well as those which merely consist in tacit understandings about price competition may be effective remedies under conditions of depression. As far as they are, they may in the end produce not only steadier but also greater expansion of total output than could be secured by an entirely uncontrolled onward rush that cannot fail to be studded with catastrophes. Nor can it be argued that these catastrophes occur in any case. We know what has happened in each historical case. We have a very imperfect idea of what might have happened, considering the tremendous pace of the process, if such pegs had been entirely absent.

Even as now extended however, our argument does not cover all cases of restrictive or regulating strategy, many of which no doubt have that injurious effect on the long-run development of output which is uncritically attributed to all of them. And even in the cases our argument does cover, the net effect is a question of the circumstances and of the way in which and the degree to which industry regulates itself in each individual case. It is certainly as conceivable that an all-pervading cartel system might sabotage all progress as it is that it might realize, with smaller social and private costs, all that perfect competition is supposed to realize. This is why our argument does not amount to a case against state regulation. It does show that there is no general case for indiscriminate "trust-busting" or for the prosecution of everything that qualifies as a restraint of trade. Rational as distinguished from vindictive regulation by public authority turns out to be an extremely delicate problem which not every government agency, particularly when in full cry against big business, can be trusted to solve. But our argument, framed to refute a prevalent *theory* and the inferences drawn therefrom about the relation between modern capitalism and the development of total output, only yields another *theory*, i.e., another outlook on facts and another principle by which to interpret them. For our purpose that is enough. For the rest, the facts themselves have the floor.

The Economics of Technical Development

JOHN KENNETH GALBRAITH

John Kenneth Galbraith, formerly United States Ambassador to India, returned in 1963 to his post as Professor of Economics at Harvard University. This essay is taken from his book American Capitalism.

CLEARLY THE drift of the accepted ideas concerning the economy of the United States has been toward a most dismal set of conclusions. They suggest that the economy does not work at its highest efficiency; incentives do not reward most the man who produces what people most want at least cost. The greatest reward may go to the crypto-monopolist or to the most skillful advertiser and salesman. The accepted ideas also expose a disagreeable problem of power. A plenary authority lies with the heads of private corporations, evidently also with leaders of unions, which enables them to make decisions affecting the wealth and livelihood of others. There is no reason for supposing that the economy works reliably. The depression of the thirties remains impressively on the record to suggest the possibility of serious breakdown. The accepted ideas make depression, or its counterpart inflation, as normal as good performance. True, the Keynesian system, which affirms the likelihood of such misfortune, carries with it a remedy. But it is one requiring a degree of government participation in the economy which many conservatives, to put it mildly, find repugnant.

Yet most Americans, and most foreigners whose sources of information bear a perceptible relation to the truth, undoubtedly consider the American economy, as it has performed in the last decade, a considerable success. In principle the economy pleases no one; in practice in the last ten years it has satisfied most. Social inefficiency, unrationalized power, intrusive government and depression are all matters for deep concern. But neither liberals nor conservatives, neither the rich nor all but the very poor, find the present intolerable.

Pessimism in our time is infinitely more respectable than optimism: the man who foresees peace, prosperity, and a decline in juvenile delinquency is a negligent and vacuous fellow. The man who foresees catastrophe has a gift of insight which insures that he will become a radio commentator, an editor of *Time* or go to Congress. Recognizing the risks in running counter to our national preference for gloom, it may still be worth while inquiring why the years of peace following World War II proved tolerable. Conceivably, from this analysis, one can learn how the future can be tolerable too. The task is to examine in turn the circumstances which have kept social inefficiency, private power, government intervention and unemployment from ruining us in the recent present.

The first reason the present is tolerable is that efficiency in the American economy appears in a deep disguise. To the man steeped in the preconceptions of the competitive model the disguise is nearly complete. The incentives in the typical American industry, the industry pre-empted by a handful of large firms, do not in fact work in the direction of maximum output at lowest prices. Subject to important restraints, which I will examine later, the market power of the individual firm is used, at any given time, to obtain prices that are higher for an output that, as a result, is smaller than would be ideal. In consumers' goods industries, great energy is, without doubt, channeled into one or another form of selling effort, which is of no perceptible benefit to the public and which is not in response to any recognizable public demand.

However, there is a major compensation for much of this inefficiency, and that is technical change. Moreover, a benign Providence who, so far, has loved us for our worries, has made the modern industry of a few large firms an almost perfect instrument for inducing technical change. It is admirably equipped for financing technical development. Its organization provides strong incentives for undertaking development and for putting it into use.[1] The competition of the competitive model, by contrast, al-

1. This point has been much overlooked by economists. A major exception was the late Professor Joseph A. Schumpeter in whose system the in-

most completely precludes technical development.

There is no more pleasant fiction than that technical change is the product of the matchless ingenuity of the small man forced by competition to employ his wits to better his neighbor. Unhappily, it is a fiction. Technical development has long since become the preserve of the scientist and the engineer. Most of the cheap and simple inventions have, to put it bluntly, been made. Not only is development now sophisticated and costly but it must be on a sufficient scale so that successes and failures will in some measure average out. Few can afford it if they must expect all projects to pay off. This was the case in the late eighteenth and the nineteenth century. Then, in the beginning stages of the applications of science and technology to industry and agriculture, there was scope for the uncomplicated ingenuities of a Hargreaves or a Franklin. The competition of the competitive model encouraged such ingenuity and assured the spreading of its fruits. As elsewhere the competitive model had great appropriateness to the industrial society which it was designed to interpret. Its designers were not abtruse theorists or dolts. It is the society they interpreted that has changed.

Because development is costly, it follows that it can be carried on only by a firm that has the resources associated with considerable size. Moreover, unless a firm has a substantial share of the market it has no strong incentive to undertake a large expenditure on development. There are, in practice, very few innovations which cannot be imitated—where secrecy or patent protection accords a considerable advantage to the pioneer. Accordingly the competitor of the competitive model must expect that his innovation will be promptly copied or imitated. Whether it be a new product or a new way of reducing the costs of producing an old one, the change will be dispersed over a market in which he has only an infinitely small share. The imitators, who haven't stood the cost of development, profit along with the pioneer. And presently prices will adjust themselves to remove entirely the advantage of the innovator. He is thus restored to a plane of equality with his imitators. Thus the very mechanism which assures the

novating role of large enterprises is strongly emphasized. See his *Capitalism, Socialism and Democracy* (New York: Harper & Bros., 2d ed., 1943), pp. 79 ff. While my analysis is in a tradition of economic theory different from his, and one of which he was frequently critical, the conclusions on this point are similar.

quick spread of any known technology in the purely competitive market—and which was a strong recommendation of that market—eliminates the incentive to technical development itself. It leaves to the pioneer, apart from the rare case of effective patent protection, only the fleeting rewards of a head start. Where the costs of development are considerable, there is no reason to suppose that the returns to the pioneer will be sufficient to compensate for the cost. On the contrary, as the costs of development increase—and with time and progress toward more sophisticated innovation they must increase—there is a diminishing likelihood that they will be recovered. The higher the level of science and technology required for change, the more nearly static an industry which conforms to the competitive model will become.

In the industry that is shared by a relatively small number of large firms, the convention that excludes price competition does not restrain technical innovation. This remains one of the important weapons of market rivalry. The firms, typically, are large. Hence resources are available on a scale appropriate to the modern requirements of technical development. Some of them in fact are the fruits of market power—of monopoly gains. And, while imitation must be assumed and expected, the convention which limits price competition also insures that the returns, whether to a new product or from cost-reducing innovation, will accrue to the innovator as well as to its rivals for a period of time. The presence of market power makes the latter time period subject to some measure of control.

Thus, in the modern industry shared by a few large firms, size and the rewards accruing to market power combine to insure that resources for research and technical development will be available. The power that enables the firm to have some influence on prices insures that the resulting gains will not be passed on to the public by imitators (who have stood none of the costs of development) before the outlay for development can be recouped. In this way market power protects the incentive to technical development.

The net of all this is that there must be some element of monopoly in an industry if it is to be progressive. This, at first glance, is shockingly at variance with accepted notions. Economists have long excoriated the comfortable domination of an industry by a single firm in the belief that such a firm will sit not only on production but on progress as well. So, far from spending money on innovation, it may even suppress patents in order to protect existing investment in plant and machinery.

Such a view of the behavior of a monopoly may not be entirely in error although, as Schumpeter has argued, it may be somewhat improbable in a world where there are always potential substitutes and where innovation is proceeding elsewhere.[2] The error has resulted from generalizing from what may be the plausible behavior of a single firm in possession of the entire output of an industry to the consequences of the monopoly power of a few firms sharing the output of an industry. Because stagnation is a plausible counterpart of monopoly in the first case it has been thought to be a likely counterpart of the monopoly power that undoubtedly exists in the second case. This generalization, so far from being valid, would appear to be almost completely in error.

To be sure, some room must be left for exceptions. One can imagine that the convention against price competition could be extended, in the industries of small numbers, to innovation. And, as in the well-publicized instances of patent suppression, this has undoubtedly happened. But to maintain a convention against innovation requires a remarkably comprehensive form of collusion. This is difficult as well as legally dangerous. While it would be going too far to say that oligopoly insures progress, technical development is all but certain to be one of the instruments of commercial rivalry when the number of firms is small. Like advertising and salesmanship—and unlike price competition which is unique in this respect—technical development is a safe rather than a reciprocally destructive method by which any one firm can advance itself against its few powerful rivals.

Moreover, in a community which sets great store by progress, technical progress is an important source of business prestige. An American business concern simply cannot afford the reputation of being unprogressive. If it has no laboratories it must imagine some; an annual report that makes no reference to research is unthinkable. Such an environment is highly unfavorable to any systematic restraint on innovation.

Thus there can be little doubt that oligopoly, both in theory and in fact, is strongly oriented toward change. There can be no serious doubt at all that the setting for innovation, which is so

2. *Ibid.*, pp. 101–2.

favorable in this market structure, disappears almost entirely as one approaches the competition of the competitive model.

These propositions can be readily verified by experience. The American farmer, the producer who most closely approaches the competitor of the model, does almost no research on his own behalf. It was the foresight of genius that caused this to be recognized at an early stage in our history, with the result that technical development within this field has been almost completely socialized. We now take for granted that technical development in agriculture as such will come from the State Experiment Stations and from the United States Department of Agriculture. Not minimizing for a moment the well-publicized efforts of the men of literature who have invested their royalties in land, there would be little technical development and not much progress in agriculture were it not for government-supported research supplemented by that of the large corporations who devise and sell products to the farmer. The individual farmer cannot afford a staff of chemists to develop an animal protein factor which makes different proteins interchangeable as feeds. So many would appropriate the innovation so quickly, without having contributed to the cost of development, that it wouldn't profit any farmer to try.

The other industries which are distinguished by a close approach to the competitive model are also distinguished, one can almost say without exception, by a near absence of research and technical development. The bituminous coal industry, apart from a handful of very large operators, the cotton textile industry, apart from a few very large groups of mills, the clothing industry, the lumber industry and the shoe industry do very little research. None of them are thought of as technically progressive industries. All of them (apart always from the few large firms they contain and which help prove the case) roughly meet the specifications of the competitive model. They also conform to the ideal which the American economist has had anciently in mind. No firm in these industries (the few special cases again excepted) has appreciable influence on prices; each is forced by circumstances which it cannot control to search for the greatest efficiency of operation; in most of them entry and exit are admirably free; few of the firms in these industries engage in extensive competitive advertising and salesmanship. Yet almost no one would select them as a showpiece of American industrial achievement. The showpieces are, with rare exceptions, the industries which are dominated by a handful of large firms. The foreign visitor, brought to the United States by the Economic Cooperation Administration, visits the same firms as do attorneys of the Department of Justice in their search for monopoly.

The reductions in cost, and the consequent increases in efficiency from technical change can be of a wholly different order of magnitude from those sacrificed as the result of the exercise of market power. Thus it comes about that a slight continuing loss of efficiency, as compared with ideal performance, from the possession of market power is regularly offset and more than offset by large gains from technical development. Economists, aided by the new market theory, have fixed their attention on the loss and have overlooked the offset. In concentrating on the inefficiency of the steam engine—specifically the fact that it is not being worked to ideal capacity—they have failed to notice that the owner was designing a gas turbine.

A comparison of the oil with the bituminous coal industry usefully illustrates the point being emphasized. The oil industry is an unquestioned oligopoly; in any market area there are a few large firms and the characteristic fringe of independents. Over the years it has been under repeated attack for violation of the antitrust laws; it has rarely been free of suspicion of holding prices above the level that would be associated with more vigorous price competition. Profits have generally been excellent. Yet few would be inclined to trade the oil industry for the bituminous coal industry which, abstracting from the stabilization operations of John L. Lewis, approaches the competition of the model.

The oil industry is clearly progressive—almost as progressive, perhaps, as the uncommonly attractive brochures of its member companies unreluctantly concede. As the result of its enterprise in petroleum exploration and recovery, in developing new products, and in engineering new methods of transporting both petroleum and products, the consumer of gasoline and fuel oil has been a far more fortunate man than the consumer of coal. The continuing shift of customers from the admirably competitive coal industry to the dubiously competitive oil industry emphasizes the point.

It seems reasonable to suppose that if the same technical talent that has been devoted to the search for oil, or to its utilization, had been brought to bear on coal-mining in the last half-century, the coal industry would be very different from what it is today. New techniques of recovery might long since have been developed. Men would no longer toil like moles in mining operations that "under the most favorable conditions are hazardous and highly inefficient . . . an unpleasant, uninspiring and none too healthy occupation." [3] It is significant, by way of verifying the technical limitations of competition, that recent efforts to raise the technology of coal production have required the co-operative effort of the industry—some three hundred operators, railroads and equipment suppliers now jointly support Bituminous Research, Inc.—and that the significant work on the hydrogenation of coal has been under government sponsorship. One of the country's experienced research administrators has observed of the coal industry that "An industry with 6,000 little units has made a terribly difficult pattern on which to develop modern industrial research programs." [4]

Thus, while the incentives in the American economy do not, at any given moment, act to encourage the largest possible production at the lowest possible price, this is not the tragedy that it appears to be at first glance. The market concentration of American industry that is affirmed by the statistics and condemned by the competitive model turns out on closer examination to be favorable to technical change. To get the ideal equilibrium of price and output of the competitive model, we should almost certainly have to forego the change. Life might be simpler were we to do so, but progress, as it is called, is a wheel to which we are all bound.

In all this there is less comfort for the businessman than might appear. He must still defend himself from the charge that he is too big and that he is partially monopolistic with the reply that he

3. "Coal I: The Industrial Darkness," *Fortune*, March 1947. Quoted from *Industrial Engineering and Chemistry*, August 1946.

4. Frank A. Howard, *ibid.*, p. 87. It must be observed that the anthracite industry, the ownership of which is considerably more concentrated than bituminous mining, has not, at least until recent times, been credited with any strongly progressive tendencies. There appear, however, to have been special reasons, relating generally to character of ownership, for this.

is really competitive in the classical sense. In the words of a leading oil company, speaking recently of the Gulf Coast refining market, he must aver that in his industry the "truest, finest form of competitive pricing exists." [5] For competition, with us, is more than a technical concept. It is also a symbol of all that is good. Even though we mightn't survive under a regime of competition of classical purity we must still worship at its throne.

5. *Competition Makes Gasoline Prices* (Philadelphia: Sun Oil Company, n.d.).

The Concentration of Research and Development in Large Firms

RICHARD NELSON, MERTON PECK,
and EDWARD KALACHEK

Richard Nelson is an economist at the RAND Corporation, Merton J. Peck is Professor of Economics at Yale University, and Edward Kalachek is Associate Professor of Economics at Washington University. This essay is taken from their book, Technology, Economic Growth, and Public Policy, *published in 1967.*

JOHN KENNETH GALBRAITH articulated the view of many people when he argued

> There is no more pleasant fiction than that technical change is the product of the matchless ingenuity of the small man forced by competition to employ his wits to better his neighbor. Unhappily, it is a fiction. Technical development has long since become the preserve of the scientist and the engineer. Most of the cheap and simple inventions have to put it bluntly, been made . . . A benign Providence . . . has made the modern industry of a few large firms an almost perfect instrument for inducing technical change.[1]

The continuing presence and importance of private individuals and small firms in invention shows that Galbraith's statement is somewhat exaggerated. Nonetheless, industrial R&D spending is much more heavily concentrated in large firms than employment or sales. In 1961, firms with more than 5,000 employees accounted for about 86 percent of industrial R&D expenditures, as compared with 41 percent of manufacturing employment and 47 percent of sales.

REASONS FOR R&D PREDOMINANCE IN LARGE FIRMS

Two principal reasons for the predominance of large firms [are as follows]. First, large firms are much more likely than

1. John Kenneth Galbraith, *American Capitalism* (Boston: Houghton Mifflin Co., 1952), p. 91.

small ones to have any R&D program at all. Second, of those firms which do have R&D programs, the larger firms spend more on R&D than do the smaller ones.

Larger firms also spend more on R&D as a fraction of sales. In 1961 the giants—those employing more than 5,000 persons—spent on R&D on the average of 5.2 percent of their sales; firms in the 1,000-5,000 range averaged 2.2 percent and firms with less than 1,000 employees, 2.0 percent. However, this largely results from certain industries, particularly aircraft, electronics and chemicals, being characterized by significantly higher than average R&D intensity for all firms in the industry regardless of size, and also by high average firm size. Within an industry the tendency for R&D spending to rise more than proportionately with sales is far less marked than in the aggregate. While in most (but not all) industries the R&D to sales ratios rise as one moves from the group of firms with less than 1,000 employees to the group in the 1,000-5,000 range, there is no clear tendency for these ratios to be larger for the giants in the above 5,000 range than for the firms in the 1,000-5,000 range.[2]

Assuming firms are interested in maximizing expected profits, this suggests three broad factors behind the distribution of R&D spending by firm size. First, in most industries there would appear to be a threshold on the size of an efficient program; if firms are not large enough to support a program of minimum efficient size, their efforts are ad hoc and informal or nonexistent. Second, large firms find it profitable to spend more on R&D than smaller firms. This in part reflects the role of market size in profitability. Because they already have a large market, the absolute gains from a given percentage reduction in cost or a given percentage increase in product attractiveness are larger for large firms, or at least come quicker. More projects then will be profitable for the large firm. In addition, large companies have more internal funds and find it easier to raise funds externally (their supply curve for external financing is more elastic). Third, in a few industries, like aircraft, large-scale projects are important sources of technical progress or there are other significant economies of scale in R&D. In these industries a firm must have a large R&D

2. National Science Foundation, *Research and Development in Industry—1961* (Washington: Government Printing Office, 1964).

program, and be of sufficient size to carry it, or fail to survive.

POLICY IMPLICATIONS

The data on R&D concentration suggest to some commentators that the way to create more R&D (and hence more technical change) is to encourage the growth of large firms or at least not discourage their growth by antitrust or other actions. There is a corollary proposition: the low R&D intensity of industries such as textiles reflects the absence of large firms. Of course, the fact that large firms spend more on R&D than small firms is not sufficient to support the implied policy conclusions. The relevant question is: for a market of given size, will an industry comprised of a large number of small firms be less progressive technologically than an industry comprised of a few firms of large size, with the same aggregate sales?

The evidence suggests that if, by the wave of a magic wand, the small firms could be aggregated into units of about 1,000 employees, the result would be an increase in R&D spending.[3] However, it is unclear how much additional spending would be achieved by expansion of minimum firm size beyond the 1,000 employee level up to say, the 5,000 employee level. There would be some effect on the percentage of firms which engage in a formal R&D program. However, while in almost all industries the proportion of firms with R&D programs is greater in the 5,000 or more employee class than in the 1,000-5,000 employee class, differences here are far less within industries than in the aggregate. Beyond increasing somewhat the percentage of firms that have an R&D program, merging middle size firms in most industries would likely increase total R&D spending little if at all. As stated earlier, within any particular industry there is no systematic tendency for firms in the over 5,000 employee class to have higher R&D to sale ratios than firms in the 1,000-5,000 range.

Merging beyond the 5,000 employee level almost certainly would be pointless in most industries. The NSF data do not seg-

3. Needless to say, this is not a sufficient justification for arguing that such a policy would be desirable.

regate firms by size above the 5,000 employee mark, but Scherer has examined R&D employment to sales ratios among 352 firms on *Fortune's* 1955 list of the 500 largest firms. Grouping these firms into industry categories and excluding major defense contractors, he found that the implication is that among firms big enough to appear on *Fortune's* 1955 list, the largest firms supported inventive and innovative activity less intensively relative to their size than did small firms.[4] It is at the high end of the size distribution that antitrust and other government actions have much of their influence, and it is with respect to such giant firms that the argument about bigness and progressivity is often made. Such arguments are not borne out by the kind of evidence just cited. A further point is, whatever the immediate effect on R&D effort, creating giants might well dilute competition and reduce the number of independent decision units. This could affect innovation by limiting the chances of a new idea getting a trial, and by reducing the competitive pressures to undertake R&D.

Further, the variable of concern is R&D output, not input. Scherer reports that in most industries patents per dollar of R&D spending among the super giants is less than for the mere giants.[5] Of course the "products" are not exactly comparable and patents per dollar of R&D input is a poor measure of productivity. In industries like aircraft and missiles, the size and complexity of the products call for massive R&D projects and require giant supporting firms. But the NSF and Scherer data, and the data on sources of inventions from Jewkes, Sawers, and Stillerman, suggest that in most industries major advances often can be achieved with modest sized programs. Medium sized companies have the capability to support these programs, and many of them do.

Mansfield has examined the relative importance of the four largest firms in several industries in being the first to introduce inventions. While not invention itself, it is closely related.[6] In petroleum and coal mining, where the costs of innovation tended to be large relative to the assets of all but the giants of the industry, the largest four firms accounted for a larger share of introduc-

4. Frederic M. Scherer, "Firm Size, Market Structure, Opportunity, and the Output of Patented Inventions," *American Economic Review*, vol. 55 (December 1965).

5. *Ibid.*

6. Edwin Mansfield, "Size of Firm, Market Structure, and Innovation," *Journal of Political Economy*, vol. 71 (December 1963).

tions than their share of the market. In steel where the required investment was much less relative to the assets of smaller firms, the largest four firms accounted for a smaller share of introductions than their share of the market. Thus the question of whether it is desirable social policy to encourage the growth of giants would appear to have different answers depending on the costs of making different kinds of inventions in different industries.

Mansfield has focused on average cost of innovation in different industries, but clearly a wide range of important R&D work exists within an industry, some projects requiring larger expenditures than others. Further, costs and uncertainties differ at various stages in the evolution of an invention. Many have low costs and high risk at the initial stages, and higher costs and lower risks at later stages. The low cost-high risk exploratory work is commonly initiated by a small company or independent inventor, with the subsequent lower risk, higher cost development work taken over by a large company. For example, Whittle was able to develop a working model of his jet engine with the financial and technical resources he could obtain on his own, but he had to turn to a larger English engine company to complete the development. Mueller reports that of the twenty-five important new products and processes introduced in America by Du Pont, fifteen were based on work initially done outside Du Pont, either by independent inventors or small companies.[7] While Du Pont's technical capabilities and financial and marketing resources played a major role in bringing the invention to market, the initial conception and early R&D work often came from smaller firms. Thus, even within an industry, there is no single answer to the question of optimum firm size for invention. Rather, optimum size appears to vary according to the kind of invention and the stage of work.

Even the notion of a distribution of firm sizes does not provide an adequate description of the optimum. The turnover of firms within any given size distribution is also important; in particular the relative ease with which new (and generally small) firms can enter the industry may be more important than the statical properties of the size distribution of firms. In many industries new entrants have been a prime source of invention; they were often

7. See Willard F. Mueller, "The Origins of the Basic Inventions Underlying DuPont's Major Product and Process Innovations, 1920 to 1950," *The Rate and Direction of Inventive Activity,* Princeton, 1962.

founded by individuals for the specific purpose of carrying out inventions and innovations. Brown, in his study of new firms established in Connecticut after World War II, found a number started by inventors whose former employers were not interested in financing their inventions.[8] Thus, ease of entry serves as a check against the risk aversion tendencies of established firms.

Such new entrants may be particularly important when sharp discontinuities in technological evolution occur. At such times, the technical competence of established and new firms tends to be equalized. Old firms may be reluctant to abandon existing technology to gamble on radical inventions because of their success in an established field. The history of airframe propulsion illustrates this point. At the outset of World War II there were five major aircraft engine firms who had brought the art of gasoline propellor engines to a high state. The wartime jet engines, however, were pioneered by two outsiders, Westinghouse and General Electric, who remained major producers after the war. Likewise, rocket engines were pioneered by relative newcomers like Aerojet General, Grand Central Rocket, and Rocketdyne.[9]

These considerations and evidence suggest quite a different conclusion than the one equating large firms and technological advances. No single size firm is an optimum for conceiving and introducing all inventions of an industry. Rather, the optimum is a size distribution composed of small, medium, and large firms varying from industry to industry and from time to time. The optimum must further include a rate of turnover among firms sufficient to accommodate enough new firms to prevent excessive traditionalism.[10]

Where cost-savings from large scale operation are not too great, or when turnover is not particularly important in stimulating or permitting desirable R&D, competition probably tends to produce a distribution of firms fairly well suited to exploiting R&D opportunities. If these opportunities shift toward high cost projects

8. Gilbert Brown, "Characteristics of New Enterprises," *New England Business Review* (June 1957 and July 1957).

9. For a further discussion, see Merton J. Peck and Frederic M. Scherer, *The Weapons Acquisition Process: An Economic Analysis* (Boston: Harvard University Graduate School of Business Administration, Division of Research, 1962), chap. 7.

10. Obviously this is only one dimension to the question of desirable industry structure.

there are incentives and pressures to create more large firms through merger and expansion. The aerospace complex, the electronics and chemical industries have evolved large firms. A shift of technological opportunities towards the high risk, low cost inventions will stimulate the formation of new firms if established firms do not exploit the opportunities and if entry is not too costly.

However, major economies of scale in production or distribution or advertising may lead to an industry consisting of a few large firms, even though a more diversified size distribution and more turnover would be desirable for technological progress. In such a circumstance, even though there may be important unexploited opportunities for low cost R&D, entry into the industry may be costly and difficult. The ability to operate multiple plant units suggests that the opposite problem—economies of scale in R&D conflicting with efficiency of smaller production units—is likely to exist, at least in the long run. However, in industries where small firms are efficient in R&D and production and few large firms exist, sometimes opportunities for fruitful large-scale effort may be lost because of lack of sufficient resources. These problems—the blocking of progressive newcomers in industries with high entry costs, and an occasional important but expensive project which is too large and complex to be handled by the firms in an industry—call for public policy attention. It hardly appears that, as Galbraith suggests, the time is ripe to encourage giantism in all industries.

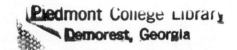

Monopoly Power, Big Business, and Technological Change

Edwin Mansfield is Professor of Economics at the Wharton School, University of Pennsylvania. This article comes from his book, Microeconomics: Theory and Applications, *published in 1970.*

ECONOMISTS LIKE Joseph Schumpeter and John Kenneth Galbraith of Harvard University [1] have argued that a perfectly competitive economy is likely to be inferior in a dynamic sense to an economy including many imperfectly competitive industries (i.e., monopolies, oligopolies, etc.). In their view, although a perfectly competitive economy will satisfy the conditions for static economic efficiency, it will not result in as high a rate of technological change and productivity increase as an imperfectly competitive economy. . . . Why [should we] expect the rate of technological change and productivity increase to be higher in an imperfectly competitive economy? This is a question that has been debated at great length. On the one hand, some economists, like Schumpeter and Galbraith, believe that there are a number of good reasons why the rate of technological change and productivity increase will be higher in an imperfectly competitive economy. On the other hand, other economists stick with the view of John Stuart Mill and J. B. Clark that this is not the case.[2]

Members of the Schumpeter-Galbraith group argue that firms under perfect competition have less resources to devote to research and experimentation than do firms under imperfect competition. Because profits are at a relatively low level, it is difficult

1. J. Schumpeter, *Capitalism, Socialism, and Democracy,* New York: Harper & Row, 1947; J. K. Galbraith, *American Capitalism,* Boston: Houghton Mifflin, 1952; and H. Villard, "Competition, Oligopoly, and Research," *Journal of Political Economy,* Dec. 1958.
2. J. S. Mill, *Principles of Political Economy,* London, 1852, Book IV, Ch. VII, p. 351; and J. B. Clark, *Essentials of Economic Theory,* New York, 1907, p. 374.

for firms under perfect competition to support large expenditures on research and development. Moreover, it is argued that, unless a firm has sufficient control over the market to reap the rewards of an innovation, the introduction of the innovation may not be worthwhile. If competitors can imitate the innovation very quickly, the innovator may be unable to make any money from the innovation.

Defenders of perfect competition retort that there is likely to be less pressure for firms in imperfect markets to introduce new techniques and products, since such firms have fewer competitors. Moreover, such firms are better able to drive out entrants who, uncommitted to present techniques, are likely to be relatively quick to adopt new ones. (Entrants, unlike established producers, have no vested interest in maintaining the demand for existing products and the profitability of existing equipment.) Also, there are advantages in having a large number of independent decision-making units, there being less chance that an important technological advance will be blocked by the faulty judgment of a few men.

It is difficult to obtain evidence to help settle this question, if it is posed in this way, since perfect competition is, of course, a hypothetical construct that does not exist in the real world. However, it does seem unlikely that a perfectly competitive industry (if such an industry could be constructed) would be able in many areas of the economy to carry out the research and development required to promote a high rate of technological change.[3] Moreover, if entry is free and rapid, firms in a perfectly competitive industry will have little motivation to innovate. Although the evidence is not at all clear-cut, this much can probably be granted the Schumpeter-Galbraith group.[4]

It is one thing to grant that a certain amount of market imperfection may promote the rate of technological change, and another thing to say, as does Galbraith, that the "modern industry

3. Even if supplier firms emerge that specialize in research and development, the members of the competitive industry must still carry out some technical work to be able to accept new technology rapidly. Moreover, there may have to be imperfect competition in the supplying industry if it is to be viable.

4. Also, technological change may result in a certain amount of market imperfection, although the extent of the market imperfection is likely to vary greatly from case to case.

of a few large firms [is] an almost perfect instrument for inducing technical change." [5] If true, this is an extremely important point. But is it true? Does the evidence indicate that an industry dominated by a few giant firms is generally more progressive than one composed of a larger number of smaller firms?

To prevent confusion, it is advisable to distinguish among several related issues. First, what is the effect of an industry's market structure on the amount it spends on research and development? Suppose that, for a market of given size, we could replace the largest firms by a larger number of somewhat smaller firms—and thus decrease concentration. If the largest firms in this industry were giants like Standard Oil of New Jersey or U. S. Steel, the available evidence, which is extremely tentative, does not suggest that total research and development expenditures are likely to decrease considerably. On the contrary, there is usually no tendency for the ratio of research and development expenditures to sales to be higher among the giants then among their somewhat smaller competitors. However, if the largest firms in the industry were considerably smaller than this or if concentration were reduced greatly, one might expect a decrease in research and development expenditures, because the size of the firm often must exceed a certain minimum for research to be profitable.

Second, to what extent would such a change in market structure be harmful because of economies of scale in research and development? Obviously, the answer to this question varies with the type of research or development being considered. In research, the optimal size of group may be fairly small in many areas; for example, the transistor, the maser, the laser, and radio command guidance were conceived by an individual or groups of not more than a dozen persons. In development, the optimal size of effort tends to be larger, particularly in the aircraft and missile industries, where tremendous sums are spent on individual projects.[6] However, in most industries, the limited data that are

5. J. K. Galbraith, *American Capitalism,* Boston: Houghton Mifflin, 1952, p. 91.
6. Development costs are sometimes very high in other industries, too. For example, du Pont spent $25 million to develop Corfam, and $50 million for Delrin. See J. Jewkes, R. Sawers, and R. Stillerman, *The Sources of Invention,* revised edition, Norton, 1970. This book also presents considerable evidence concerning the importance of independent inventors as sources of inventions. This is an important point.

available do not seem to indicate that only the largest firms can support effective research and development programs; there is generally no indication that the largest programs have any marked advantage over somewhat smaller ones.

Third, is there any evidence that research and development programs of given scale are carried out more productively in large firms than in small ones? The data are extremely limited, but they seem to indicate that, in most industries for which we have information, the answer is no. In most of these industries, when the size of research and development expenditures is held constant, increases in the size of the firm are associated with decreases in inventive output. The reasons for this are by no means obvious. Some observers claim that it is because the average capabilities of technical people are higher in the smaller firms, research and development people in smaller firms are more cost-conscious than those in larger firms, and the problems of communication and coordination tend to be less acute in smaller firms.

Fourth, what is the effect of an industry's market structure on how rapidly new processes and products, both those developed by the industry and those developed by others, are introduced commercially? The answer seems to depend heavily on the types of innovations that happen to occur. If they require very large amounts of capital, it appears that the substitution of fewer large firms for more smaller ones may lead to more rapid introduction; if they require small amounts of capital, this may not be the case. Another important factor is the ease with which new firms can enter the industry. If increased concentration results in increased barriers to entry, it may also result in slower application of new techniques, since innovations often are made by new firms. Indeed, many new firms are started for the specific purpose of carrying out innovations.

Fifth, what is the effect of an industry's market structure on how rapidly innovations, once introduced, spread through an industry? The fact that large firms often are quicker, on the average, than small firms to use a new technique does not imply that increased concentration results in a faster rate of diffusion. On the contrary, the very small amount of evidence bearing on this question seems to suggest that greater concentration in an industry may be associated with a slower rate of diffusion.

Contrary to the allegations of Galbraith, Schumpeter, and

others, there is little evidence that industrial giants are needed in all or even most industries to insure rapid technological change and rapid utilization of new techniques. Moreover, there is no statistically significant relationship between the extent of concentration in an industry and the industry's rate of technological change. Of course, this does not mean that industries composed only of small firms would necessarily be optimal for the promotion and diffusion of new techniques. On the contrary, there seem to be considerable advantages in a diversity of firm sizes, no single firm size being optimal in this respect. Moreover, the optimal average size is likely to be directly related to the costliness and scope of the inventions that arise. However, in general, these factors do not make giantism necessary. To repeat, there is little evidence that industrial giants are needed in all or even most industries to promote rapid technological change and rapid utilization of new techniques.

Monopoly and the Social Responsibility of Business and Labor

Milton Friedman is Professor of Economics at the University of Chicago. This article is taken from his book Capitalism and Freedom, *published in 1963.*

COMPETITION HAS two very different meanings. In ordinary discourse, competition means personal rivalry, with one individual seeking to outdo his known competitor, In the economic world, competition means almost the opposite. There is no personal rivalry in the competitive market place. There is no personal higgling. The wheat farmer in a free market does not feel himself in personal rivalry with, or threatened by, his neighbor, who is, in fact, his competitor. The essence of a competitive market is its impersonal character. No one participant can determine the terms on which other participants shall have access to goods or jobs. All take prices as given by the market and no individual can by himself have more than a negligible influence on price though all participants together determine price by the combined effect of their separate actions.

Monopoly exists when a specific individual or enterprise has sufficient control over a particular product or service to determine significantly the terms on which other individuals shall have access to it. In some ways, monopoly comes closer to the ordinary concept of competition since it does involve personal rivalry.

Monopoly raises two classes of problems for a free society. First, the existence of monopoly means a limitation on voluntary exchange through a reduction in the alternatives available to individuals. Second, the existence of monopoly raises the issue of the "social responsibility," as it has come to be called, of the monopolist. The participant in a competitive market has no appreciable power to alter terms of exchange; he is hardly visible as a separate entity; hence it is hard to argue that he has any "social responsibility" except that which is shared by all citizens to obey the law of the land and to live according to his lights. The monopolist is visible and has power. It is easy to argue that he should discharge his power not solely to further his own interests but to further socially desirable ends. Yet the widespread application of such a doctrine would destroy a free society.

Of course, competition is an ideal type, like a Euclidean line or point. No one has ever seen a Euclidean line—which has zero width and depth—yet we all find it useful to regard many a Euclidean volume—such as a surveyor's string—as a Euclidean line. Similarly, there is no such thing as "pure" competition. Every producer has some effect, however tiny, on the price of the product he produces. The important issue for understanding and for policy is whether this effect is significant or can properly be neglected, as the surveyor can neglect the thickness of what he calls a "line." The answer must, of course, depend on the problem. But as I have studied economic activities in the United States, I have become increasingly impressed with how wide is the range of problems and industries for which it is appropriate to treat the economy as if it were competitive.

The issues raised by monopoly are technical and cover a field in which I have no special competence. In consequence, this essay is limited to a fairly cursory survey of some of the broader issues: the extent of monopoly, sources of monopoly, appropriate government policy, and the social responsibility of business and labor.

THE EXTENT OF MONOPOLY IN INDUSTRY

The most important fact about enterprise monopoly is its relative unimportance from the point of view of the economy as a whole. There are some four million separate operating enterprises in the United States; some four hundred thousand new ones are born each year; a somewhat smaller number die each year. Nearly one-fifth of the working population is self-employed. In almost any industry that one can mention, there are giants and pygmies side by side.

Beyond these general impressions, it is difficult to cite a satisfactory objective measure of the extent of monopoly and of competition. The main reason is one already noted: these concepts as used in economic theory are ideal constructs designed to analyze particular problems rather than to describe existing situations. As a result, there can be no clear-cut determination of whether a particular enterprise or industry is to be regarded as monopolistic or as competitive. The difficulty of assigning precise meanings to such terms leads to much misunderstanding. The same word is used to refer to different things, depending on the background of experience in terms of which the state of competition is judged. Perhaps the most striking example is the extent to which an American student will describe as monopolistic, arrangements that a European would regard as highly competitive. As a result, Europeans interpreting American literature and discussion in terms of the meaning attached to the terms competition and monopoly in Europe tend to believe that there is a much greater degree of monopoly in the United States than in fact exists.

A number of studies, particularly by G. Warren Nutter and George J. Stigler, have tried to classify industries as monopolistic, workably competitive, and governmentally operated or supervised, and to trace changes over time in these categories.[1] They conclude that, as of 1939, roughly one quarter of the economy could be regarded as governmentally operated or supervised. Of the three-quarters remaining, at most one-quarter and perhaps as little as 15 per cent can be regarded as monopolistic, at least three-quarters and perhaps as much as 85 per cent, as competitive. The governmentally operated or supervised sector has of course grown greatly over the past half-century or so. Within the private sector, on the other hand, there appears not to have been any tendency for the scope of monopoly to have increased and it may well have decreased.

There is, I suspect, a widespread impression that monopoly is both far more important than these estimates suggest and has been growing steadily over time. One reason for this mistaken

1. G. Warren Nutter, *The Extent of Enterprise Monopoly in the United States, 1899–1939* (Chicago: University of Chicago Press, 1951) and George J. Stigler, *Five Lectures on Economic Problems* (London; Longmans, Green and Co., 1949), pp. 46–65.

impression is the tendency to confuse absolute and relative size. As the economy has grown, enterprises have become larger in absolute size. This has been taken to mean also that they account for a larger fraction of the market, whereas the market may have grown even faster. A second reason is that monopoly is more newsworthy and leads to more attention than competition. If individuals were asked to list the major industries in the United States, almost all would include automobile production, few would include wholesale trade. Yet wholesale trade is twice as important as automobile production. Wholesale trade is highly competitive, hence draws little attention to itself. Few people could name any leading enterprises in wholesale trade, though there are some that are very large in absolute size. Automobile production, while in certain respects highly competitive, has many fewer firms and is certainly closer to monopoly. Everyone can name the leading firms producing automobiles. To cite one other striking example: domestic service is a vastly more important industry than the telegraph and telephone industry. A third reason is the general bias and tendency to overemphasize the importance of the big versus the small, of which the preceding point is only a particular manifestation. Finally, the main characteristic of our society is taken to be its industrial character. This leads to overemphasis on the manufacturing sector of the economy, which accounts for only about one-quarter of output or employment. And monopoly is far more prevalent in manufacturing than in other sectors of the economy.

The over-estimation of the importance of monopoly is accompanied, for much the same reasons, by an over-estimation of the importance of those technological changes that promote monopoly by comparison with those that extend competition. For example, the spread of mass production has been greatly stressed. The developments in transportation and communication that have promoted competition by reducing the importance of local regional markets and widening the scope within which competition could take place have been given much less attention. The growing concentration of the automobile industry is a commonplace; growth of the trucking industry which reduces dependence on large railroads passes with little notice; so does the declining concentration in the steel industry. . . .

THE SOURCES OF MONOPOLY

There are three major sources of monopoly: "technical" considerations, direct and indirect governmental assistance, and private collusion.

1. *Technical Considerations* · Monopoly arises to some extent because technical considerations make it more efficient or economical to have a single enterprise rather than many. The most obvious example is a telephone system, water system, and the like in an individual community. There is unfortunately no good solution for technical monopoly. There is only a choice among three evils: private unregulated monopoly, private monopoly regulated by the state, and government operation.

It seems impossible to state as a general proposition that one of these evils is uniformly preferable to another. The great disadvantage of either governmental regulation or governmental operation of monopoly is that it is exceedingly difficult to reverse. In consequence, I am inclined to urge that the least of the evils is private unregulated monopoly wherever this is tolerable. Dynamic changes are highly likely to undermine it and there is at least some chance that these will be allowed to have their effect. And even in the short run, there is generally a wider range of substitutes than there seems to be at first blush, so private enterprises are fairly narrowly limited in the extent to which it is profitable to keep prices above cost. Moreover, as we have seen, the regulatory agencies often tend themselves to fall under the control of the producers and so prices may not be any lower with regulation than without regulation.

Fortunately, the areas in which technical considerations make monopoly a likely or a probable outcome are fairly limited. They would offer no serious threat to the preservation of a free economy if it were not for the tendency of regulation, introduced on this ground, to spread to situations in which it is not so justified.

2. *Direct and Indirect Government Assistance* · Probably the most important source of monopoly power has been government assistance, direct and indirect. Numerous examples of reasonably direct government assistance have been cited above. The indi-

rect assistance to monopoly consists of measures taken for other purposes which have as a largely unintended effect the imposition of limitations on potential competitors of existing firms. Perhaps the three clearest examples are tariffs, tax legislation, and law enforcement and legislation with respect to labor disputes.

Tariffs have of course been imposed largely to "protect" domestic industries, which means to impose handicaps on potential competitors. They always interfere with the freedom of individuals to engage in voluntary exchange. After all, the liberal takes the individual, not the nation or citizen of a particular nation, as his unit. Hence he regards it just as much a violation of freedom if citizens of the United States and Switzerland are prevented from consummating an exchange that would be mutually advantageous as if two citizens of the United States are prevented from doing so. Tariffs need not produce monopoly. If the market for the protected industry is sufficiently large and technical conditions permit many firms, there can be effective competition domestically in the protected industry, as in the United States in textiles. Clearly, however, tariffs do foster monopoly. It is far easier for a few firms than for many to collude to fix prices, and it is generally easier for enterprises in the same country to collude than for enterprises in different countries. Britain was protected by free trade from widespread monopoly during the nineteenth and early twentieth centuries, despite the relatively small size of her domestic market and the large scale of many firms. Monopoly has become a much more serious problem in Britain since free trade was abandoned, first after World War I and then more extensively in the early 1930's.

The effects of tax legislation have been even more indirect yet not less important. A major element has been the linkage of the corporate and individual income tax combined with the special treatment of capital gains under the individual income tax. Let us suppose a corporation earns an income of $1 million over and above corporate taxes. If it pays the whole million dollars to its stockholders as dividends, they must include it as part of their taxable income. Suppose they would, on the average, have to pay 50 per cent of this additional income as income tax. They would then have available only $500,000 to spend on consumption or to save and invest. If instead the corporation pays no cash dividends to its stockholders, it has the whole million dollars to invest internally. Such reinvestment will tend to raise the capital value of its stock. Stockholders who would have saved the funds if distributed can simply hold the stock and postpone all taxes until they sell the stock. They, as well as others who sell at an earlier date to realize income for consumption, will pay tax at capital gains rates, which are lower than rates on regular income.

This tax structure encourages retention of corporate earnings. Even if the return that can be earned internally is appreciably less than the return that the stockholder himself could earn by investing the funds externally, it may pay to invest internally because of the tax saving. This leads to a waste of capital, to its use for less productive rather than more productive purposes. It has been a major reason for the post-World-War-II tendency toward horizontal diversification as firms have sought outlets for their earnings. It is also a great source of strength for established corporations relative to new enterprises. The established corporations can be less productive than new enterprises, yet their stockholders have an incentive to invest in them rather than to have the income paid out so that they can invest it in new enterprises through the capital market.

A major source of labor monopoly has been government assistance. Licensure provisions, building codes, and the like, have been one source. Legislation granting special immunities to labor unions, such as exemption from the antitrust laws, restrictions on union responsibility, the right to appear before special tribunals, and so on, are a second source. Perhaps of equal or greater importance than either is a general climate of opinion and law enforcement applying different standards to actions taken in the course of a labor dispute than to the same actions under other circumstances. If men turn cars over, or destroy property, out of sheer wickedness or in the course of exacting private vengeance, not a hand will be lifted to protect them from the legal consequences. If they commit the same acts in the course of labor dispute, they may well get off scot free. Union actions involving actual or potential physical violence or coercion could hardly take place if it were not for the unspoken acquiescence of the authorities.

3. Private Collusion · The final source of monopoly is private collusion. As Adam Smith says, "People of the same trade seldom meet together, even for merriment and diversion, but the conversation ends in a conspiracy against the public, or in some contrivance to raise prices." [2] Such collusion or private cartel arrangements are therefore constantly arising. However, they are generally unstable and of brief duration unless they can call government to their assistance. The establishment of the cartel, by raising prices, makes it more profitable for outsiders to enter the industry. Moreover, since the higher price can be established only by the participants' restricting their output below the level that they would like to produce at the fixed price, there is an incentive for each one separately to undercut the price in order to expand output. Each one, of course, hopes that the others will abide by the agreement. It takes only one or at most a few "chiselers"—who are indeed public benefactors—to break the cartel. In the absence of government assistance in enforcing the cartel, they are almost sure to succeed fairly promptly.

The major role of our antitrust laws has been to inhibit such private collusion. Their main contribution in this respect has been less through actual prosecutions than by their indirect effects. They have ruled out the obvious collusive devices—such as the public get-together for this specific purpose—and have therefore made collusion more expensive. More important, they have reaffirmed common law doctrine that combinations in restraint of trade are unenforceable in the courts. In various European countries, the courts will enforce an agreement entered into by a group of enterprises to sell only through a joint selling agency, committing the enterprises to pay specified penalties if they violate the agreement. In the United States, such an agreement would not be enforceable in the courts. This difference is one of the major reasons why cartels have been more stable and widespread in European countries than in the United States.

APPROPRIATE GOVERNMENT POLICY

The first and most urgent necessity in the area of government policy is the elimination of those measures which directly support

2. *The Wealth of Nations* (1776), Bk. I, chap. x, Pt. II (Cannan ed. London, 1930). p. 130.

monopoly, whether enterprise monopoly or labor monopoly, and an even-handed enforcement of the laws on enterprises and labor unions alike. Both should be subjected to the antitrust laws; both should be treated alike with respect to laws about the destruction of property and about interference with private activities.

Beyond this, the most important and effective step toward the reduction of monopoly power would be an extensive reform of the tax laws. The corporate tax should be abolished. Whether this is done or not, corporations should be required to attribute to individual stockholders earnings which are not paid out as dividends. That is, when the corporation sends out a dividend check, it should also send a statement saying, "In addition to this dividend of ——— cents per share, your corporation also earned ——— cents per share which was reinvested." The individual stockholder should then be required to report the attributed but undistributed earnings on his tax return as well as the dividend. Corporations would still be free to plough back as much as they wish, but they would have no incentive to do so except the proper incentive that they could earn more internally than the stockholder could earn externally. Few measures would do more to invigorate capital markets, to stimulate enterprise, and to promote effective competition.

Of course, so long as the individual income tax is as highly graduated as it is now, there is strong pressure to find devices to evade its impact. In this way as well as directly, the highly graduated income tax constitutes a serious impediment to the efficient use of our resources. The appropriate solution is the drastic scaling down of the higher rates, combined with an elimination of the avoidance devices that have been incorporated in the law.

SOCIAL RESPONSIBILITY OF BUSINESS AND LABOR

The view has been gaining widespread acceptance that corporate officials and labor leaders have a "social responsibility" that goes beyond serving the interest of their stockholders or their members. This view shows a fundamental misconception of the character and nature of a free economy. In such an economy, there is one and only one social responsibility of business—to use its resources and engage in activities designed to increase its profits so long as it stays within the rules of the game, which is to say, engages in open and free competition, without deception or fraud. Similarly, the "social responsibility" of labor leaders is to serve the interests of the members of their unions. It is the responsibility of the rest of us to establish a framework of law such that an individual in pursuing his own interest is, to quote Adam Smith again, "led by an invisible hand to promote an end which was no part of his intention. Nor is it always the worse for the society that it was no part of it. By pursuing his own interest, he frequently promotes that of the society more effectually than when he really intends to promote it. I have never known much good done by those who affected to trade for the public good." [3]

Few trends could so thoroughly undermine the very foundations of our free society as the acceptance by corporate officials of a social responsibility other than to make as much money for their stockholders as possible. This is a fundamentally subversive doctrine. If businessmen do have a social responsibility other than making maximum profits for stockholders, how are they to know what it is? Can self-selected private individuals decide what the social interest is? Can they decide how great a burden they are justified in placing on themselves or their stockholders to serve that social interest? Is it tolerable that these public functions of taxation, expenditure, and control be exercised by the people who happen at the moment to be in charge of particular enterprises, chosen for those posts by strictly private groups? If businessmen are civil servants rather than the employees of their stockholders then in a democracy they will, sooner or later, be chosen by the public techniques of election and appointment.

And long before this occurs, their decision-making power will have been taken away from them. A dramatic illustration was the cancellation of a steel price increase by U.S. Steel in April 1962 through the medium of a public display of anger by President Kennedy and threats of reprisals on levels ranging from antitrust suits to examination of the tax reports of steel executives. This was a striking episode because of the public display of the vast powers concentrated in Washington. We were all made aware of how much of the power needed for a police state was already available. It illustrates the present point as well. If the price of steel is a public decision, as the doctrine of

3. *Ibid.*, Bk. IV, chapter ii, p. 421.

social responsibility declares, then it cannot be permitted to be made privately.

The particular aspect of the doctrine which this example illustrates, and which has been most prominent recently, is an alleged social responsibility of business and labor to keep prices and wage rates down in order to avoid price inflation. Suppose that at a time when there was upward pressure on prices— ultimately of course reflecting an increase in the stock of money —every businessman and labor leader were to accept this responsibility and suppose all could succeed in keeping any price from rising, so we had voluntary price and wage control without open inflation. What would be the result? Clearly product shortages, labor shortages, gray markets, black markets. If prices are not allowed to ration goods and workers, there must be some other means to do so. Can the alternative rationing schemes be private? Perhaps for a time in a small and unimportant area. But if the goods involved are many and important, there will necessarily be pressure, and probably irresistible pressure, for governmental rationing of goods, a governmental wage policy, and governmental measures for allocating and distributing labor.

Price control, whether legal or voluntary, if effectively enforced would eventually lead to the destruction of the free-enterprise system and its replacement by a centrally controlled system. And it would not even be effective in preventing inflation. History offers ample evidence that what determines the average level of prices and wages is the amount of money in the economy and not the greediness of businessmen or of workers. Governments ask for the self-restraint of business and labor because of their inability to manage their own affairs—which includes the control of money—and the natural human tendency to pass the buck.

One topic in the area of social responsibility that I feel duty-bound to touch on, because it affects my own personal interests, has been the claim that business should contribute to the support of charitable activities and especially to universities. Such giving by corporations is an inappropriate use of corporate funds in a free-enterprise society.

The corporation is an instrument of the stockholders who own it. If the corporation makes a contribution, it prevents the individual stockholder from himself deciding how he should dispose of his funds. With the corporation tax and the deductibility of contributions, stockholders may of course want the corporation to make a gift on their behalf, since this would enable them to make a larger gift. The best solution would be the abolition of the corporate tax. But so long as there is a corporate tax, there is no justification for permitting deductions for contributions to charitable and educational institutions. Such contributions should be made by the individuals who are the ultimate owners of property in our society.

People who urge extension of the deductibility of this kind of corporate contribution in the name of free enterprise are fundamentally working against their own interest. A major complaint made frequently against modern business is that it involves the separation of ownership and control—that the corporation has become a social institution that is a law unto itself, with irresponsible executives who do not serve the interests of their stockholders. This charge is not true. But the direction in which policy is now moving, of permitting corporations to make contributions for charitable purposes and allowing deductions for income tax, is a step in the direction of creating a true divorce between ownership and control and of undermining the basic nature and character of our society. It is a step away from an individualistic society and toward the corporate state.

The Social Responsibility of Business and Environmental Pollution

FORTUNE

This article appeared in the December 1970 issue of Fortune *magazine. It is an interesting contrast to the point of view expressed in the previous article by Milton Friedman.*

THE CHIEF EXECUTIVE of an automobile company, talking recently in his Detroit office about the prospect of having to redesign his product around antipollution devices, repeated the question a visitor had asked: "Why wasn't all this anticipated?" After a few moments' reflection, he said, "Issues don't get dealt with until they become issues."

A few miles away, on the shore of Lake St. Clair, the owner president of one of the country's largest marinas sat in his office and brooded over the empty pleasure boats rolling in their wells and the deserted expanse of water damned for its mercury-poisoned fish. "Michigan is a resort state," he said, "and what we sell is enchantment. Business is way off, and a lot of operators of all kinds around the lake are hurting. I'm going to survive, but a lot of people aren't. Now we are trying to do something about it politically and perhaps legally, but why, you ask, didn't we do something before to prevent this from happening? I don't know. What could we have done? Who's used to coping with problems like this?"

Many top executives in U. S. business could well ask that question today. They are suddenly meeting a whole array of social issues—pollution, racial discrimination, consumerism, and the like—that seriously and directly affect their corporate operations. Expectations of the future of the automobile market, for example, will be drastically affected by government decisions regulating engine exhaust emissions. In many other industries the resolution of specific problems of controlling pollution in production threatens to rearrange patterns of competition and payoff. Planning is contingent upon such potential effects. The intertwined state of markets and society is not a new phenomenon, but this may be the first time in U. S. business history that so much *conscious* thought has been given to reconciling what happens in markets with what is happening in society.

WHY THEY'RE SPEAKING A NEW LANGUAGE

Not only are the rules changing, giving rise to new business games with unpredictable consequences, but so also are the customs—the commonly accepted standards—of U. S. society, which are normally adopted by business without question. Until quite recently no public opprobrium attached to dumping waste chemicals into rivers, or refusing to hire uneducated blacks. As long as the old customs prevailed, businessmen never had to speak the language of corporate "social responsibility." But with social standards changing, they are forced to remember an old but muted truth: although the corporation in its markets pursues hard economic goals headed by profit, it lives and breathes in society and is shaped to some extent by law and custom.

The law, representing the formal injunction of the collective society, gives business its man-made rules, but a society governed only by explicit rules would be overburdened by rigorous procedures. Hence the importance of customs. Social standards—convention, tradition, mores, habits, norms—do not always have quite the force of law, but when they are stable over long periods, they offer broad and flexible "solutions" to social-economic problems, that is, ways of identifying, understanding, and meeting issues without formal rules or consciously detailed decisions. That some standards are clearly unfair to somebody does not alter this fact. It is difficult to survive in markets without having a feel for the subtle relationships of law, custom, and hard economics.

Standard modes of economic thought do not deal adequately with this interrelationship. For this reason they are not able to cope well with the issues that are troubling executives today. The standard classical ideal of a market postulates a society of individuals, each pursuing his own interests. Large numbers of small decentralized economic units—both buyers and sellers—are governed by an impersonal price mechanism that automatically regulates supply and demand, and so efficiently clears the market of its goods. As a theory, this model market has been admired for its elegance and great generality. It has served as a basic analytic tool for professional economists and perhaps always will; no other theory can safely go altogether against it.

WHAT NADER CHANGED

In real life, there is a reasonable approximation of the standard market in the clothing industry, the stock market, banking, hotels, and numerous other service industries, and a lot of detailed everyday transactions. But the standard concept does not help much in understanding markets with small numbers of either buyers or sellers, nor how markets got bent and molded into the multifarious forms of unions, trade associations, "fair trade," the presence of the government as a gargantuan buyer, and the labyrinthine alterations represented by taxes, subsidies, tariffs, and quotas.

Consumers typically have adhered to the individual, passive, decentralized conduct prescribed for all participants in the standard market. The great body of legislation put on the books in their behalf has been prompted largely by the sensitivity of professional politicians to unorganized consumer interests. Now the movement called "consumerism" promises to change that traditional situation. If it succeeds in its aims, it will have an impact analogous to the establishment of organized labor as a major institutional force in both markets and politics.

The consumer advocate, Ralph Nader—following intuition rather than theory—has become an ex officio national figure whom politicians and businessmen have had to reckon with ever since, single-handed, he brought down the market for the Corvair. It is not clear just where the movement he represents is going, but its early, unprecedented effectiveness seems to stem from the increasing dissemination of information through mass communication. It appears to be seeking to invent novel forms of consumer coalition power, as in the proposed federal consumer "class action" law, which would bring fleeting forms of concerted action to bear upon particular cases. From the strict point of view of the standard market this sort of thing is an exasperating aberration. Least of all does the ideal standard market offer an understanding of how the whole social environment influences real markets.

THE SEARCH FOR STABLE STANDARDS

Milton Friedman, the leading fundamentalist of classical economic thought today, has accused those corporate executives who talk about "social responsibilities" of something akin to fraud and subversion of free enterprise. He maintains that since executives are fiduciaries enjoined to make money, they are misappropriating the shareholders' investments and usurping the functions of politics and government if they choose to get involved with pollution control and urban problems. Friedman does acknowledge that, in seeking to maximize their profits, businessmen must abide by law and "ethical custom," but he does not seem to see the new issues that have arisen in this area.

By and large, the men who run the nation's major corporations do see these issues. In the preparation of this article, *Fortune* interviewed thirty-one top executives, mostly chiefs, of corporations whose 1970 sales will aggregate about $100 billion. They were encouraged to talk frankly, on a not-for-attribution basis, so that they would reveal their real feelings. Their remarks reflect a deep concern about how to fulfill social responsibilities. They observe a weakening of a number of old customs and the emergence of new ones. They find no settled custom today that says they may pollute or discriminate to the extent permitted by present law. Wherever they find social standards in flux, they are unable to adopt a standard unthinkingly and still look forward to a profitable future. They regard it as their fiduciary duty to try to cope with the instability of standards where they find evidence of it. Many of them have called this search for a stable standard of behavior "social responsibility."

The classical concept of the market will not aid them in their quest. For, in dealing with social pressures, they will have to solve problems in ways that are not governable by the market alone. The awkward thing about the standard mode of economic thought has always been that it is forced to contend with a vast region of exceptions—kinds of behavior that are not in fact controlled by an impersonal market mechanism. These have come to be regarded as "market failures." Market failures do not represent either a fall into chaos or a movement toward socialism, but only a recognition of the tangible realities of a relatively free exchange economy in a diverse society.

Market failures appear to have had many different origins. At some earlier time a judgment of value may have been made which indicated that, for certain kinds of activities, the alternative of a non-market was more economic than a market. Some have become so institutionalized that they now appear to be part of the natural order of things. No one would think, for example, of "marketing" the light from a lighthouse. How could the lighthouse keeper collect fees from passing ships—or exclude non-paying ships from using the light? And if he could, would the costs of the transaction be worth it? Presumably by some such reasoning, lighthouses were made a "public good." The presumption about all public goods, debatable as it might be in a particular instance, is that it is preferable to keep them out of a market because that course seemed to represent a better payoff to society. Air, water, public land and forests, dams, streets, police, schools, and libraries represent goods that were consciously plucked or unconsciously kept out of putative markets. Some of them are known to have had a pre-existence as markets. The roads of ancient Rome, for example, were public goods. In the decline and fall of the empire, private turnpikes came into being and remained until the nineteenth century, when their owners went broke.

The standard market may also fail even when an actual market exists, owing to manipulations of the rules. Getting the rules changed through law is a political act—a game on another level. Some of these manipulations may originate from the demands of society at large, but more striking is the phenomenon that occurs because participants in markets—notably major corporations—are not always satisfied with the results of a free market. The oil industry, for example, prefers production controls, quotas, and subsidies to a free market in oil; it lobbies for the view that the "failure" of this market is in the public interest as well as their own. Oil companies are unique only in the standout success they have had in inducing a failure of the standard market for nearly a half century. Although most of these manipulations of the rules have been secured by appeal to some public principle

—national security, the balance of trade, education—they have been sought and welcomed not only by oilmen but also by textile manufacturers, publishers, farmers—indeed by almost everyone in business. Much of the money redirected by these manipulations eventually flows through the economy, but there is a marked effect on the allocation of the benefits.

One might wonder how markets have survived all that interference. But even a market manipulated by changes in rules is still a market with a large base in hard economics. The standard market conforms with real life when the numbers of actors are quite large on both the buying and selling sides; they are unable to form groups, and the limits of bargaining and negotiating become quite small. No one has much choice but to take the price as given by the market. But as the number of actors becomes relatively small, the freedom to interact grows greater. This situation prevails in many manufacturing industries, in part because of the rewards of scale or the thinness of markets. Each party knows that what he does will influence what the others do, and that knowledge in turn influences his own action. Each can make a choice among alternative kinds of interaction with others. Many of the strategies of the marketplace consist of competitive interactions whereby each party, though taking account of move and countermove, acts against the other parties. But rules permitting—in the U. S. this means whenever antitrust rules don't interfere—all parties may interact cooperatively.

THE COST OF NEGATIVE PRODUCTS

Of all the large social issues pressing on business today the most novel bears upon the changing social standards concerning the environment. The issue looms large not only because industry has produced an increasing amount of undesirable goods (i.e., pollutants) along with the increasing amount of desirable ones, but also because the basic U. S. philosophy of economic growth is no longer accepted without qualification.

The problem that industry and society face is how to distribute the costs of these negative products, since the market fails to do it. The old norm allocating the cost of pollution to society at large was so well established that no one even tried to compute the social cost. Each producer had to keep polluting or suffer a competitive disadvantage.

A measure of the strength of a social standard is whether laws that conflict with it are enforced. By that measure the old standard scored very high—until recently, the 1899 federal law against water pollution was as ineffective as prohibition. The confused reaction to present changes in environmental standards ranges from the negative extreme—ignore it—all the way to a pastoral dream of a natural earth. But businessmen sense that something very real is happening and they are viewing it as a serious operational issue.

Although most chief executives take for granted that the consumer will pay for pollution control in the end, they also recognize that that doesn't say much about what is happening or may happen to them in business as a result of the solutions adopted or in prospect. The chief of a leading forest-products company described a common view of some of the internal complexities of the problem: "We want to clean up air and water, but we don't want to be at a competitive disadvantage. Suppose you've already put money into pollution control while others in the industry haven't, and along comes a proposal for a new state standard. I might be better off with a higher one, because it would put my competitor at a disadvantage. But everybody knows the public is going to force it, and big polluters know that they're going to have to do something about the problem, that it's only a question of timing. I think much of this will have to be settled by federal law. You've got to go outside of industry to do it fairly."

This tendency of executives to try to resolve pollution problems at the political level reveals the difficulties that follow the breakdown of a broad social norm. Society appears no longer to want industry to allocate the social costs of production to society at large. Not being a player in this game at the economic level, society can only seek political solutions. That means a rule change—a new game. Business, too, is going the political route to obtain some influence over what the new game is to be.

This may be the only option it has left. But other solutions, developed by a new generation of game theorists, are also possible. One of these (called "the core") emphasizes cooperative hard economics. Its line of thought can be illustrated by the situation on Lake St. Clair, Michigan, which was mentioned at the beginning of this article. Pollution by business on the lake is interfering with business; several hundred fishing and resort enterprises have been damaged, most seriously by mercury from one big industrial polluter. The lake was also being polluted by the victims themselves, who included thousands of pleasure-boat owners. The market failed to offer a solution, and there was no new standard of behavior to rely on. Now that the damage is done, the victims are seeking relief at government levels.

A COALITION FOR CLEAN WATER

As in most pollution situations, no effort by any one individual would avail. Voluntary cooperative economic action to control the pollution at its sources was not actually considered. But such an approach might have given the victims a way of getting a clean lake even in the absence of a social standard and without having to resort to politics. Cooperative action would involve trying to find the economic basis of a lake coalition. For the effort to work, the advantages to each member would have to be commensurate with the cost to each. This could happen if the loss each suffered as a result of lake pollution were greater than what each would have to spend to clean up his own effluent; or if those who gained disproportionately to their costs were willing to offer a settlement to those who gained less than their costs.

In this case, the fishing and resort businesses might have found that they could afford collectively to reimburse the industrial polluter, who otherwise had little motive to join the lake coalition and control his effluent. Either arrangement would internalize the economics of the pollution cooperatively and would be stable.

Each player or group of players should be willing to join the over-all lake coalition if each does better that way. If this is the situation, the *total* lake society is doing the best it can. This solution doesn't say precisely what distribution of costs and benefits will finally be made; other game-theory solutions can carry it further—for example, through the bargaining process.

The lake coalition will have stability if it has control of a decisive amount of pollution. If there is one holdout whose pollution is decisive, the solution falls apart. In sum, unless the lake businesses arrive at a voluntary cooperative arrangement with this kind of hard economic rationale, or the rationale of a standard of behavior, they will be vulnerable to a coercive resolution by politics and law, over which they would have some influence but not control.

PART TWO

Industrial Concentration,
Business Behavior, and
the New Industrial State

Concentration in Manufacturing

WILLARD F. MUELLER

*Willard F. Mueller is chief economist and Director of the Bureau
of Economics of the Federal Trade Commission. The following
piece is derived from his testimony in 1965 before a subcommittee
of the Senate Judiciary Committee.*

IN 1962, THE POPULATION OF American manufacturing enterprises
consisted of about 180,000 corporations and 240,000 partnerships
and proprietorships. These approximately 420,000 business units
had combined assets of about $296 billion as of the fourth quarter
of 1962. About 98.4 percent of these assets were held by corporations.

Table 1 shows the ownership distribution of manufacturing assets. The 20 largest manufacturing corporations (all of which had
assets of more than $1.5 billion at year-end 1962) had $73.8
billion in assets, or an estimated 25 percent of the total assets of
all U.S. manufacturing companies. The 50 largest corporations accounted for 35.7 percent, the 100 largest for 46.1 percent, the 200
largest for 55.9 percent, and the 1,000 largest for almost three-fourths (74.8 percent) of the total assets of all manufacturing
companies. These data demonstrate quite clearly the high degree
of concentration in American manufacturing. In fact, whereas the
20 largest companies held 25 percent and the 1,000 largest held
74.8 percent of all manufacturing assets, the 419,000 smallest

companies accounted for only 25.2 percent of total manufacturing assets. Thus, the total assets of the 20 largest manufacturing corporations were approximately the same as those of the 419,000 smallest.

TABLE 1.   *Concentration of Total Manufacturing Assets, 4th Quarter, 1962*

Corporate size group	Assets (millions)	All manu- facturing (percent)	Corpora- tions only (percent)
5 largest	$36,447	12.3	12.5
10 largest	54,353	18.4	18.7
20 largest	73,825	25.0	25.4
50 largest	105,421	35.7	36.2
100 largest	136,222	46.1	46.8
200 largest	165,328	55.9	56.8
500 largest	199,894	67.6	68.7
1,000 largest	221,279	74.8	76.0
Corporations with assets over $10,000,000 [1]	237,410	80.3	81.6
All corporations [2]	291,022	98.4	100.0
Total manufacturing businesses [3]	295,690	100.0	

1. There were 2,041 manufacturing corporations in operation the 1st quarter of 1963.

2. This group includes about 180,000 manufacturing corporations.

3. Includes asset estimates for approximately 240,000 manufacturing proprietorships and partnerships.

SOURCE: Bureau of Economics, Federal Trade Commission.

Considerable variations in the degree of concentration exist among industry groups. For example, the four largest producers of motor vehicles and parts accounted for 79.7 percent of that industry's total assets and 89.1 percent of its net profits; the four largest producers of tobacco products accounted for 72.7 percent of total assets and 72.5 percent of total net profits of that industry group (Table 2). Both industries are highly concentrated and there is considerable disparity between the size of the four largest and all other producers of these products.

Rather high degrees of concentration also exist in rubber and miscellaneous plastic products, dairy products, primary iron and steel, alcoholic beverages, petroleum refining, industrial chemicals, other transportation equipment, and instruments and related products. In each one of these relatively broad industry groups,

TABLE 2.   *Concentration of Sales, Total Assets, Net Capital Assets, and Profits after Taxes for the 4 Largest Firms in 28 Selected Industry Groups, 4th Quarter, 1962*

| | Percent of total | | | |
Industry	Sales	Total Assets	Net Capital Assets	Profits
Motor vehicles	80.8	79.7	83.1	89.1
Aircraft	47.3	41.9	32.6	46.6
Other transportation equipment	30.3	44.2	59.9	51.6
Electrical machinery	34.4	35.6	41.5	44.4
Metalworking machinery	14.5	16.3	18.5	19.1
Other machinery	20.6	24.3	31.5	39.6
Primary iron and steel	40.2	48.0	48.8	44.3
Primary nonferrous metals	27.3	41.1	47.7	37.1
Other fabricated metal products	14.7	19.9	30.3	17.7
Stone, clay, and glass products	18.1	19.9	19.8	23.4
Furniture and fixtures	5.2	8.4	9.6	5.3
Lumber and wood products	21.2	31.0	41.5	48.6
Instruments	37.9	41.2	50.2	56.6
Miscellaneous manufacturing	16.3	33.1	34.3	25.2
Dairy products	42.9	48.8	47.4	73.9
Bakery products	33.6	39.6	38.2	52.8
Other food	12.5	13.2	14.9	20.1
Textile mill products	22.0	26.1	25.7	30.5
Apparel	4.9	7.7	11.4	7.4
Paper	20.7	23.2	22.3	35.0
Basic industrial chemicals	42.0	45.5	44.6	64.6
Drugs and medicines	31.0	29.2	33.3	32.6
Other chemicals	28.5	30.0	33.6	35.8
Petroleum refining	50.3	50.1	47.7	54.3
Rubber	48.1	55.0	56.4	51.6
Leather	26.7	32.1	35.4	28.8
Alcoholic beverages	41.4	47.2	30.8	58.3
Tobacco	70.9	72.7	69.8	72.5

SOURCE: Bureau of Economics, Federal Trade Commission.

the four largest companies accounted for more than 40 percent of the total assets and more than 50 percent of the profits after taxes (Table 2).

On the other hand, there are seven industry groups in which the four largest companies accounted for less than 20 percent of total assets. These include stone, clay, and glass products, fabricated metal products, textile products, metalworking machinery, other food products (except alcoholic beverages, dairy and bakery products), furniture and fixtures, and apparel. However, in all but 2 of the above industry groups the 20 largest companies in each group accounted for 40 percent or more of the profits after taxes.

In addition to the above estimates of concentration in 1962, we have prepared estimates of the share of total manufacturing assets held by the 200 largest manufacturing corporations in 1950 (Table 3). These data show that between 1950 and 1962 a substantial increase in total manufacturing assets occurred in this country. During the period, the total assets of all manufacturing businesses increased by 106 percent and the total assets of all manufacturing corporations grew by 111 percent. However, the assets of the 200 largest manufacturing corporations increased by 141.3 percent during the same period.

The data presented in Table 3 reflect the relatively more rapid growth of the 200 largest American manufacturing corporations (all with assets of $200 million or more in 1962). In 1950, for example, the 20 largest companies accounted for 21.5 percent of total *corporate* assets. By 1962, the 20 largest companies' share had grown to 24.8 percent—an increase of 3.3 percentage points. The share of the 100 largest companies increased from 40.2 percent in 1950 to 45.7 percent in 1962—an increase of 5.5 percentage points, while that of the 200 largest companies increased from 48.9 percent in 1950 to 55 percent in 1962—an increase of 6.1 percentage points. These data show that concentration in manufacturing has increased substantially since 1950.

When noncorporate manufacturing companies are included in the comparison, the increase in concentration is even more pronounced. Whereas in 1950 the 100 largest corporations held 38.6 percent of all manufacturing assets, by 1962 they held 45 percent of such assets—an increase of 6.4 percentage points. The share of the 200 largest companies increased from 46.7 to 54.6 percent, an increase of 7.9 percentage points. Hence, in just 12 years, their share of all manufacturing assets grew by about 17 percent.

TABLE 3. *Concentration of total assets, 200 largest*
manufacturing corporations, 1950 and 1962
[in millions of dollars]

| Corporate size group | 1950, total assets [1] | Percent of total | | 1962, total assets [1] | Percent of total | |
		All corporations	All manufacturing		All corporations	All manufacturing
5 largest	13,711	10.0	9.6	35,299	12.3	11.9
10 largest	20,759	15.7	14.5	52,924	18.9	17.9
20 largest	29,682	21.5	20.7	72,179	24.8	24.4
50 largest	43,353	31.8	30.2	103,560	35.8	35.0
100 largest	55,388	40.2	38.6	133,000	45.7	45.0
200 largest	66,931	48.9	46.7	161,531	55.0	54.6
All corporations	[2] 137,719			[2] 291,022		
All manufacturing	[3] 143,396			[3] 295,690		

1. These asset figures differ from those appearing in tables 1 and 2 because the asset data used here are those reported in *Moody's Industrial Manual* rather than those reported in the *FTC-SEC Quarterly Financial Report.*

2. Estimate.

3. Estimate of the total assets of all incorporated and unincorporated manufacturing corporations.

SOURCE: Bureau of Economics, Federal Trade Commission.

Changes in Industrial Concentration

MORRIS A. ADELMAN

Morris A. Adelman is Professor of Economics at Massachusetts Institute of Technology. This essay comes from his testimony in 1965 before a subcommittee of the Senate Judiciary Committee.

TABLE 1 PRESENTS a summary view of concentration over the past 60-odd years. The technique is simple. For each comparison, for example, between 1901 and 1947, or between 1954 and 1958, the industries are classed in the same groups, or as near to them, as the data will permit. For each industry we compute the "concentration ratio"; that is, the percentage of sales accounted for by the four largest firms. The weighting factor of each industry is its value added, the difference between its purchases and its sales, which measures its own contribution to the national product. For 1901, where the figures are more rough, we must make do with using the value added by the individual industries with a concentration ratio over 50 as a percent of value added by all industries in the large industry group. But for later years we are able to use a more precise measure. If we multiply each industry's concentration ratio by its weighting factor, then add up all the resulting numbers and divide by the total value added, we have a weighted average concentration ratio. Table 1 shows the weighted average concentration ratio for the 20 large industry groups, and, in the bottom line, shows the weighted average for all census industries.

The measure appears to have declined substantially from 1901 to 1947, and not to have changed much since then. I say "appears to have" advisedly: we must be cautious in interpreting data as imperfect as those we have for the early period. The error should not be exaggerated: they were published estimates, subject to informed criticism by people who knew enough of the industries to question a radically wrong estimate and suggest a better. One might not know anything about the sales or assets of the old Standard Oil Co., but one could have some rough idea of their share of the market, and say so in a published place. Hence the estimates in the old table cannot be called wide of the mark. But

TABLE 1.   *Average Concentration Ratios*

Industry Group	% of value added in industries with concentration over 50 [1]		Average concentration		
	1901	1947	1947	1954	1958
Food and kindred products	39.1	18.8	34.9	33.8	32.6
Tobacco manufactures	49.9	77.7	76.2	73.4	74.1
Textile mill products	20.3	9.0	24.3	26.5	29.2
Apparel and related products		2.2	12.6	13.0	13.4
Lumber and wood products	.5	2.0	11.2	10.8	12.8
Furniture and fixtures		8.1	21.9	20.3	19.0
Pulp, paper, and products	71.0	1.6	21.2	24.8	25.9
Printing and publishing	1.0	0	19.7	17.7	17.6
Chemicals and related products	24.3	33.7	51.0	48.6	45.7
Petroleum and coal products	46.8	13.6	39.5	36.6	31.6
Rubber products	100.0	59.9	58.6	54.1	51.3
Leather and leather products	26.3	0	26.2	26.4	25.0
Stone, clay, and glass products	13.3	43.9	43.4	46.4	40.3
Primary metal products	45.7	21.0	43.8	49.5	46.8
Fabricated metal products		8.4	25.3	26.1	25.5
Machinery, except electrical	41.4	18.5	38.0	33.2	35.5
Electrical machinery		53.2	54.1	48.2	46.9
Transportation equipment	57.3	84.2	54.4	58.7	61.3
Instruments and related products		45.0	45.3	47.4	47.8
Miscellaneous manufactures	2.7	21.2	34.9	16.1	22.6
Total, all industries	32.9	24.0	35.3	36.9	37.0

1. In the absence of complete data for 1901, this measure was substituted for average concentration with value-added weights. The correspondence between these 2 measures depends upon the extent to which the frequency distribution of 4 digit concentration ratios, with value added measuring frequency, retained the same general shape in 1947 as in 1901.

SOURCES:
1. U.S. Bureau of the Census, "Historical Statistics of the United States, Colonial Times to 1957," Washington, D.C., 1960, p. 573.
2. U.S. Bureau of the Census, "U.S. Census of Manufactures: 1958," vol. 1, Summary Statistics, Washington, D.C., 1961, app. C.
3. "Concentration Ratios in Manufacturing Industry: 1958," Washington, D.C., 1962, table 2.

they do retain a substantial possibility of error and I think the apparent decrease is within the limits of that error. Therefore, I would hesitate to conclude that there really was a substantial decline. The only safe conclusion, I believe, is that there was at least no increase over that time. Since 1947, it is apparent that there has been a considerable change in many four-digit industries, but the ups have about offset the downs, so that we are about where we started. . . .

I turn now to a very different subject, "concentration" not in individual industries or industry groups, but in very broad classifications such as all nonfinancial corporations, or manufacturing, and so forth. It is unfortunate that the same term "concentration" should be applied to statistics of this kind, for there is no logical relation between the two kinds of measurements. However, we are stuck with this customary usage, and I will therefore follow it. "Overall concentration" has little connection with industry concentration. In economic theory, the fewer the firms, everything else being equal, the nearer to monopoly. There is no such rationale in the aggregating of several dozen or hundred firms into such broad groups as manufactures, public utilities, and so forth. There may be some other perfectly good reasons for such aggregations. But we can say nothing about market structure, market behavior, competition, prices, production, and so forth, after viewing statistics of overall concentration.

Our data really begin in 1931, when the Internal Revenue Service began publishing corporate balance sheets by asset-size classes and industry groups. These we have for every year, but with a 1934–41 gap, because of a change in the tax laws. These figures are all entered subject to the same set of accounting definitions, and of course, with some substantial penalties for false statements. For corporate financial statistics, prehistory ends in 1931, and history begins.

Table 2 shows the share of assets held by the largest firms in manufacturing for every available year since 1931. You will note immediately that the number of companies in the largest size class tends to increase because of economic growth and often price increases. Twice the lower limit was increased, from $50 to $100 million, then to $250 million, and the number in the topmost class drops abruptly. Hence, we must look pretty carefully for years which are close together in number, and then a small adjustment to estimate an addition to the class cannot throw us far off, when we add the proper number of firms and credit them with the minimum value for the class just above it. Table 3 shows the share of the largest 117 firms from 1931 to the present, but omits all the years for which we either have no data or for which the number

TABLE 2.   *Largest Manufacturing Firms*

Year	Largest asset class (thousands of dollars)	Number of largest firms	Total assets (thousands of dollars)	Largest firms' assets (thousands of dollars)	Largest firms' share of assets (percent)
1931	50,000	139	63,802	29,646	46.5
1932	50,000	117	59,023	27,295	46.2
1933	50,000	119	57,753	26,436	45.8
1942	100,000	112	85,092	35,285	41.5
1943	100,000	127	94,767	41,597	43.9
1944	100,000	126	95,999	41,774	43.5
1945	100,000	120	91,030	38,470	42.3
1946	100,000	116	96,300	37,310	38.7
1947	100,000	133	111,355	45,082	40.5
1948	100,000	144	121,708	51,458	42.3
1949	100,000	144	123,755	53,628	43.3
1950	100,000	170	141,600	63,073	44.5
1951	100,000	199	160,876	75,700	47.1
1952	100,000	215	170,282	84,031	49.3
1953	100,000	223	176,805	90,024	50.9
1954	250,000	91	181,891	74,437	40.9
1955	250,000	97	201,360	84,246	41.8
1956	250,000	101	216,363	91,406	42.2
1957	250,000	107	224,910	99,634	44.3
1958	250,000	114	235,836	104,808	44.4
1959	250,000	121	252,134	113,202	44.9
1960	250,000	125	262,308	118,993	45.4

SOURCE: Internal Revenue Service, Statistics of Income; Corporation Returns.

of firms are so different that we cannot safely compare them. We use the number of 117 firms merely because that permits us to make the most comparisons with the least adjustments, but if we also were to try 107 firms, 119 firms, or 133 firms, the picture would not change. As you can see there was an increase from 1931 to 1932 and then a decrease. There was an increase from 1942 to 1943, and then a decrease through 1946. There was a decrease from 1957 through 1959 and then a slight increase to 1960.

How are we to interpret these observations? There is room for at least three hypotheses: first, as suggested by Willard F. Mueller, a cyclical movement. But this implies a regular recurrent motion, for which in my opinion there is too little evidence. The second hypothesis is an irregular fluctuation. The third would be

TABLE 3. *Assets for the Equivalent of 117 Firms*

Year	Number of largest firms	Unadjusted share of total assets	Required adjustment	Adjusted share (117 firms)
1931	139	46.5	Subtract 22	44.7
1932	117	46.2	None	46.2
1933	119	45.8	Subtract 2	45.6
1942	112	41.5	Add 5	42.0
1943	127	43.9	Subtract 10	42.8
1944	126	43.5	Subtract 9	42.6
1945	120	42.3	Subtract 3	41.9
1946	116	38.7	Add 1	38.8
1947				
1948				
1949				
1950				
1951				
1952				
1953				
1954				
1955				
1956				
1957	107	44.3	Add 10	45.4
1958	114	44.4	Add 3	44.8
1959	121	44.9	Subtract 4	44.5
1960	125	45.4	Subtract 8	44.6

no real change in the underlying data, but the disturbances of depression, war, and reconstruction generated some meaningless change in the observations. My own feeling is that the truth lies somewhere between the second and third hypotheses, but there is no way of rigorously disproving the others. Perhaps later research will tell us more, though it would take a large-scale effort at best.

One result can under no circumstances be gotten out of these data, and that is the notion of any long-term increase in "overall concentration." If there was a cyclical movement, with a decline from about 1935 to about 1947, as Mueller thinks, then we ought to measure from peak to peak, 46.2 percent in 1932 and 45.4 percent in 1957. Or if we simply use terminal years, that would be from 44.7 in 1931 to 44.6 in 1960. If we preferred to use groups of 3 years, in order to avoid single-year fluctuations we still have a mild decrease from 1931–33 to 1958–60.

I do not see any possible escape from the conclusion that "over-all concentration" in the largest manufacturing firms has remained quite stable over a period of 30 years, from 1931 to 1960. I cannot conceive of any circumstances which could so affect the statistics that they failed to register an increasing concentration, taking place over so long a period of time.

The General Explanation of the Development of Concentration

JOE S. BAIN

Joe S. Bain is Professor of Economics at the University of California, Berkeley. The following selection is taken from his book Industrial Organization, *published in 1959.*

WHAT SORTS of forces determine the degree of business concentration [i.e., the number and size distribution of firms] which is attained, or "explain" existing concentration patterns? One thing stands out clearly—there is no one simple force determining concentration and no especially simple explanation. There is instead a multiplicity of considerations determining the degrees of concentration which will be reached at any time in various industries, and the degree of overall concentration in the whole economy. The same multiplicity of considerations, of course, determines the directions and rates of change of concentration as it evolves through time.

The variety of considerations or forces involved may be summarized in the following way:

1. First, there is generally a drive on the part of firms in the various industries to attain efficient sizes by exploiting existing economies of large-scale production and distribution, and thus effective degrees of seller concentration (and patterns of vertical integration) which are at least roughly consistent with efficiency. This inclination to move toward efficient market structure, sometimes said to reflect mainly *technological considerations*, tends to bring degrees of seller concentration in the various markets within certain limits—that is, roughly, concentrated enough to exploit available economies of large-scale production, and not so con-

centrated that firms become inefficiently large. But fulfillment of this condition in the usual industry allows a substantial range of alternative degrees of seller concentration to develop, so that the degree of seller concentration ordinarily is not at all closely determined by technological considerations alone.

2. Parallel to the drive for productive efficiency, there is a drive on the part of firms in some industries (largely consumer-good industries) to develop scales which are most effective or profitable for sales promotion. Operation of this force may lead to the development of larger firms and higher degrees of seller concentration than would be required for technological reasons alone—and also to more vertical integration. Response to these *sales promotion considerations*, however, still does not leave the degree of seller concentration at all closely determined.

3. In addition, there is a group of "concentration-increasing" forces always at work with one degree of vigor or another. These are stimuli for firms to increase concentration progressively without any necessary limit, either within the industry or through the growth of firms exceeding the bounds of single industries. Principal among them are:

(*a*) Drives to restrict competition by reducing the number of firms, whether by mergers or by elimination or exclusion of rivals—either at the horizontal level of one industry, or by vertical integration. These may be called, for convenience, *monopolization considerations*.

(*b*) Tendencies for certain firms to acquire dominant market positions and thus impose high seller concentration because of their acquisition and possession of strategic advantages over all actual or possible competitors—of patent controls over strategic techniques or products, or monopolistic ownership of strategic resource supplies, and of strong stable buyer preferences for their products as compared to actual or potential competitive products. These *specific entry barrier considerations* are important in explaining the development of high seller concentration in a number of industries.

(*c*) Tendencies of "outsider" financial interests to wish to perpetrate mergers (within industries or across industry lines) in order to reap financial profits from the formation of the merger. And, parallel to these, tendencies of corporations with large liquid funds from undistributed profits to acquire other firms, within or outside their own industries, mainly as a means of investing these funds. Both of these tendencies may be included under the head of *financial considerations,* and both are concentration-increasing in essence, though they do not always result in increased concentration just within individual industries.

4. Opposing these concentration-increasing forces are certain concentration-deterring ones, which tend to check, limit, offset, or virtually discourage increases in concentration. The most important of these are three:

(*a*) *Legal considerations,* principally in the form of the antitrust laws, especially the Sherman Act and the Clayton Act. These tend to place certain limits on mergers, on extremely high concentration, and on the development of high concentration through the employment of predatory and exclusionary tactics toward actual or potential competitors. (In the very early days of the Sherman Act these considerations may have worked in a reverse direction, but this, in general, is no longer so.)

(*b*) *Enterprise sovereignty considerations,* by which we refer to the virtual deterrent force to mergers inhering in the difficulty of potential participants in agreeing on terms, and fundamentally to the reluctance of individual ownership-management units to yield up their sovereign controls over their operations to a larger combined unit. This is certainly not an insignificant force in retarding the increase of concentration via mergers.

(*c*) *Market-growth considerations,* which refer to the tendency of the steady growth of markets, and of the economy, to reduce concentration unless the larger business units grow as rapidly, and to offset the virtual concentration-increasing effects of the merger and internal growth of larger firms.

5. Operation of all these considerations or forces of course takes place within a certain institutional and legal framework or environment, important parts of which include the tariff laws, the tax laws, and the laws governing incorporation of businesses (as well as the patent law and the antitrust laws). *The legal framework* of course has at least a conditioning influence on the results, in terms of concentration, which will ensue from the operation of the various positive forces or considerations just enumerated.

What happens to business concentration, either within an industry or in the whole economy, is a resultant of the simultaneous operation of all these various complementary and opposing forces. Exactly what patterns of concentration will emerge at any particular date cannot be predicted *a priori* unless we acquire more information than we now possess concerning the relative strength and detailed nature of the various forces. And, as to changes in concentration over time, we must recognize that the relative force of various concentration-increasing or concentration-deterring forces may alter significantly through time. Scale economies may become more or less important because of technological changes; entry barriers based on patent or resource control may wither away, or new ones may emerge; product developments may undercut old product-differentiation barriers to entry; legal restrictions on concentration may be tightened or slackened; markets may grow more or less rapidly. The future course of changes in concentration cannot be predicted until future changes in all of the preceding respects can be predicted, and their probable consequences appraised. In our present state of knowledge, therefore, we cannot fully explain or rationalize the evolution of concentration in the past, or accurately predict its future course. General identification of the various qualitative forces at work, however, provides us with a better understanding of the complex phenomena of structural change observed in the past, and a better basis for appraising the alternative possibilities of future development.

Moreover, this analysis of complex forces enables us to reject two incomplete and erroneous theories about economic concentration, and to make some sort of probability judgment about the relationship of existing concentration patterns to economic efficiency, as follows:

1. *It is not true* that we should necessarily expect a never-ending process of increasing concentration, toward fewer and fewer firms controlling more and more of individual industries and of the economy. The "monopolization considerations," or desire to combine and concentrate to restrict competition, is, to be sure, always operative, and it is reinforced in a degree by other considerations favoring higher concentration. But there are powerful opposing or countervailing considerations—law, market growth, protection of enterprise sovereignty—and it is quite possible that these will over time tend to balance (or even overbalance) the drives to-

ward increasing concentration so that in the net concentration will not increase (or may even decline) over time. The experience of the last twenty years is consistent with predictions to this effect.

2. *It is not true* that existing degrees of business concentration are adequately explained simply as the result of adjustments to attain maximum efficiency in production and distribution. More broadly, they are in part the result of adjustments to attain maximum profits (in a context where profits are influenced by things in addition to efficiency); and in part the result of other things (see financial considerations, and legal and sovereignty restraining factors). As a result, existing degrees of business concentration necessarily reflect the operation of many considerations in addition to that of technological efficiency. And although market structures may still turn out to be relatively efficient on the average (since the limits of efficient structure are fairly broad), the precise degrees of concentration attained are likely to reflect importantly the operation of these other forces.

3. Although, as seems probable, the degrees of seller concentration observed in various industries are reasonably efficient—that is, somewhere within the efficient range—the strength of the various concentration-increasing forces enumerated appears to have been such that concentration will frequently tend to be higher than the minimum required for efficiency. Industries probably tend to be "more concentrated than necessary" for efficiency —and the larger firms bigger than necessary—because of the operation of monopolization, sales-promotion, and financial motives, and because of specific entry barriers favoring a few firms in certain industries. And excessive, or inefficiently high, concentration is not ruled out in a certain proportion of cases.

Collusion Among Electrical
Equipment Manufacturers

WALL STREET JOURNAL

*In 1961, the electrical equipment producers—General Electric,
Westinghouse, Allis Chalmers, and others—pleaded guilty to
charges of violating the antitrust laws. The following article, taken
from the* Wall Street Journal, *January 10, 12, 1962, is an interesting case study of collusion.*

THE TERM "organization man" may well be looked on with suspicion as a too simple, too pat summation of a personality that is
complex as any. But the term is meaningful. And while Judge
Ganey and some of the attorneys involved in the Government's
criminal antitrust cases against various members of the electrical
equipment industry sought to dodge the word, they found it a
useful one in referring to some individual defendants.

Here were men of substance in their communities and in the
business world who were pleading guilty or "no contest" to serious charges of conspiracy. From the court record and from some
of the pleas it can hardly be argued that most of them did not
know what they were doing. Yet the overwhelming impression is
that these men hardly fit the stereotype of law evaders. Almost
as pervasive as the almost undisputed evidence of wrong-doing
was the question of why. And the simplest, if not the complete,
answer goes back to the organization man.

It would seem that in these cases the term not only concerned
solid and respectable businessmen, however, but also the whole
mores and what was taken for the mores of an entire industry.
One charge sometimes leveled against the organization man is
that he is strong on conformity. If, in the case of the individuals
in the electrical cases, what was to be conformed to was a large-
scale system of law evasion, they evidently conformed to that too.

Potentials for Trouble · Certainly the climate in which the individuals and companies in the heavy electrical equipment industry operated was loaded with potentials for trouble, and these may well have been the genesis of the legal difficulties which came to afflict a large segment.

The industry is a relatively compact one. Its members range from very large enterprises to relatively small ones. For example, among those indicted in the case were General Electric with $4 billion annual sales and Joslyn Manufacturing and Supply Co. of Chicago with annual sales of less than $2 million and only 45 production employees.

The industry is tightly-knit with many friendships among executives of competing firms; indeed, officials of smaller firms sometimes are former General Electric or Westinghouse Electric executives. The men involved oftentimes had similar educational backgrounds also—college graduates in engineering with a rise through technical ranks into the world of sales. There sometimes existed on the part of the men with the bigger companies an almost protective, big brother attitude toward the smaller companies; this was reciprocated.

And the friendships were not only professional but often quite personal. Trade association meetings fostered these. It was perhaps easy in the camaraderie of these meetings at upper bracket hotels, amid speeches typical of any association lauding the industry's members and "mission," to draw even closer than business and background indicated. It was perhaps easy, with wives and children present, and acquainted from past conventions, to drift into the belief that nothing could be very wrong in such an atmosphere.

Darkening Grays · Indeed, many of the meetings took place at the conventions of the National Electrical Manufacturers Association and other trade groups. Rather typically, after a conventional and perfectly lawful meeting of some kind, certain members would adjourn for a rump session and a few drinks in someone's suite. It seemed natural enough that mutual business problems would be discussed—specifications, for example—and like as not prices would come up. In time it was easy enough to drift from general talk about prices into what should be done about them—and finally into separate meetings to fix them for everyone's mutual benefit.

Thus purely legal gatherings might have drifted into ones with increasingly dark shades of gray and finally into ones that were pretty black; more than one moralist has noted that it isn't the blacks and whites of situations that get initially law-abiding citizens into trouble; rather it is a progressive inability to distinguish between shades of gray.

It was especially easy in this industry to get into price discussions.

The economic position of the various companies has often been one of feast or famine—large orders or none at all for the gigantic pieces of equipment manufactured. Widespread overcapacity after World War II brought intermittent price warring. In 1955, for example, there occurred a price war, known throughout the industry as the "white sale," which saw some prices cut as much as 50%. Profit losses resulted and in some cases red ink. Again in 1957 there was a lesser wave of competitive cutting. At least during the "white sale" General Electric and Westinghouse wound up with most of the business. By reports then current some smaller companies were seeking Government intervention under the Sherman Act's anti-monopoly provisions.

The case has a number of ironic aspects but one of the great ones is that men in the large companies believed they had to protect the position of the smaller companies or run the risk of antitrust prosecution. Another is that much of the overcapacity underlying the "need" to fix prices was Government spurred. Fast tax write-offs, growing out of two wars in two decades, brought the greater capacity for defense that the Government wanted, but they also left the manufacturers with an embarrassing amount of plant.

As a result of this industry makeup, the friendships, and the price-capacity situation, there evidently developed in wide segments the philosophy that collusive activity was ethical, illegal though it might be.

Perhaps an extreme exponent of this view, though expressing a widespread one, is F. F. Loock, president, general manager and sales manager of Allen-Bradley Co. of Milwaukee, who has pleaded guilty.

Looking back on what happened, he says: "No one attending the gatherings [in the electrical controls industry] was so stupid he didn't know [the meetings] were in violation of the law. But it is the only way a business can be run. It is free enterprise."

Price fixing is not usually associated with the idea of free enterprise, with the idea that the market mechanism is to be the ultimate controlling factor, and that this mechanism must remain unimpaired either by individuals or governments. But there is a rationale for the cartel system which permits the general type of collusive activity the electrical men were engaged in. According to it, markets are divided and prices fixed so everyone involved can "get along." Even the consumer is supposed to benefit because stable markets aid stable production and supposedly costs can thus be stabilized.

"Protection Against Buyers" · Price competition is anathema to such a setup. Mr. Loock says one reason for the gatherings in his industry was "we also need protection against buyers" and the "illegal meetings gave us such protection."

Elaborating on the need for "protection," Mr. Loock cites one instance in which the purchasing agent of a major Detroit manufacturer told the electrical manufacturer another one had offered a lower price. "By discussing the matter, which was not true, among ourselves, we were able to iron out the problem." He concludes: "I believe that in an industry where money is necessary to continue research and development of products we should have some protection against the crookedness of some buyers."

There was also a feeling in the industry that the antitrust laws were unjust. With a rationale developed of friendly live and let live among competitors, laws designed to force competition seemed "Government interference." The question was also asked in the industry: If such getting together was all right under the old N.R.A. why isn't it all right now? Of course the N.R.A. of the 1930's was declared unconstitutional by the Supreme Court, but some say the industry's philosophy of "getting together" has roots in that era.

But if illegal "stabilization" was an industry way of life, it should not be assumed that relations were continually rosy among competitors, or that all authority in the industry was bent on collusive activity.

Getting together to fix prices did not alter the basically competitive situation prevailing in the industry's markets. Indeed, it often seems some attendance at the collusive meetings was with tongue in cheek as to stabilizing prices, with a real reason of finding out what the rest of the industry was up to in order to get the jump in the next price cutting wave. Too, some of the conspirators pretty much inherited their roles from predecessors, older men who may have felt more of a tug from the industry's "way of life" than they did. In fact there was personal dislike among some of the individual conspirators; perhaps an individual who did not like himself for conspiring had little respect for others also so engaged. . . .

It is plain that many of the individuals involved in the conspiracy were under, or felt they were under, heavy pressure to produce and basically believed their meetings, however clandestine, were ethically justifiable.

An attorney for one company sums it up: "Most of the businessmen and attorneys involved don't think there's a moral issue. This isn't a blind spot in American business. These people honestly think they were getting a fair profit and weren't hurting their customers. An unenforced law isn't respected. The Government should have given the companies a warning before cracking down. Now either the companies will conform to the law or the law will be changed."

A look at some individual stories, and at some of these meetings, illustrates the pressures and difficulties—the law aside—that these organization men ran into.

The Problems of Price Fixing · For a number of years various electrical companies and individuals successfully evaded the antitrust laws. They periodically met to fix prices, divide up markets and otherwise cartellize their industry.

But examination of court records of the case indicates the conspiracy was not a very successful one. Prices were not fixed except temporarily—some one of the conspirators was forever evading the intent of conspiracy.

Markets were divided somewhat more successfully, but here again the planners of the market were always running afoul of new circumstances which did not fit into the master plan. Certainly the attempt to evade the give and take of the market place meant for the people and companies involved a good deal of unforeseen trouble—the law aside. Red tape flourished; bureaucracy, unofficial and perhaps illegal though it may have been, grew apace. The need for conspiratorial gatherings mounted, all as man-made rules were substituted for competition.

For example, the circuit breaker conspiracy involving General Electric, Westinghouse, Allis-Chalmers and Federal Pacific ran into this problem in 1958—what to do about the entrance onto the scene of a new company? While a new competitor is never an easy matter for an individual company, it was also quite complex for the conspirators.

What happened was that I-T-E Circuit Breaker Co., a factor in other aspects of the electrical equipment business, in 1958 bought out a small company and wanted to enter the circuit breaker field where prices were being fixed and markets allotted on a percentage basis.

"Now, room had to be made for I-T-E," Antitrust Chief Bicks noted in remarks at the arraignment of the defendants. "So a series of meetings began in January of 1958, at which I-T-E indicated its desire for some business. I-T-E had bought a company; it wanted to get into the business.

"The knowledge by I-T-E that it was entering into a pre-existing conspiracy is clear beyond doubt from the pattern of events in early 1958. I-T-E began meeting with the four conspirators that had been going, going more or less smoothly, it's true, with greater or less success, with greater or less mutual confidence that each of the conspirators was living up to his part of the deal, but, nonetheless, one constant conspiracy I-T-E sought to get in.

Over-all Policy · "In early 1958 I-T-E secured an agreement as to the over-all pricing policy leaving the allocation aside.

"The nature of that agreement arrived at in early 1958 at a series of meetings was roughly this, that general pricing would be tied to G.E.'s book price, that I-T-E in the southern part of California would be allowed 15% off, that I-T-E nationally would be allowed 5% off . . . Remaining to be finalized was I-T-E's allocation share of the sealed bid business. This was discussed . . . I-T-E was cut in for a share of 4% following a series of conferences, and so from 1958 on everybody cut back a bit except Federal Pacific. . . .

"The three big companies, G.E., Westinghouse, Allis-Chalmers . . . cut down their percentage. Federal Pacific came up from 10 to 15. I-T-E was cut in for 4. That was roughly the pattern of the conspiracy that kept on until the date of the indictment."

I-T-E, seeking to plead no contest in this case, said among other things that it was charged with being only a small factor in the industry for a short period of time. It has told its men to stay away from competitors, that if they're caught in such activities again they'll be fired.

It was one thing, as in the circuit breaker case, to agree that a certain company would get a specific piece of sealed-bid business. It was something else again to see that the designated company actually got the job. Here, again according to Mr. Bicks' statement to the court, is how that worked, amid burgeoning red tape.

"At a working level meeting where a particular big job was up for discussion the percentages initially would be reviewed in light of what was known as the ledger list, which had on it recent sealed-bid jobs given to the other defendants. In light of that ledger list it was decided which of the companies, to keep the percentages constant, would get the job. Now if that company was prepared to say the price at which it was going to bid, then the other companies could discuss among themselves what they would bid, add on for accessories, to make sure to give . . . the company . . . whose turn it was to get the job, the best shot at it.

Numbers Code · " If the company whose job the particular rigged job was supposed to be did not know the price, there would be later communication, either by phone to homes with just the first names used, or by letter to homes with just first names of senders, with no return address, and this wonderful code. . . . The numbers were 1, General Electric; 2, Westinghouse; 3, Allis-Chalmers; and 7, Federal Pacific. What happened to 4 or 5 and 6 until I-T-E came in remains a mystery."

One of the great ironies of the conspiracies was that no matter how hard the participants schemed, no matter how friendly their meetings and communications might be, there was an innate tendency to compete. Someone was always violating the agreements to get more business and this continually called for new illegal plans. For example, price-cutting in sales of power switching equipment to Government agencies was getting out of hand in late 1958. This led to the "quadrant" system of dividing markets.

"So," declared Baddia Rashid, chief of the trial section of the antitrust division, "at a meeting in November of 1958 at Philadelphia . . . they decided that the best way to handle the sealed-bid market was to allocate the business; however, since there were sixteen companies involved in this particular conspiracy it would have been difficult to try to allocate the business as in other cases on a percentage basis, and therefore it was decided that it would be best to divide the country into four separate geographical areas which were called quadrants—the northwest quadrant, the southwest quadrant, the southeast quadrant, and the northeast quadrant.

"Four companies were assigned to participate in each quadrant, and one of the company representatives in that quadrant was designated as a secretary for the purpose of handling the allocation within the particular quadrant. [For example,] in the northeast quadrant . . . meetings were held and it was decided that the business within that quadrant would be allocated in an alphabetical rotation. . . ."

This plan did not work to everyone's satisfaction, but rather than fall back on the give and take of the market place which the law requires, the conspirators formulated another plan.

"In September of 1959, however, there were some complaints that had arisen because some companies felt they were not getting a sufficient share of the business . . . it appeared that certain of the quadrants were obtaining more sealed-bid business than other quadrants. Therefore, they held a meeting in Pittsburgh . . . in September, 1959 . . . and they discussed this situation. . . . After some discussion it was finally decided that perhaps the best way to do it would be to go back to a national allocation scheme at which every company would be allotted a certain percentage of the business. They all agreed to that plan and each company was then asked to indicate what percentage of the sealed-bid market it felt it should obtain. . . . An individual from one of the . . . companies was designated to act as secretary. . . ."

But the basic problem, in this industry where price fluctuations were sometimes drastic, was "stabilizing" prices and efforts to bring this about spawned many a difficulty. . . . No matter how diligently plans and schemes were laid, they somehow could not defeat the basic economic factors, which insisted on responding to the inherent forces of the free market.

THE STEEL PRICE
CONTROVERSY, 1962

Attack on the Steel Price Increase

*In his news conference on April 11, 1962, the day after the
U. S. Steel Corporation announced a $6 per ton increase in the
price of steel, President Kennedy charged that U. S. Steel had
acted in disregard of its "public responsibilities." The statement
which he made relating to this action is reproduced here.*

THE SIMULTANEOUS and identical actions of United States Steel
and other leading steel corporations increasing steel prices by
some $6 a ton constitute a wholly unjustifiable and irresponsible
defiance of the public interest.

In this serious hour in our nation's history, when we are confronted with grave crises in Berlin and Southeast Asia, when we
are devoting our energies to economic recovery and stability, when
we are asking reservists to leave their homes and families for
months on end, and servicemen to risk their lives—and four were
killed in the last two days in Vietnam—and asking union members
to hold down their wage requests, at a time when restraint and
sacrifice are being asked of every citizen, the American people
will find it hard, as I do, to accept a situation in which a tiny
handful of steel executives whose pursuit of private power and
profit exceeds their sense of public responsibility can show such
utter contempt for the interest of 185 million Americans.

If this rise in the cost of steel is imitated by the rest of the industry, instead of rescinded, it would increase the cost of homes,
autos, appliances and most other items for every American family. It would increase the cost of machinery and tools to every
American businessman and farmer. It would seriously handicap

102

our efforts to prevent an inflationary spiral from eating up the pensions of our older citizens, and our new gains in purchasing power. It would add, Secretary McNamara informed me this morning, an estimated one billion dollars to the cost of our defenses, at a time when every dollar is needed for national security and other purposes.

It will make it more difficult for American goods to compete in foreign markets, more difficult to withstand competition from foreign imports, and, thus, more difficult to improve our balance-of-payments position and stem the flow of gold. And it is necessary to stem it, for our national security, if we are going to pay for our security commitments abroad.

And it would surely handicap our efforts to induce other industries and unions to adopt responsible price and wage policies.

The facts of the matter are that there is no justification for an increase in steel prices.

The recent settlement between the industry and the union, which does not even take place until July 1, was widely acknowledged to be noninflationary, and the whole purpose and effect of this Administration's role, which both parties understood, was to achieve an agreement which would make unnecessary any increases in prices.

Steel output per man is rising so fast that labor costs per ton of steel can actually be expected to decline in the next 12 months. And, in fact, the acting Commissioner of the Bureau of Labor Statistics informed me this morning that, and I quote: "employment costs per unit of steel output in 1961 were essentially the same as they were in 1958." The cost of major raw materials— steel scrap and coal—has also been declining.

And, for an industry which has been generally operating at less than two thirds of capacity, its profit rate has been normal, and can be expected to rise sharply this year in view of the reduction in idle capacity. Their lot has been easier than that of 100,000 steelworkers thrown out of work in the last three years.

The industry's cash dividends have exceeded 600 million dollars in each of the last five years, and earnings in the first quarter of this year were estimated in the February 28 "Wall Street Journal" to be among the highest in history.

In short, at a time when they could be exploring how more efficiency and better prices could be obtained, reducing prices in this industry in recognition of lower costs, their unusually good labor contract, their foreign competition and their increase in production and profits which are coming this year, a few gigantic corporations have decided to increase prices in ruthless disregard of their public responsibilities.

The Steelworkers Union can be proud that it abided by its responsibilities in this agreement, and this Government also has responsibilities which we intend to meet. The Department of Justice and the Federal Trade Commission are examining the significance of this action in a free, competitive economy.

The Department of Defense and other agencies are reviewing its impact on their policies of procurement.

And I am informed that steps are under way by those members of the Congress who plan appropriate inquiries into how these price decisions are so quickly made and reached, and what legislative safeguards may be needed to protect the public interest.

Price and wage decisions in this country, except for very limited restriction in the case of monopolies and national-emergency strikes, are and ought to be freely and privately made. But the American people have a right to expect, in return for that freedom, a higher sense of business responsibility for the welfare of their country than has been shown in the last two days.

Some time ago I asked each American to consider what he would do for his country, and I asked the steel companies. In the last twenty-four hours we had their answer.

Defense of the Steel Price Increase

ROGER BLOUGH

On the day following President Kennedy's news conference Roger Blough, Chairman of the Board of U. S. Steel, defended the price rise. His statement is given below.

WHEN THE President of the United States speaks as he did yesterday regarding our corporation and its cost-price problems, I am sure a response is indicated and desirable.

Let me say respectfully that we have no wish to add to acrimony or to misunderstanding. We do not question the sincerity of anyone who disagrees with the action we have taken.

Neither do we believe that anyone can properly assume that we are less deeply concerned with the welfare, and the strength, and the vitality of this nation than are those who have criticized our action.

As employes and stockholders, we, along with thousands of other employes and stockholders, both union and nonunion, must discharge faithfully our responsibilities to United States Steel.

But as citizens we must also discharge fully our responsibilities to the nation. The action we have taken is designed to meet both those responsibilities.

One of the nation's most valuable and indispensable physical assets is its productive machinery and equipment, because its strength depends upon that. I, among others, share the responsibility of keeping a portion of that plant machinery and equipment in good working order. To do that our company, like every other employer, must be profitable. The profit which any company has left over after paying its employes, its other expenses, the tax collector and its stockholders for the use of their resources, are the main source of the plants and equipment that provide the work that thousands of workers have now.

Had it not been for those profits in the past, the millions with jobs in many varieties of business would not have those jobs.

But the machinery and equipment must be kept up to date, or no sales will be made, no work provided, no taxes available, and our international competitive position, our balance of payments, our gold reserves, and our national growth will seriously suffer.

None of us is unaware of the serious national problem and no one is unsympathetic with those in the Executive Branch of Government attempting to conduct the affairs of the nation, nationally and internationally.

But certainly, more rapid equipment modernization is one of the nation's basic problems as outlined by Secretary of the Treasury Douglas Dillon.

Speaking before the American Bankers Association last October, he said:

"More rapid equipment modernization by industry is vital to the success of our efforts to remain competitive in world markets, and to achieve the rate of growth needed to assure us prosperity and reasonably full employment."

"I think it highly significant," says Mr. Dillon, "that all the industrial countries of Western Europe, except Belgium and the United Kingdom, are now devoting twice as much of their gross national product to purchases of industrial equipment as are we in the United States."

"And Belgium and the United Kingdom," continues Mr. Dillon, "the two European countries whose economic growth has lagged in comparison with the rest of Western Europe, are devoting half again as much of their G.N.P. to the purchase of equipment as we are."

Now what this all means is that as a nation, we keep ahead in the race among nations through machinery and equipment through good productive facilities, through jobs that are vitally linked to the industrial strength. Surely our workmen are as good as any in the world, but they must have the tools with which to compete.

In other words, we compete as a company, as an industry and as a nation with better costs and better ways of production. Proper pricing is certainly part of that picture. And that is what is involved here, however it may be portrayed. For each individual company in our competitive society has a responsibility to the public, as well as to its employes and to its stockholders, to do the things that are necessary price-wise, however unpopular that may be at times to keep in the competitive race. And that is all we have attempted to do.

Now may I say several things with respect to any misunderstandings that have been talked about.

First, the President said when questioned regarding any arrangement not to increase prices, and I quote, "We did not ask either side to give us any assurance because there is a very proper limitation to the power of the Government in this free economy." So the effect of this statement is quite right. No assurances were asked and none were given regarding price action so far as I am concerned or any other individual connected with our corporation.

Furthermore, at least in my opinion, it would not have been proper for us under those circumstances to have had any understanding with anyone regarding price.

Second, I have said a number of times over the past months that the cost-price relationship in our company needed to be remedied.

As recently as Feb. 16, while the labor negotiations were going on, I referred in an interview made public to the steadily rising costs which we have experienced.

And I said, and I quote: "And you're asking me how long that can continue to increase, and how long it can be borne without any kind of a remedy? I would give you the answer that it is not reasonable to think of it as continuing. In other words, even now there should be a remedy. If any additional cost occurs, the necessity for the remedy becomes even greater."

And that was said in February.

This very real problem has been discussed in recent months with a number of individuals in Washington, and I am at a loss to know why anyone concerned with the situation would be unaware of the serious deterioration in the cost-price relationship.

In this connection President Kennedy in his letter of last Sept. 6 addressed to the executives of the steel companies said:

"Now I recognize too that the steel industry by absorbing increases in employment cost since 1958 has demonstrated a will to halt the price-wage spiral in steel."

I am sure that anyone reading the reply made on Sept. 13 to

that letter could not infer any commitment of any kind to do other than to act in the light of all competitive factors. So it is useful to repeat here that hourly employment costs have increased since 1958 by a total of about 12 per cent and that other costs have risen too. The net cost situation, taking into account employment and other costs, has risen about 6 per cent since 1958.

All this is without regard to the new labor contract. When costs keep moving upward, and prices remain substantially unchanged for four years, the need for some improvement in the cost-price relationship should be apparent.

Fourth, the thought that it costs no more to make steel today than it did in 1958 is quite difficult to accept, in view of the cost increases since that time. For U. S. Steel costs since 1958 have gone up far more than the announced price increase of yesterday.

Fifth, higher costs at the same selling prices obviously mean lower profit. Our own profits of 5.7 per cent on sales in 1961 were the lowest since 1952.

Sixth, the increase of three-tenths of a cent per pound in the price of steel adds almost negligibly to the cost of the steel which goes into the familiar everyday products that we use. Here for example is the amount by which this price change would increase the cost of steel for the following items:

A refrigerator, 65 cents; a domestic gas range, 70 cents; a wringer-type washing machine, 35 cents; a toaster, 3 cents; a compact-size car, $6.83; an intermediate-size car, $8.33; and a standard-size car, $10.64.

Seventh, it must be remembered that the process by which the human needs of people are met, and the process by which jobs are created, involves, importantly, the role of the investor.

Only when people save and invest their money in tools of production can a new productive job be brought into existence.

So our nation cannot afford to forget its obligations to these investors. Nor can we in United States Steel, who are responsible to more than 325,000 stockholders, forget the many Americans who have a stake in our enterprise, directly or indirectly.

Over half of our shares are held by individuals in all walks of life. And no one of these individuals owns as much as two-tenths of 1 per cent of the total stock. Most of the rest is held by pension funds, insurance companies, charitable and educational institutions, investment companies and trustees representing the direct or indirect ownership of large numbers of people in America.

These are the owners of United States Steel.

Now, I have touched upon a few matters here in the hope that those who are so seriously interested with these matters, and the public at large, will recognize that there was nothing irresponsible about the action we have taken.

My hope is that this discussion of our responsibilities, as we see them, will lead to a greater understanding, and a more thoughtful appraisal of the reasons for that action.

On April 13, 1962, two days after President Kennedy's attack on the steel price increase, U. S. Steel rescinded its announced increase. Shortly after, the five companies that had followed its lead in raising their prices took the same action. But one year later, in April, 1963, smaller across-the-board increases in steel prices were announced by the corporations. The government voiced no objections.

The Large Conglomerate Firm:
A Critical Appraisal

CORWIN EDWARDS

Corwin Edwards, Professor of Economics at the University of Oregon, was formerly chief economist of the Federal Trade Commission. The following essay is taken from the testimony in 1965 before a subcommittee of the Senate Judiciary Committee.

A BIG FIRM has advantages over a smaller rival just because it is big. Money is power. A big firm can outbid, outspend, and outlose a small firm. It can advertise more intensively, do more intensive and extensive research, buy up the inventions of others, defend its legal rights or alleged rights more thoroughly, bid higher for scarce resources, acquire the best locations and the best technicians and executives. If it overdoes its expenditures, it can absorb losses that would bankrupt a small rival.

Some of these advantages express economies of scale. They constitute real economies. Others are bargaining advantages which do not appear to have any particular advantage to the economy as a whole, and some of them are advantages of being able to live for a time on accumulated fat.

Such advantages of bigness are derived from the total size of the enterprise, whether that size is attained in one market or in many. Because they are to be found in large monopolies, they are relatively familiar. Please note, however, that so far as diversification increases the possibility for some firms to become big relative to others, it increases the possibility that they will obtain such advantages.

The power that is derived from dispersion of resources is peculiar to conglomerate enterprise. The aspects of such power that are most important have to do with: (*a*) subsidization; (*b*) reciprocity; (*c*) full line selling; and (*d*) the forbearance that prevails among large conglomerates.

Because a large conglomerate operates in many markets, it can divert income from one market to another. It can subsidize its losses in one market from its profits in another, or make investments in production for one market with resources derived from another. This fact gives a conglomerate exceptional leeway in market policy and exceptional possibility of imposing its will upon its more specialized rivals.

Whereas a specialized firm dependent upon a single market cannot afford to lose substantial amounts of money for a substantial period of time, a conglomerate can do so in a selected market if it chooses. It can pursue long-run profit regardless of short-run loss. It is thus immunized from some of the competitive pressures to which its specialized rivals must respond.

Similarly, a conglomerate can subsidize some of its products indefinitely. It can adjust its prices so that products upon which it encounters vigorous competition are not asked to carry much of the overhead costs or joint costs, nor to provide much of the total profit, while products that are less competitive carry more of the load. If there is a later change in relative competition, price policy can change likewise. So long as competition is not uniformly vigorous over the conglomerate's entire field of activity, such subsidization can be an enduring handicap for specialized competitors. The conglomerate can maintain its place in those parts of its field of operation in which other enterprises are more efficient.

At first glance, the likelihood of such enduring subsidization seems slight, because it reduces the total profit of the conglomerate enterprise. But profit is not necessarily reduced by carrying the overhead on certain products and selling others at something more than out-of-pocket costs. That conglomerates persist in their subsidized activities appears to be the result of four other influences also. First, because of the prevalence of joint costs and the arbitrary nature of cost allocation, large enterprises seldom segregate costs and profits on a market-by-market basis, and have little faith in the reliability of costs thus segregated. Hence, they are uncertain what markets are profitable. Second, difference of profit from one product to another is regarded as normal in a large enterprise; relatively unprofitable lines of business are dropped infrequently and only when the evidence against them appears to be very strong. Third, each effort to drop an unprofitable line is likely to be resisted by persons in the enterprise whose jobs depend directly on that line. It is somewhat like the effort of the

Congress to drop a redundant Government bureau. Fourth, in the strategy of the enterprise as a whole, unprofitable business activities are sometimes desirable as supplements to others, and the ability to subsidize them from other activities contributes to flexibility and strength.

Because of its obvious ability to accept temporary losses, a conglomerate may also be able to impose its will upon its specialized competitors. It can discipline or destroy them by selective price cutting. A geographically dispersed conglomerate can cut prices locally; a diversified conglomerate can use loss leaders. Where such tactics are crude—that is, where a small firm is told what to do and punished for not doing it—they are likely to be illegal. But subtler differences in price policy, particularly differences between prices on one product and another, can be described as responses to competition, and are likely to be beyond the law's reach. Knowing themselves to be exposed to the possibility of such pressures, small specialized firms are likely to acquiesce in the policies of their large conglomerate rivals. A big conglomerate that becomes a price leader seldom needs to use threats, and even more seldom needs to take overt disciplinary action. Most small rivals can be coerced by their own imaginations.

So far as subsidies are prevalent in conglomerate enterprise, they reduce the effectiveness of markets in allocating resources. Markets are expected to serve as automatic correctives of misapplied effort—to discourage the production of goods that are not worth their cost and to stimulate the production of profitable goods. For various reasons, including the prevalence of public and private subsidies, markets fail to do this adequately. So far as conglomerate business structures make the relative costs of different products more uncertain or increase the amount of subsidized production, they make the functioning of markets less adequate.

So much for subsidization.

Reciprocal buying appears to be common among conglomerates. As a diversified enterprise, a large conglomerate buys a large and varied assortment of goods and services. These purchases can be used as leverage in making sales. When a conglomerate adopts such a policy, it is likely to instruct its various buyers to report all purchases, classified by the name of the supplier; to compile totals for each source of supply, and to report these totals to an official who bears some such title as "director of trade relations." The director then approaches his counterparts in other enterprises with the argument that his company's purchases should be recognized by reciprocal purchases—an argument that implies a threat that if satisfactory reciprocal purchases are not made, he will divert his own company's purchases to other sources. Such reciprocity tends to stultify competition in the same way that intergovernmental barter deals stultify it in international trade. Particular sources of goods obtain reciprocal special favors, to the detriment of excluded third parties. Since leverage in reciprocity increases with the enterprise's aggregate purchases, small firms may become satellites of their largest customers, and large firms reciprocally derive strength as sellers from their bigness as buyers. Bigness fosters still more bigness.

In relations with distributors and customers, a conglomerate enterprise can use the sale of one product as a source of leverage to sell another. In its crudest form, such a policy consists of tying or full-line forcing—refusal to sell a product that cannot readily be obtained elsewhere unless the buyer accepts other products also. Such crude tactics violate our own antitrust laws and are widely considered abuses of economic power in Western Europe. But subtler ways of accomplishing similar results are available to a conglomerate enterprise. Most of them consist of various methods of using coordinated sales activity and coordinated advertising to promote the full line of products. By spreading sales expense over more products, the seller can often diminish the selling cost for each product. From the point of view of the enterprise, this is an economy. From the point of view of the community as a whole, it is a bargaining advantage available to large diversified enterprises, that does not necessarily reduce the total cost of selling or redound to the consumer's advantage.

When one large conglomerate enterprise competes with another, the two are likely to encounter each other in a considerable number of markets. The multiplicity of their contacts may blunt the edge of their competition. A prospect of advantage from vigorous competition in one market may be weighed against the danger of retaliatory forays by the competitor in other markets. Each conglomerate competitor may adopt a live-and-let-live policy designed to stabilize the whole structure of the competitive relationship. Each may informally recognize the other's primacy of interest in markets important to the other, in the expectation that its own important interests will be similarly respected. Like national states, the great conglomerates may come to have recognized spheres of influence and may hesitate to fight local wars vigorously because the prospect of local gain are not worth the risk of general warfare.

The foregoing considerations lead me to conclude that large conglomerate enterprises possess kinds of power that may involve jeopardy to competition. In some instances a direct anticompetitive effect is apparent. In other instances, magnitude of resources, internal subsidy, coordinated sales effort, and reciprocity may significantly increase the obstacles to entry by new firms into the affected markets, and may thus significantly diminish competition. In still other instances, use of conglomerate power may give sufficient advantage to foster an increase in diversification and in size, and may thus tend through time toward a more concentrated and less competitive economy.

I doubt that many small conglomerates create these problems. I doubt that all large ones do. I believe that the likelihood of anticompetitive effect increases with the size of the conglomerate and also with the proportion of the economy in which similar conglomerate power is exercised.

The Large Conglomerate Firm: A Different View

JESSE MARKHAM

Jesse Markham is Professor of Economics at Princeton University. This short piece is taken from his testimony in 1965 before a subcommittee of the Senate Judiciary Committee.

PROFESSOR CORWIN EDWARDS pointed out that "conglomerate enterprise does not have a well-defined place either in public policy or economic theory," and that partly for this reason we know relatively little about the subject. This deficiency in our knowledge will remain with us for some time unless the subject is explored with greater depth and circumspection than has been accorded it in the past. Lacking the requisite analytical framework for assessing the behavior of business enterprises simultaneously engaged in the production and/or marketing of ostensibly unrelated products, economists have tended to obscure the problem by covering it with the relatively meaningless label "conglomerate firm." This would have been harmless, albeit unproductive, had the same economists conformed to George Gaylord Simpson's observation on the social researcher set forth in his provocative "The Meaning of Evolution" some years ago:

> Each student thus actually puts his theory into the data, and it is not surprising that each then gets his own theory out of these data when he is through.

But in inquiring into conglomerateness we appear to have gotten out of the inquiry much more than we put into it. We coined the phrase to describe an economic phenomenon we know relatively little about; but once we had the handy title we seem to have imparted to it far greater capabilities for explaining how large diversified firms operate than were available to us when we called such firms by other names. I myself seriously doubt that switching the labels in any way altered the contents of the package.

What I mean is this: The argument goes that the conglomerate firm, simply by virtue of the fact that it actively engages in producing and selling in two or more reasonably distinct markets, somehow acquires a special advantage over its single-product competitors in each. This thesis, stated in its harshest, boldest, and simplest form asserts that the conglomerate firm can elect to take its profits where it chooses, and can therefore use its earnings in one market to wage unfair competitive warfare against its smaller rivals in another; it can be less efficient in producing a product than its single-product competitors who also produce that product because it can draw on pools of resources available to it from other markets; in short, the conglomerate firm is really several firms at once, operating under several distinct sets of managerial rules; in some markets it is intent on earning maximum profits, in others on maximizing the discomfiture of its competitors. It strives for efficiency in some operations so that it can indulge in carelessness in others.

The slight note of acidity that may possibly be detected in the foregoing remarks is not entirely unintentional. There is fairly persuasive evidence that the practices enumerated above are indeed pursued in American industry; they are even pursued by the U.S. Government in the sense that revenues from first-class mail and other sources are used to "sell" lower classes of postal service at substantially "below cost." But such practices in neither Government nor private industry can be satisfactorily explained simply by showing that both can appropriately be described as conglomerate.

What I shall now endeavor to do is to provide a more meaningful way of looking at and analyzing the multiproduct firm. Probably the most accepted proposition in economic theory is that capital tends to flow into those economic activities where it receives the highest reward. If nothing impedes this flow, and if innovations do not occur with such rapidity that the economy remains in a state of general disequilibrium, the rates of return on capital in all lines of productive effort will tend toward equality, with appropriate allowance for the differential risks involved. Hence, in an economy devoid of differential rates of industrial innovation and monopoly power, the competitive forces of the capital market should tend to bring the rate of return on investment in all industries into a state of equality, except for risks. In such a workably competitive economy, no firm, irrespective of the number of individual product markets in which it may be engaged—irrespective of its degree of "conglomerateness"—would be in a position "unfairly" to subsidize one of its product lines from profits earned on other products. Such profits by definition are only sufficient to reward the capital employed at the competitive rate of return. Hence conglomerateness and nothing more raises no public policy issue; the term is simply a synonym for industrial diversification and bestows on the business entity to which it is frequently applied no more nor no less special significance than that of a group of independent firms competing in the same markets. Perhaps this point can be made clearer by reflecting on the economic position of a small textile mill operator who may also at the same time operate a wheat farm, a local fertilizer dealership, and be in the broiler industry. If all of these industries are in fact as competitive as various definitive economic studies show them to be, the conglomerateness of the firm bestows on it no special advantage over its competitors in any one of its four markets—it cannot use above-normal profits from its broiler business to wage unfair competition against its textile competitors for the simple reason that it does not possess the market power required to earn monopoly rewards.

It should be noted that the foregoing conclusion rests on the assumptions that (1) all markets are effectively competitive—no firms earn monopoly rewards, and (2) technological change is not going on at so rapid a rate that firms of necessity lag significantly in adjusting to it. If either or both of these assumptions are not fulfilled there are opportunities in the system for some business firms to exercise power over the market and to earn more than competitive rates of return, and hence to accumulate uncommitted surpluses. It is this discretionary power over the market unchecked effectively by market forces, and not "conglomerateness," or for that matter, "bigness," that makes possible the anticompetitive tactics often erroneously assigned to the large multiproduct firm as such.

The New Industrial State

JOHN KENNETH GALBRAITH

John Kenneth Galbraith is Paul M. Warburg Professor of Economics at Harvard University. This paper was presented in 1967 before a subcommittee of the Senate Committee on Small Business, the purpose being to discuss some of the ideas in Galbraith's The New Industrial State, *published in 1967.*

IN THE LECTURES that precipitated this discussion and the book I have just published,[1] I took it for granted that American business has become very big. The element of surprise in this conclusion is very small; I doubt that this conclusion will be much disputed. There are still a large number of small firms and small farms in the United States. They are, however, no longer characteristic of the American economy. In 1962, the five largest industrial corporations in the United States, with combined assets in excess of $36 billion, possessed over 12 percent of all assets used in manufacturing. The 50 largest corporations had over a third of all manufacturing assets. The 500 largest corporations had well over two-thirds. Corporations with assets in excess of $10 million, some 2,000 in all, accounted for about 80 percent of all the resources used in manufacturing in the United States.

In the mid-1950's, 28 corporations provided approximately 10 percent of all employment in manufacturing, mining, and retail and wholesale trade. Twenty-three corporations provided 15 percent of all the employment in manufacturing. In the first half of that decade—June 1950–June 1956—a hundred firms received two-thirds by value of all defense contracts; 10 firms received one-third. In 1960 four corporations accounted for an estimated 22 percent of all industrial research and development expenditure. Three hundred and eighty-four corporations employing 5,000 or more workers accounted for 85 percent of these research and development expenditures; 260,000 firms employing fewer than 1,000 accounted for only 7 percent.

1. "The New Industrial State" (Boston: Houghton Mifflin Co., 1967).

If I might continue this somewhat exaggerated dose of statistics for just a minute, in 1965, three industrial corporations, General Motors, Standard Oil of New Jersey, and Ford Motor Co. had more gross income than all of the farms in the country. This is relevant to my statement that these are the typical, characteristic parts of the economy. The income of General Motors, of $20.7 billion, about equalled that of the 3 million smallest farms in the country—around 90 percent of all farms. The gross revenues of each of the three corporations just mentioned far exceed those of any single State. The revenues of General Motors in 1963 were 50 times those of Nevada, eight times those of New York, and slightly less than one-fifth those of the Federal Government.

These figures, like all statistics, are subject to minor query on matters of detail. As orders of magnitude they are not, I believe, subject to any serious question. Nor are the consequences.

The large firms that dominate the nonservice and nonagricultural sector of the economy have extensive power over their prices. They have large influence over the prices that they pay— at least those costs that are important to their operations. And also the wages they pay. They supply themselves with capital; some three-quarters of all savings now come from the retained earnings of corporations, which is to say that the latter have largely exempted themselves from dependence on the capital market. And, with varying degrees of success, firms with the resources to do so go beyond the prices that they set to persuade their customers as to what they should buy. This is a persuasion that, in various and subtle ways, extends to the State. There is great room for difference of opinion, and accordingly for debate, on how decisive are these several manifestations of power. But nearly all will agree that "There is a large correlation between the concentration of output in the hands of a small number of large producers and the existence of firms with significant degrees of market power." The observation just cited is that of Mr. Carl Kaysen and Mr. Donald F. Turner in their authoritative volume, "A Policy for Antitrust Law." [2]

They add, as would I, that a policy that deals with "the existence and significance of market power is not aimed at *merely marginal or special phenomena, but at phenomena spread widely*

2. Harvard University Press, 1959, pp. 8–9.

through the economy." [3] Still quoting Professor Kaysen and Mr. Turner.

In my own volume I have gone on, at no slight length, to argue that this trend to the large corporation and this resulting exercise of substantial power over the prices, costs, wages, capital sources, and consumers is part of the broad sweep of economic development. Technology; the extensive use of capital; affluent and hence malleable customers; the imperatives of organization; the role of the union; the requirements imposed by public tasks, including arms development and space exploration, have all weakened the authority of the market. At the same time, these developments have both enabled and required firms to substitute planning with its management of markets for a simple response to the market. Bigness and market power, in other words, are but one part of a much larger current of change. To see them in isolation from other change is artificial. In part it is what results when a social discipline passes however partially from the custody of scholars to that of specialists and mechanics.

I have also been concerned in this book with the problem of how we are to survive, and in civilized fashion, in a world of great organizations which, not surprisingly, impose both their values and their needs on the society they are assumed to serve. But these further matters . . . do not directly involve the question of the antitrust laws.

The issue of the antitrust laws arises in response to a prior question. That question is whether we can escape the concentration and the attendant market control and planning which I have outlined and whether the antitrust laws, as now used, are an effective instrument for this escape. The present hearings materialized when I urged the contrary—when I said that the trend to great size and associated control was immutable, given our desire for economic development, and that the present antitrust efforts to deal with size and market power were a charade. I noted that the antitrust laws legitimatize the real exercise of market power on the part of the large firms by a rather diligent harassment of those who have less of it. Thus, they serve to reassure us on the condition they are assumed to correct.

The facts which lead to the foregoing conclusions are not at all

3. *Ibid.,* p. 41. (Emphasis is Dr. Galbraith's.)

obscure. Nor are they matters of great subtlety. They are accepted by most competent economists and lawyers. Only the rather obvious conclusions to be drawn from these facts encounter a measure of resistance. This, no doubt, is purely temporary, but while it persists it does cause a measure of confusion.

The most effective manifestation of economic power, all must agree, is simply the big firm. To be big in general and big in an industry is by far the best way of influencing prices and costs, commanding capital, having access to advertising, and selling resources, and possessing the other requisites of market power. And, as we have seen, by common agreement the heartland of the industrial economy is now dominated by large firms. The great bulk of American business is transacted by very large corporations.

And here enters the element of charade in the antitrust laws. If a firm is already large it is substantially immune under the antitrust laws. If you already have the basic requisite of market power, you are safe. The assistant Attorney General in Charge of the Antitrust Laws [Donald F. Turner] in the distinguished book to which I have already adverted argues that the market power of the large firm should now be made subject to the antitrust laws. This indeed is the main thrust of Mr. Turner's and Mr. Kaysen's book. If something needs to be done, he would not, of course, argue that it has been done. And in responding to the questions of this committee on May 2 of this year he affirmed the point, if in slightly more cautious language:

> It is more difficult under present law to bring a case attacking *existing* concentration in an industry than to prevent further concentrations which firms attempt to realize through merger.

But this we see is no minor qualification. If firms are already large—if concentration is already great—if the resulting power to use Mr. Turner's own words, is not "merely marginal" but is "spread widely through the economy" as he says, then it means that all so favored have won immunity or virtual immunity from the antitrust laws. And this, of course, is the case.

Meanwhile, the antitrust laws are effective in two instances where the firms do not have market power but are seeking to achieve it. Where firms are few and large they can, without overt collusion, establish and maintain a price that is generally satisfactory to all participants. Nor is this an especially difficult calculation, this exercise of power. This is what we economists with our genius for the neat phrase have come to call oliogopolistic rationality. And this market power is legally immune or very nearly so. It is everyday practice in autos, steel, rubber, and virtually every other industry shared or dominated by, relatively, a few large firms. But if there are 20 or 30 or more significant firms in the industry, this kind of tacit pricemaking—this calculation as to what is mutually advantageous but without overt communication —becomes more difficult, maybe very difficult. The same result can only be achieved by having a meeting or by exchanging information on prices and costs and price intentions. But this is illegal. It is also legally vulnerable. And it is, in fact, an everyday object of prosecution as the Department of Justice will confirm. What the big firm in the concentrated industry can accomplish legally and effortlessly because of its size, the small firm in the unconcentrated industry does at the pain of civil and even criminal prosecution. Moreover, with this my colleagues will, I believe, agree.

The second manifestation of the charade has to do with mergers. If a firm is already large, it has as a practical matter nothing to fear under antimerger provisions of the Clayton Act. It will not be demerged. It can continue to grow from its own earnings; if discreet, it can even, from time to time, pick up a small and impecunious competitor, for it can reasonably claim that this does little to alter the pattern of competition in the industry. But if two medium-sized firms unite in order to deal more effectively with this giant, the law will be on them like a tiger. Again if large, you are exempt. If you seek to become as large, or even if you seek to become somewhat larger, although still much smaller, you are in trouble. And again I doubt that the committee will encounter a great deal of dissent.

Here we have the nature of modern antitrust activity. It conducts a fairly effective war on small firms which seek the same market power that the big firms already, by their nature, possess. Behind this impressive facade the big participants who have the most power bask in nearly total immunity. And since the competitive market, like God and a sound family life, is something that no sound businessman can actively oppose, even the smaller entrepreneurs who are the natural victims of this arrangement do not actively protest. It is possible that they do not know how they are being used.

As I say all of this is agreed—or at least is supported by the past writings and speeches of participants in this discussion. All I have done—I wish I could lay claim to greater novelty—is to state the rather disagreeable conclusion flowing from this agreement. The antitrust laws give the impression of protecting the market and competition by attacking those who exercise it most effectively, I wonder if the committee thinks that charade is an unjust word?

Now let me clear up two or three secondary matters which may seem to affect this discussion but really do not. The first requires me, I think for the first time—in substance as distinct from terminology—to quit company with Attorney General Turner. Mr. Turner, while conceding that the law is largely helpless in attacking achieved as distinct from aspired-to power, holds that it is important to act preventatively to keep smaller firms from getting larger. This he has emphasized in his responses to this committee. It will surely have occurred to the committee, as it must have occurred to Mr. Turner, that this does not meet the issue of gross discrimination as between those who already have and those who aspire to market power. Nor, one imagines, can a major law officer of the Government be entirely happy about such discrimination. It condones professional and accomplished wrongdoing, as it were, but stresses the importance of cracking down on amateur wickedness. Surely this is bad law. Also, given the size and market power that has already been achieved, and given its immunity, it will be evident that this justification amounts to locking the stable door not alone after the horse has been stolen but after the entire stud has been galloped away.

Next, I must correct a misapprehension of Attorney General Turner. His responses to the committee and his extremely interesting lecture attacking my general position in London convey the impression that I am concerned with making the economic case for the large corporation. I am, he suggests, especially concerned to defend its efficiency and technical virtuosity. To this he responds by arguing that, while the big corporation is more efficient than the small firm, there is no great difference between the big corporation and the giant corporation. He doesn't make altogether clear, incidentally, how big a big as distinct from a giant corporation is. All would, I imagine, be among the five hundred or thousand firms that dominate industrial activity. But I have a more fundamental objection. He attacks me on a point that concerns me little and which is of no importance for my case.

I am not concerned with making the case for big business. Nor am I especially concerned about its efficiency or inefficiency. Doubtless efficiency is worth having. But, like truth, regular bathing and better traffic regulation, it has an adequate number of exponents. I have always thought it unwise to compete with the commonplace. Mr. Turner may be correct in his conclusions about the giants. I am content to argue that we have big business, and that the antitrust laws notwithstanding we will continue to have it, and that they give an impression of alternative possibilities that do not exist.

I conclude also that while big business and giant business may not be more efficient, their market power as manifested only on what they sell and what they buy and over buyers does give them advantages in planning their own future and insuring their own survival. Since big business is inevitable and will not be affected by the antitrust laws, I naturally go on to consider how we may come to terms with it. Much of my book is concerned with that. If my colleagues this morning disagree, as is their right, they must tell you how the antitrust laws are to be brought effectively to bear on the large corporation. Otherwise—and here let me interpolate an important point—there is no escape from the conclusion that the antitrust laws, so far from being a threat to business are a facade behind which it operates with yet greater impunity. They create the impression, the antitrust laws, that the market is a viable control. Then, if a drug firm has exorbitant profits, it can say this is what the market allows. Or if an automobile firm does not want to install safety appliances, it can say that the market does not demand it. Or if there is resistance to Government price guideposts to prevent inflation, it can be said that these interfere with the market.

In each case, the antitrust laws effectively protect the large business from social pressure or regulation by maintaining the myth that the market does the regulating instead.

Finally, I agree that the antitrust laws have purposes other than those related to the structure of industry and the resulting power and planning. I agree in particular they are a code of what is deemed fair and decent as between seller and buyers. They exclude the resort to activities—naked aggression, as in the case of the old Standard Oil Co. in the last century—based on superior economic resources, favoritism, surreptitious and unfair discounts, numerous other practices which the civilized commercial community holds in disesteem. I have no complaint about these aspects of the antitrust laws. On the contrary, I consider them serviceable. But only in the most marginal fashion do they thus affect the structure of industry. They are, in large part, a separate matter and do not affect the discussion here.

To what then does this all lead? It is possible that my distinguished colleagues here this morning will call for an all-out attack on achieved market power along the lines which Attorney General Turner has adumbrated in his book, which Prof. Walter Adams has long favored, and which I have just said would be necessary if they disagree with my conclusions on the inevitability of market power. This means action, including enabling legislation leading to all-out dissolution proceedings against General Motors, Ford, the oil majors, United States Steel, General Electric, IBM, Western Electric, Du Pont, Swift, Bethlehem, International Harvester, North American Aviation, Goodyear, Boeing, National Dairy Products, Procter & Gamble, Eastman Kodak, and all of comparable size and scope. For there can be no doubt: All are giants. All have market power. All enjoy an immunity not accorded to those who merely aspire to their power. Such an onslaught, tantamount, given the role of the big firms in the economy as I described it, to declaring the heartland of the modern economy illegal, would go far to make legitimate the objections to my position. It would mean that achieved market power was subject to the same legal attack as that which is only a matter of aspiration.

But I will be a trifle surprised if my distinguished colleagues from the Government are willing to proclaim such a crusade. I am frank to say I would not favor it myself; as I indicated at the outset, I do not think that the growth of the modern corporation can be isolated from other and intricately related changes in modern economic development. I doubt that one can operate on one part of this fabric. The political problems in proclaiming much of the modern economy illegal will also strike many as impressive.

If this crusade is not to be launched, then my good friends have no alternative but to agree with me. They are good men; they cannot acquiesce in a policy which by their own admission attacks the small man for seeking what the bit firm enjoys with impunity. I readily concede that it would be quixotic to ask the repeal of the antitrust laws although other industrial countries function quite competently without them. But the antitrust laws are part of the American folklore. They receive strong support from the legal profession and vice versa. They have a reserve value for dealing with extreme and sanguinary abuse of power as occasionally occurs. I would be content were we simply to withdraw our faith from the antitrust laws—were we to cease to imagine that there is any chance that they will affect the structure of American industry or its market power and, having in mind the present discrimination in their application, were we then to allow them quietly to atrophy. Then we would face the real problem, which is how to live with the vast organizations— and the values they impose—that we have and will continue to have. This being so, nostalgia will no longer be a disguise for that necessity.

Another View of the New Industrial State

WALTER ADAMS

Walter Adams is Professor of Economics at Michigan State University. This paper, with the preceeding paper by John Kenneth Galbraith, was presented in 1967 before a subcommittee of the Senate Committee on Small Business, the purpose being to discuss some of the ideas in Galbraith's The New Industrial State.

TIME PRECLUDES more than a cursory tribute to an eminently civilized and literate political economist—a leader in that small but brave army of men who "prefer to see the truth imperfectly and obscurely rather than to maintain error, reached indeed with clearness and consistency and by easy logic, but based on hypotheses inappropriate to the facts." It is Galbraith's cardinal virtue to focus on real problems and vital issues. His questions are invariably to the point. Regrettably, his answers are sometimes wrong.

In *The New Industrial State,* Galbraith once again examines the reality of corporate giantism and corporate power, and outlines the implications for public policy. He finds that the giant corportion has achieved such dominance of American industry, that it can control its environment and immunize itself from the discipline of all exogenous control mechanisms—especially the competitive market. Through separation of ownership from management it has emancipated itself from the control of stockholders. By reinvestment of profits (internal financing), it has eliminated the influence of the financier and the capital market. By brainwashing its clientele, it has insulated itself from consumer sovereignty. By possession of market power, it has come to dominate both suppliers and customers. By judicious identification with, and manipulation of the state, it has achieved autonomy from government control. Whatever it cannot do for itself to assure survival and growth, a compliant government does on its behalf—

assuring the maintenance of full employment; eliminating the risk of, and subsidizing the investment in, research and development; and assuring the supply of scientific and technical skills required by the modern technostructure.

In return for this privileged autonomy, the industrial giant performs society's planning function. And this, according to Galbraith, is not only inevitable (because technological imperatives dictate it); it is also good. The market is dead, we are told; and there is no need to regret its passing. The only remaining task, it seems, is to recognize the trend, to accept it as inexorable necessity, and, presumably, not to stand in its way.

Mr. Chairman, here is a blueprint for technocracy, private socialism, and the corporate state. The keystone of the new power structure is the giant corporation, freed from all traditional checks and balances, and subject only to the countervailing power of the intellectual in politics—those Platonic philosopher-kings who stand guard over the interests of the Republic. Happily, this blueprint need not cause undue alarm: first, because Galbraith's analysis rests on an empirically unsubstantiated premise; and second, even if this analysis were correct, there would be more attractive public policy alternatives than Galbraith suggests.

Galbraith's contention that corporate giantism dominates American industry requires no adumbration. On that there is consensus. But Galbraith fails to prove that this dominance is the inevitable response to technological imperatives, and hence beyond our control. Specifically, he offers little evidence to demonstate that Brobdingnagian size is the prerequisite for, and the guarantor of—

(1) operational efficiency;
(2) invention, innovation, and technological progress; and
(3) effective planning in the public interest.

Let me comment briefly on each of these points, and in so doing indicate that the competitive market need not be condemned to the euthanasia which Galbraith thinks is inexorable, and perhaps even desirable.

EFFICIENCY

In the mass-production industries, firms must undoubtedly be large, but do they need to assume the dinosaur proportions of some present-day giants? The unit of technological efficiency is the plant, not the firm. This means that there are undisputed advantages to large-scale integrated operations at a single steel plant, for example, but there is little technological justification for combining these functionally separate plants into a single administrative unit. United States Steel is nothing more than several Inland Steels strewn about the country, and no one has yet suggested that Inland is not big enough to be efficient. A firm producing such divergent lines as rubber boots, chain saws, motorboats, and chicken feed may be seeking conglomerate size and power; it is certainly not responding to technological necessity. In short, one can favor technological bigness and oppose administrative bigness without inconsistency.

Two major empirical studies document this generalization. The first, by Dr. John M. Blair, indicates a significant divergence between plant and company concentration in major industries dominated by oligopoly. It indicates, moreover, that between 1947 and 1958, there was a general tendency for plant concentration to decline, which means that in many industries technology may actually militate toward optimal efficiency in plants of "smaller" size.

The second study, by Professor Joe Bain, presents engineering estimates of scale economies and capital requirements in 20 industries of above-average concentration. Bain finds that—

o o o Concentration by firms is in every case but one greater than required by single-plant economies, and in more than half of the cases very substantially greater.

In less precise language, many multiplant industrial giants have gone beyond the optimal size required for efficiency. Galbraith acknowledges the validity of Bain's findings, but dismisses them by saying:

The size of General Motors is in the service not of monopoly or the economies of scale, but of planning. And for this planning o o o there is no clear upper limit to the desirable size. It could be that the bigger the better.

If size is to be justified, then, this must be done on grounds other than efficiency. I shall return to this point in a moment.

TECHNOLOGICAL PROGRESS

As in the case of efficiency, there is no strict correlation between giantism and progressiveness. In a study of the 60 most important inventions of recent years, it was found that more than half came from independent inventors, less than half from corporate research, and even less from the research done by large concerns. Moreover, while some highly concentrated industries spend a large share of their income on research, others do not; within the same industry, some smaller firms spend as high a *percentage* as their larger rivals. As Wilcox points out:

The big concern has the ability to finance innovation; it does not necessarily do so. There is no clear relationship between size and investment in research.

Finally, as this committee well knows, roughly two-thirds of the research done in the United States is financed by the Federal Government, and in many cases the research contractor gets the patent rights on inventions paid for with public funds. The inventive genius which ostensibly goes with size would seem to involve socialization of risk and privatization of profit and power.

The U.S. steel industry, which ranks among the largest, most basic, and most concentrated of American industries, certainly part of the industrial state that Professor Galbraith speaks of, affords a dramatic case in point. It spends only 0.7 percent of its revenues on research and, in technological progressiveness, the giants which dominate this industry lag behind their smaller domestic rivals as well as their smaller foreign competitors. Thus, the basic oxygen furnace—considered the "only major breakthrough at the ingot level since before the turn of the century" was invented in 1950 by a miniscule Austrian *firm* which was less than one-third the size of a single *plant* of the United States Steel Corp. The innovation was introduced in the United States in 1954 by McLouth Steel which at the time had about 1 percent of domestic steel capacity—to be followed some 10 years later by the steel giants: United States Steel in December 1963, Bethlehem in 1964, and Republic in 1965. Despite the fact that this revolutionary invention involved an average operating cost saving of $5 per ton and an investment cost saving of $20 per ton of installed capacity, the steel giants during the 1950's according to Business Week, "brought 40 million tons of the wrong capacity—the open-hearth furnace" which was obsolete almost the moment it was put in place.

Only after they were subjected to actual and threatened competition from domestic and foreign steelmakers in the 1960's did the steel giants decide to accommodate themselves to the oxygen revolution. Thus, it was the cold wind of competition, and not the catatonia induced by industrial concentration, which proved conducive to innovation and technological progress.

PLANNING IN THE PUBLIC INTEREST

Modern technology, says Galbraith, makes planning essential, and the giant corporation is its chosen instrument. This planning, in turn, requires the corporation to eliminate risk and uncertainty, to create for itself an environment of stability and security, and to free itself from all outside interference with its planning function. Thus, it must have enough size and power not only to produce a "mauve and cerise, air-conditioned, power-steered, and power-braked automobile"—unsafe at any speed—but also enough power to brainwash customers to buy it. In the interest of planning, producers must be able to sell what they make—be it automobiles or missiles—and at prices which the techno-structure deems remunerative.

Aside from the unproved premise—and I keep coming back to this: technological necessity—on which this argument rests, it raises crucial questions of responsibility and accountability. By what standards do the industrial giants plan, and is there an automatic convergence between private and public advantage? Must we, as a matter of inexorable inevitability, accept the proposition that what is good for General Motors is good for the country? What are the safeguards—other than the intellectual in politics —against arbitrary abuse of power, capricious or faulty decision-making? Must society legitimatize a self-sustaining, self-serving, self-justifying, and self-perpetuating industrial oligarchy as the price for industrial efficiency and progress?

The high price need not and should not be paid. The competitive market is a far more efficacious instrument for serving society—and far more viable—than Galbraith would have us believe.

Let me illustrate:

(1) In the electric power industry, a network of local monopolies, under Government regulation and protection, was long addicted to the belief that the demand for electric power was inelastic—that rates had little to do with the quantity of electricity used. It was not industrial planning, carried on by private monopolists under public supervision, but the yardstick competition of TVA which demonstrated the financial feasibility of aggressive rate reductions. It was this competitive experiment which proved that lower electric rates were not only possible but also profitable —both to the private monopolists and to the customers they served.

(2) In the airline oligopoly, also operating under the umbrella of Government protectionism, the dominant firms long suffered from the same addiction. They refused to institute coach service on the grounds that it would eliminate first-class service and— through a reduction in the rate structure—bring financial ruin to the industry. Again it was the force and discipline of competition —from the small, nonscheduled carriers, operating at the margin of the industry—which proved that the giants and their overprotective public regulators were wrong. As this committee observed, it was the pioneering and competition of the nonskeds which "shattered the concept of the fixed, limited market for civil aviation. As a result, the question is no longer what portion of a fixed pie any company will get, but rather how much the entire pie can grow."

Again, a bureaucracy-ridden, conservative, overcautious, overprotected industry was shown to have engaged in defective planning—to its own detriment as well as the public's.

(3) In the steel industry, after World War II, oligopoly planning resulted in truly shabby performance. There was an almost unbroken climb in steel prices, in good times and bad, in the face of rising or falling demand, increasing or declining unit costs. Prices rose even when only 50 percent of the industry's capacity was utilized. Technological change was resisted and obsolete capacity installed. Domestic markets were eroded by substitute materials and burgeoning imports. Steel's export-import balance deteriorated both in absolute and relative terms; whereas the industry once exported about five times as much as it imported, the ratio today is almost exactly reversed, and steel exports are

confined almost exclusively to AID-financed sales guaranteed by "Buy American" provisos. We may be confident that if this deplorable performance is to be improved, it will come about through the disciplining force of domestic and foreign competition, and not through additional planning or an escalation of giant size. It will come about through an accommodation to the exigencies of the world market, and not by insensitive monopolist pricing, practiced under the protectionist shelter of the tariffs which the industry now seeks.

Without multiplying such examples, it is safe to say that monopoloid planning is done in the interest of monopoly power. Seldom, if ever, is society the beneficiary.

In conclusion, I would note that industrial giantism in America is not the product of spontaneous generation, natural selection, or technological inevitability. In this era of "Big Government," it is often the end result of unwise, manmade, discriminatory, privilege-creating governmental action. Defense contracts, R. & D. support, patent policy, tax privileges, stockpiling arrangements, tariffs, subsidies, etc., have far from a neutral effect on our industrial structure. Especially in the regulated industries—in air and surface transportation, in broadcasting and communications—the writ of the State is decisive. In controlling these variables the policymaker has greater freedom and flexibility than is commonly supposed; the potential for promoting competition and dispersing industrial power is both real and practicable.

It seems to me that Professor Galbraith keeps coming back to the charade of antitrust, but a competitive society is the product not simply of negative enforcement of the antitrust laws; it is the product of a total integrated approach on all levels of government —legislative, administrative, and regulatory. An integrated national policy of promoting competition—and this means more than mere enforcement of the antitrust laws—is not only feasible but desirable. No economy can function without built-in checks and balances which tend to break down the bureaucratic preference for letting well enough alone—forces which erode, subvert, or render obsolete the conservative bias inherent in any organization devoid of competition. Be it the dictates of the competitive market, the pressure from imports or substitutes, or the discipline of yardstick competition, it is these forces which the policymaker must try to reinforce where they exist and to *build into* the economic system where they are lacking or moribund. The policy objective throughout must be to promote market *structures* which will *compel* the conduct and performance which is in the public interest.

The disciplining force of competition is superior to industrial planning—by the private or public monopolist, the benevolent or authoritarian bureaucrat. It alone provides the incentives and compulsions to pioneer untried trails, to explore paths which may lead to dead ends, to take risks which may not pay off, and to try to make tomorrow better than the best.

PART THREE

The Antitrust Laws:
Provisions, Effectiveness,
and Standards

Substantive Provisions of the Antitrust Laws

CLAIR WILCOX

*Clair Wilcox is Joseph Wharton Professor of Political Economy
at Swarthmore College. The following article is taken from his
book* Public Policies Toward Business.

IN THE NATIONAL campaign of 1888, the two major parties, while differing on the tariff, competed for the votes of farmers by professing opposition to monopoly. The Democrats, then in office, denounced the tariff as the mother of the trusts. The Republicans, proposing higher duties, replied that they could compel competition at home while preventing competition from abroad. Both party platforms promised enactment of legislation against monopoly. Following the Republican victory, President Harrison sent a message to Congress, in 1889, asking that this pledge be redeemed. A number of antimonopoly bills were introduced, one of them by Senator Sherman of Ohio. There was little active interest in the legislation; Congress was preoccupied with other matters, including the elevation of the tariff and the passage of the Silver Purchase Act. No hearings were held; the bill that finally emerged from the Congressional committees was enacted, following a brief debate that raised no fundamental issues, with only one dissenting vote in the Senate and without a record vote in the House. It was signed by the President on July 2, 1890. Bearing little or no resemblance to the bill originally introduced by Senator Sherman, it was given his name.

THE SHERMAN ACT

The Sherman Act, unlike most Acts of Congress, is short and simple. Its major provisions could easily be memorized:

Sec. 1. Every contract, combination in the form of a trust or otherwise, or conspiracy, in restraint of trade or commerce among the several states, or with foreign nations, is hereby declared to be illegal. Every person who shall make any such contract or engage in any such combination or conspiracy, shall be deemed guilty of a misdemeanor. . . .

Sec. 2. Every person who shall monopolize, or attempt to monopolize, or combine or conspire with any other person or persons, to monopolize any part of the trade or commerce among the several states, or with foreign nations, shall be deemed guilty of a misdemeanor. . . .

The Act thus took over the concepts of restraint of trade and monopolization from the common law, without attempting further to define their meaning. Its first section applies only to agreements in which two or more persons are involved. Its second section is broader, applying also to individual efforts to monopolize.

In substance, the legislation contained nothing that was new. Its real contribution was to turn restraint of trade and monopolization into offenses against the federal government, to require enforcement by federal officials, and to provide for the imposition of penalties. United States district attorneys, acting under the direction of the Attorney General, were instructed to institute proceedings in equity to compel observance of the law. It was also their duty to bring criminal suits against those who violated its terms. Such violations were made punishable by fines up to $5,000, imprisonment up to one year, or both. Persons injured by illegal restraints or monopolies were entitled to sue for triple damages.

The Sherman Act, with the continued support of both major parties, remained the only important antitrust law to be enacted for nearly a quarter of a century. In the Wilson Tariff Act of 1894, similar provisions were applied to persons importing goods into the United States. In legislation granting rights to certain lands, in 1908 and 1910, violation of the Sherman Act was made a basis for cancellation of these rights. In the Panama Canal Act of 1912, violators operating boats were denied the privilege of passing through the canal. But it was not until 1914 that major additions to the law were made.

THE CLAYTON AND FEDERAL TRADE COMMISSION ACTS

There was increasing dissatisfaction, in the years before 1914, with the operation of the Sherman Act. During the administrations of Cleveland and McKinley, the laws had scarcely been enforced. Powerful new combinations had been formed in steel, tin cans, corn products, farm machinery, and many other industries. During the administrations of Roosevelt and Taft, monopolistic abuses had been disclosed in hearings before committees of Congress, in the reports of public agencies, and in the evidence presented in cases brought before the courts. Though it was shown that competition had been eliminated by particular business practices, these practices had not been held to be in violation of the law. And in 1911 the Supreme Court had declared that combinations that were not unreasonable would be allowed to stand. Following these developments, the trusts again became an issue in the national campaign of 1912. Monopoly was denounced and further legislation promised by the Democrats, the Roosevelt Progressives, and the Republicans.

In 1913 the new Democratic Congress reduced the tariff, set up the Federal Reserve System, and inaugurated the income tax; in 1914 it turned to the problem of monopoly. Consideration of the problem was now more thorough than that accorded it a quarter-century before: the issues raised were subjected to exhaustive hearings and extended debate. President Wilson had recommended that uncertainty concerning the meaning of the Sherman Act be removed by prohibiting, item by item, each of the devices by which competition might be eliminated and monopoly obtained. He had also proposed that a specialized administrative agency be established to strengthen the observance and enforcement of the law. An Act setting up such a body—the Federal Trade Commission—was eventually forthcoming. But agreement on a comprehensive list of monopolistic practices was not to be obtained: opinions differed with respect to particular practices; it was difficult to define existing practices and impossible to frame definitions that would cover future practices; there was fear that such definitions would be so narrowly interpreted as to limit the scope of the law and seriously to impair its effectiveness. The attempt was finally abandoned; the list of devices to be specifically outlawed was reduced to four and provisions forbidding them were written into the Clayton Act; the other devices that had been debated were covered by a general prohibition of unfair methods of competition which was incorporated in the Federal Trade Commission Act. The two Acts, with Democratic and Progressive support, were passed by substantial majorities in both houses of Congress and signed by the President in the fall of 1914.

The particular devices that were outlawed by the Clayton Act were discrimination in prices, exclusive and tying contracts, intercorporate stockholdings, and interlocking directorates. Section 2 of the Act forbade sellers "to discriminate in price between different purchasers of commodities," but permitted such discrimination where there were "differences in the grade, quality, or quantity of the commodity sold," where the lower prices made "only due allowance for differences in the cost of selling or transportation," and where they were offered "in good faith to meet competition." Section 3 forbade sellers to "lease or make a sale or contract for sale of . . . commodities . . . on the condition that the lessee or purchaser thereof shall not use or deal in the . . . commodity . . . of a competitor. . . ." Section 7 forbade any corporation engaged in commerce to acquire the shares of a competing corporation or to purchase the stocks of two or more corporations that were competitors. It should be noted that none of these prohibitions was absolute; the three practices were forbidden only where their effect, in the words of the law, "may be to substantially lessen competition or tend to create a monopoly. . . ." Section 8 prohibited interlocking directorates between corporations engaged in commerce where one of them had a capital and surplus of more than $1 million and where "the elimination of competition . . . between them would constitute a violation of any of the provisions of the antitrust laws." The broader prohibition contained in Section 5 of the accompanying Federal Trade Commission Act provided, simply, "that unfair methods of competition in commerce are hereby declared unlawful."

In substance, these statutes added little to the content of the law. The specific practices that were prohibited might well have been attacked, as conspiracies in restraint of trade or as attempts to monopolize, under the provisions of the Sherman Act. Unfair methods of competition were already condemned, moreover, by the common law. There were, however, important differences. The Sherman Act was general in its terms; the Clayton Act was explicit. The older law dealt with monopoly as an accomplished fact; the new laws were concerned with the methods through which monopoly was attained. The one placed emphasis on punishment; the others were directed toward prevention. Practices that had not been held to violate the law unless pursued as part of a proved conspiracy were now forbidden in and of themselves. Even more important was the fact that enforcement was strengthened, as we shall, see by other provisions of the Clayton and Trade Commission Acts. Under the latter Act, moreover, attacks on unfair methods of competition, instead of being left to suits brought by private litigants on their own initiative and at their own expense, were to be made by public officials and financed by appropriations from the federal treasury. It is in these respects that the new legislation made its most significant contribution to the force of the law.

THE ROBINSON-PATMAN ACT

Section 2 of the Clayton Act, relating to price discrimination, was completely revised with the passage, in 1936, of the Robinson-Patman Act. The original section had been designed primarily to prevent large manufacturers from eliminating their smaller rivals by temporarily cutting prices on particular products and in particular markets while prices elsewhere were maintained, a notorious practice of certain of the early trusts. The new law was an outgrowth of a different situation. Independent wholesalers and retailers, in the years following World War I, found themselves faced with increasing competition from chain stores and other mass distributors. The lower prices that these organizations charged were to be attributed, in part at least, to the lower prices that they paid. Their bargaining power enabled them to obtain concessions from suppliers in many forms: brokers' commissions where no broker was employed, services provided by suppliers in addition to the delivery of goods, allowances for advertising the suppliers' products and rendering them other services, and discounts for purchasing in large quantities. The independents, contending that these concessions were larger than could be justified, demanded that the freedom of suppliers to discriminate be more strictly limited. The Robinson-Patman Act was passed in response to their demands.

Section 1 of the Act, amending Section 2 of the Clayton Act, flatly forbids the payment of a broker's commission in cases where an independent broker is not employed. It forbids sellers to provide supplementary services to buyers or to make allowances for services rendered them by buyers unless such concessions are available to all buyers "on proportionally equal terms." Other forms of discrimination, such as quantity discounts, are prohibited in cases where the effect (in the words of the Clayton Act, with the split infinitive corrected) "may be substantially to lessen competition or tend to create a monopoly in any line of commerce," either among sellers or among buyers. Persons accused of such discrimination may defend themselves by proving that their lower prices made only "due allowance" for differences in cost or were offered "in good faith to meet an equally low price of a competitor. . . ." But even where larger discounts can be justified by lower costs, the Federal Trade Commission is authorized to establish quantity limits beyond which discounts cannot be given, if such action is required to prevent large buyers from obtaining a monopoly. The section makes it unlawful, finally, for any person "knowingly to induce or receive" a prohibited discrimination in price.

Section 3 of the Act provides criminal penalties for three offenses. It flatly forbids giving or receiving a larger discount than that made available to competitors buying the same goods in the same quantity. It also forbids the establishment, in one locality, of prices lower than those charged elsewhere, and prohibits the sale of goods "at unreasonably low prices" where either of these practices is adopted "for the purpose of destroying competition or eliminating a competitor." Violation of any of these provisions is punishable by fines up to $5,000, or imprisonment up to one year, or both.

THE WHEELER-LEA ACT

The ability of the Federal Trade Commission to prevent the use of unfair methods in competition was seriously restricted by a decision handed down by the Supreme Court in 1931. (*FTC v. Raladam Co.*, 283 U.S. 643.) In this case, the Commission had ordered the Raladam Company, manufacturers of Marmola, to cease and desist from representing their product as a remedy for obesity. The court recognized that consumers had been deceived by Raladam's advertisements, but it vacated the order, finding that misrepresentation was common among the vendors of such nostrums and concluding, on this basis, that no injury had been done to Raladam's competitors. The Commission was thus denied authority to protect consumers in cases where injury to competitors could not be shown.

This loophole was closed when Section 5 of the Federal Trade Commission Act was amended by the passage of the Wheeler-Lea Act in 1938. The section, as thus amended, now outlaws not only "unfair methods of competition," but also "unfair or deceptive acts or practices."

THE CELLER ANTIMERGER ACT

The effectiveness of Section 7 of the Clayton Act—forbidding one corporation to acquire the shares of a competing corporation or to buy the stocks of two or more corporations that were competitors, where such action might substantially lessen competition or tend toward monopoly—was similarly impaired by subsequent decisions of the Supreme Court. In 1926 the court decided, in the Swift and Thatcher cases (*Thatcher Manufacturing Co. v. FTC, Swift & Co. v. FTC*, 272 U.S. 554), that the Federal Trade Commission could not order a company to divest itself of the assets of a competitor if it had effected a merger, while the proceeding was pending, by voting stock which it had unlawfully acquired. And again in 1934 the court decided, in the Arrow-Hart & Hegeman case (*Arrow-Hart & Hegeman Electric Co. v. FTC*, 291 U.S. 587), that the Commission was powerless to act when a holding company, after acquiring the shares of two competing corporations, had distributed them to its stockholders who had thereupon voted to merge the two concerns. In the years that followed there was heavy traffic over the detour that the court had built around the law.

This situation was finally corrected, after repeated efforts, by the enactment of an amendment extending the prohibitions of Section 7 to cover not only the acquisition of stock, but also "the use of such stock by the voting or granting of proxies or otherwise" and the acquisition of "the whole or any part of the assets" of a competing corporation or those of two or more corporations in competition with one another. This amendment (81st Cong., 2d Sess., Public Law No. 889) was passed over Republican opposition by Democratic votes and signed by President Truman on December 29, 1950.

SUMMARY

The prohibitions contained in the antitrust laws may now be summarized. It is illegal:

1. To enter into a contract, combination, or conspiracy in restraint trade (Sherman Act, Sec. 1);
2. To monopolize, attempt to monopolize, or combine or conspire to monopolize trade (Sherman Act, Sec. 2).

In cases where the effect may be substantially to lessen competition or tend to create a monopoly, it is illegal:

3. To acquire the stock of competing corporations (Clayton Act, Sec. 7);
4. To acquire the assets of competing corporations (Clayton Act, Sec. 7 as amended in 1950);
5. To enter into exclusive and tying contracts (Clayton Act, Sec. 3);
6. To discriminate—to an extent that cannot be justified—among purchasers (Clayton Act, Sec. 2 as amended by Robinson-Patman Act, Sec. 1).

And, in general, it is also illegal:

7. To engage in particular forms of price discrimination (Robinson-Patman Act, Sec. 1 and 3);
8. To serve as a director of competing corporations (Clayton Act, Sec. 8);
9. To use unfair methods of competition (Federal Trade Commission Act, Sec. 5);

10. To employ unfair or deceptive acts or practices (Federal Trade Commission Act, Sec. 5 as amended by Wheeler-Lea Act, Sec. 3).

In the main these provisions are designed to prevent monopoly and to maintain a competitive economy. But some of them have other purposes. It is the purpose of the Robinson-Patman Act, for instance, less to maintain competition than to preserve the small competitor. In some cases the law may check the growth of monopoly by controlling discrimination; in others, it may merely moderate the force of competition by reducing the competitive advantage of the larger firm. It is the purpose of Section 5 of the Federal Trade Commission Act, not only to preclude the attainment of monopoly through unfair methods of competition, but also to prevent the employment of such methods where no danger of monopoly exists. And it is the purpose of the Wheeler-Lea amendment, not to maintain competition, but to protect the consumer against deceptive practices. . . . It should be noted, too, that Congress has acted, from time to time, to except certain practices and to exempt particular industries from the provisions of these laws, subjecting some of them to other methods of control. . . .

The Effectiveness of the Antitrust Laws

THURMAN ARNOLD *et al.*

The following selections are from a symposium which appeared in the June, 1949, issue of the American Economic Review. *Thurman Arnold was Assistant Attorney General of the United States in charge of antitrust enforcement during 1938–1943. Arthur R. Burns is Professor of Economics at Columbia University. Edward H. Levi is Provost of the University of Chicago. Edward S. Mason is Professor of Economics at Harvard University. George W. Stocking is Professor of Economics at Vanderbilt University.*

THURMAN ARNOLD

THE ANTITRUST laws have not been effective in the real world. Therefore, the temptation of an academician is to substitute an administration which looks well on paper and compare it with the antitrust laws as they operate. This seems to me very naïve political thinking. My belief is that the only instrument which has a chance to preserve competition in America is antitrust enforcement through the courts. Traditionally we accept the courts as an institution which cannot be criticized or badgered as we badger an administrative bureau. A grand jury investigation can be conducted without public protest in a way that is impossible for an administrative tribunal to function. That is because there is a judge in a robe sitting over it. An administrative tribunal taking drastic action against a powerful political group cannot survive. We have watched the Labor Board swing too far under union pressure and then we see Congress destroying its public prestige and power. Under our tradition and habits you cannot do that to courts.

Theoretically, of course, there are many other ways to preserve a competitive system. You could arrange a tax system to regulate the amount of business which large concerns may profitably do. For instance, Fred Raymond has worked it all out along these lines in a book, which John Chamberlain endorses, entitled "The Limitist." However, my political guess is that we will not depart from the traditional ways of enforcing antitrust laws. ·

Unfortunately, all antitrust law enforcement under any plan depends on the public attitude. It does not make much difference what your instrument for carrying out antitrust policy is, it will not be effective unless there is a strong demand. There was such a demand when I was in office. Today, in an economy entirely dependent on government spending we are sufficiently prosperous that there is little demand. However, I expect the demand to grow as the consequences of the present centralization of economic power make themselves felt in the business world.

ARTHUR R. BURNS

ALTHOUGH FEDERAL antitrust legislation has been on the books since 1890, there is very little doubt that we have failed to achieve a competitive system at all closely resembling that which was in the minds of the economists of the last century and which provided the background for the legislation. The reasons for this failure lie partly in the forces within the economic system operating in a contrary direction to the legislation and partly to difficulties of achieving competition by law.

The primary pressure away from an organization of industry likely to operate competitively is the industrial technique of production. This technique often requires plants of considerable size for most economical operations. Where considerations affecting the most economical location of industry involve the scattering of plants throughout the country, local monopolies tend to develop from this cause alone. Even in other industries relatively few plants sometimes emerge as a result of efforts toward the most economical scale of operation.

EDWARD H. LEVI

I THINK there are three principal reasons for the relative ineffectiveness of the antitrust laws:

1. The courts are not sufficiently aware of the monopoly problem. As an aspect of this, the courts have not sufficiently considered size rather than the abuse of monopoly position to be the violation of the law. And as another aspect of this, they have tended to think that a finding of violation and an injunction against further monopolistic actions constitute sufficient relief. I believe that this point is the result of points (2) and (3).

2. The Department of Justice has never had a sufficiently sustained and energetic policy of enforcement. Enforcement is sporadic; vigorous enforcement is branded as witch hunting and is followed by a "period of reasonableness." One result of this is that the courts are not forced to face the problems of size in monopoly. Because there are so few monopoly cases, the courts are relatively uninformed as to economic conditions in key industries and the law itself does not develop as rapidly as it would if more cases were brought. Enormous gaps in the law are permitted to remain and this makes it much easier to have an ineffective enforcement policy.

3. Economists in general, I think, must bear a great share of the blame. The general impression of the public is that monopoly is inevitable and since it is inevitable, it is silly to try to prevent it. A variation of this is the popular opinion that it is childish to be against monopoly (perhaps because it is inevitable) and that, therefore, a monopoly cannot be said to be "bad" or a violation. In other words, I think economists have failed to distinguish between descriptions of our present economy and analyses of what can or ought to be done. Thus, even critical essays on the present state of the economy become a basis for a weak enforcement policy and for a lack of understanding on the part of the courts.

EDWARD S. MASON

THE GREAT difficulty in answering the question [raised here] lies in the interpretation one is to put on the phrase "broadly competitive economic system." There are at least two sources of confusion: (1) Is competition to be understood strictly in the market sense of the term or does it also embrace considerations having to do with the structure of the *political* economy, *i.e.*, concentration of economic control? (2) In so far as attention is concentrated on competition in the market sense, how does one measure departures from competition, *i.e.*, the degree of monopoly.

1. When people speak of a decline of competition, they frequently are thinking of such phenomena as the rise of the large corporation and the relative decline in the importance of sectors of the economy associated with small scale enterprise, *e.g.*, agriculture, which may or may not have anything to do with competition in the market sense of the term. One way of characterizing the phenomena they have in mind is "concentration of economic control."

There are various ways concentration may be measured, each of which has its own significance. Among them is a number of employees per business unit. It is, of course, obvious that the ratio between the number of business units and number of employees is continually declining as a result of the continued shift from agricultural to industrial employment, the relatively rapid growth of sectors of industry characterized by large-scale enterprise, and the increase in the size of the optimum unit in almost all branches of industry.

There is, furthermore, little doubt that this changing ratio of number of firms to number of employees has great significance for the functioning of the *political* economy. It affects the location of political power, the character and size of pressure groups, employer-employee relationships, etc. It is certainly true that it is changing the character of American democracy and it may be true that it threatens the continued existence of democratic institutions.

But it has no necessary or even obvious connection with competition in the market sense of the term. No one has been able to show as yet that monopoly is more important in the economy than it was fifty or one hundred years ago or that competition has declined. Partly this has to do with ambiguities in the interpretation of competition and in difficulties connected with the measurement of departures from competition in whatever sense the term is used.

2. The most precise notion of competition is pure or atomistic

competition but this is (a) a limiting concept in (b) a purely static analysis. Although it is possible to measure *conceptually* departures from pure competition in various ways such as ratio of price to marginal cost, ratio of actual to competitive profits, ratio of actual to competitive output, etc., each of these conceptual measures is firstly only a partial measure even on its own terms and assuming static conditions, and secondly, is not susceptible to statistical application.

Moreover, this whole conception of competition and monopoly is purely static. In the American economy new products, new techniques, new locations, changing consumer tastes, etc., are continually breaking the existing patterns of market relationships and forming new ones which in turn emerge only to be broken. How is this process to be fitted into conceptions of monopoly and competition? No one has as yet provided any satisfactory answer.

In default of answers running in terms of the degree or extent of departure from pure competition people have recently sought an answer to the question whether various industries are or are not "workably competitive." Presumably this notion fastens attention on the *results* of a particular market structure. Is the existing set-up accompanied by a progressive technology, the passing on to consumers of the results of this progressiveness in the form of lower prices, larger output, improved products, etc.? Although there is a certain attractiveness to this conception, it must be admitted that no one as yet has given it any precision. Whether a given industry is judged to be workably competitive will depend to a very substantial extent on the "ideology" of the judges. And who is to say in these terms whether the American economy is or is not more "broadly competitive" now than it was in 1890?

Whatever answer is given to this question, I believe myself that the American economy is in fact substantially more "workably competitive" than it would have been without the existence of the antitrust acts. This is due, I believe, not so much to the contribution that particular judgments have made to the restoring of competition as it is to the fact that the consideration of whether a particular course of business action may or may not be in violation of the antitrust acts is a persistent factor affecting business judgment, at least in large firms.

It is frequently stated that the greatest defects of antitrust policy are in handling the monopolistic or monopsonistic bargaining power of the large firm and the problem of mutual inter-dependence which may exist when a few large firms are pre-dominant in a market. This judgment, however, usually will be found to emanate from those who have a static approach to the problem of monopoly and competition. Until it is clearer to me than it is now (a) that the large firm in the presence of manifestly dynamic influences exerts an adverse monopolistic influence on the functioning of the economy and (b) that any possible action under existing (or a modified) antitrust policy would remedy the situation, I have my fingers crossed.

GEORGE W. STOCKING

I BELIEVE the chief reason the antitrust laws have not been more successful is that no politically powerful economic group wants them to be generally enforced. This is partly due to ignorance and partly to vested interests. But regardless of the reasons neither big business, nor labor, nor the farmers believe in a free-enter-prise system. A paraphrase of Pope expresses the trend in public attitudes:

> Monopoly is a monster of such frightful mien
> That to be hated needs but to be seen (Sherman Law 1890)
> But seen too oft, familiar with her face
> We first endure (Rule of Reason 1911; *U.S.* v. *U.S. Steel Corpora-tion*, 1920), then pity (Federal Trade Commission trade practice conferences and codes; trade association activities, etc.), then embrace (NRA).

Big Business has failed to distinguish between free enterprise and private enterprise and apparently is unwilling to admit that the former is essential to the preservation of the latter. Whether this is due to ignorance or hypocrisy does not affect business' stubborn insistence that it must be left alone. The most recent illustration is the National Association of Manufacturers' charac-terization of the Federal Trade Commission's recommendation for amending Section 7 and 11 of the Clayton Act as a witch hunt.

Labor professes to oppose business monopolies, but shouts to high heaven against any proposal to curb its own monopoly power.

Farmers have become so used to subsidies for output restric-tion and destruction that they regard them as constitutional rights.

Under these circumstances not the failure of antitrust but the basic vigor of competition is amazing. Between 1911 and 1930 the oil industry's monopoly had been transformed into competition so ruinous that the states stepped in to forbid it. Between 1897 when the Supreme Court came to the rescue of the sugar trust (E. C. Knight case) and the late 'twenties sugar refining had become highly competitive—American control having declined from 97 per cent to about 40 per cent—and the industry was "demoralized" by "ruinous" competition.

Bear in mind that the technique of competitive readjustment is ruin and bankruptcy, but among modern social groups nobody wants to be the sacrificial lamb even for the good of the tribe.

If we really wanted a competitive economy it would be necessary to:

1. Revise our patent laws so as to give venture capital easier access to modern technology.

2. Prohibit mergers so as to make business firms as small and numerous as is consistent with the economies of mass production.

3. Require federal incorporation for firms the assets of which exceed a specified minimum and which do business in interstate commerce, and limit the use of the holding corporation.

4. Supply more adequate funds for the enforcement of antitrust. Eternal vigilance is the price of liberty.

5. Curb labor monopolies. Specifically, prohibit industry-wide bargaining. The ideal unit of bargaining would probably be the firm and the size of the firm would be limited in accordance with the principle set forth under (2) above.

6. Lower tariffs.

7. Through monetary and fiscal policies, stabilize the general price structure; but leave individual prices to seek competitive levels and perform their proper function of allocating resources and distributing income.

8. Curb monopolies of prestige created by advertising where the main effect is to increase costs by diverting customers from one product to a substantially similar product. This might involve limiting or taxing advertising expenditures, government grading to prevent misleading advertising, or service by a Bureau of Standards like that of Consumers' Research.

In brief, it would be necessary to create an environment conducive to the operation of a free economy. If we could solve the problem of industrial stability, *i.e.*, insure an expanding economy, the readjustments in use of resources which competition would require would be relatively painless.

This obviously is a big order and while the broad goal is generally attractive—a maximization of economic freedom, a high level of employment and income, and economical use of productive agents—its specific objectives encounter serious obstacles on every hand.

Standards for Antitrust Policy

ALFRED E. KAHN

*Alfred E. Kahn is Professor of Economics at Cornell University.
The following article first appeared in the* Harvard Law Review,
November, 1953.

ACADEMIC ECONOMISTS have in the past frequently criticized the
antitrust authorities for their inactivity and the laws themselves
for their impotence in dealing with big business. Recently, however, increasing numbers of them have been attacking antitrust
policy from the opposite direction, asserting that the application
of the laws is too strict and the zeal of enforcement agencies excessive and misdirected, insofar as the treatment of business size,
integration, and competitive tactics is concerned.

A number of interrelated historical developments explain this
relatively novel line of criticism. One was the depression of the
1930's, which reinforced a skepticism, earlier voiced by the "in-
stitutionalists," concerning the efficiency, stability, and recuper-
ative power of an uncontrolled, purely competitive market economy and hence cast doubt on the basic validity of any attempt to
limit monopolies. A second factor has been the dynamism of the
American economy since 1940, shared, and in some instances led,
by its most clearly oligopolistic industries. Another factor has been
the pressure, greatly intensified during the depression, on legis-
latures and courts to broaden the scope of "unfair competition" to
the point where established business units are protected from
competitive extinction, no matter how well deserved. All these
developments have helped educate economists to the inadequacy
of pure competition as a condition of effective market performance or as a goal of public policy. Recent antitrust suits and decisions, because they appear to some to have been guided by the
norms of purely competitive market structure and behavior, have

helped to crystallize these developing attitudes into open criticism of the Department of Justice and the Federal Trade Commission. Though no consensus representing a consistent critique of the laws has emerged, there is fairly widespread agreement that the economist's conception of workable competition calls for a re-orientation of antitrust policy.

LEGAL AND ECONOMIC APPROACHES TO THE MONOPOLY PROBLEM

The "New Sherman Act"—No Revolution · In a society grounded in individualism, the function of government consists very largely of setting boundaries to individual action. For the free enterprise area of the economy, the law merely fixes the rules of the game. The antitrust laws involve the Government in no entrepreneurial activity proper and require no detailed review of either basic investment commitments or run-of-the-mill business decisions. Instead, appropriately, they proscribe specific actions deemed socially undesirable: contracting, combining, or conspiring to rig the market, as well as monopolizing, discriminating, selling under tie-in schemes, and competing unfairly, whether in concert or independently. These prohibitions may be summarized as embracing the substantial elimination of competition by collusion or exclusion. Of these offenses "monopolizing" is by all odds the most equivocal. It might be taken to forbid mere possession of monopoly power and hence to outlaw a market situation rather than a course of conduct. In fact it has been clear, at least until recently, that monopolizing meant the acts incident to attempts to acquire or maintain substantial monopoly power.

Has the "new Sherman Act" abandoned this conception of monopolizing? Does it now attack monopoly power itself, as many of its friends and foes alike proclaim? It would appear not.

The two cases in which the courts have come closest to condemning monopolies *per se* were those involving Alcoa and the United Shoe Machinery Corporation. However, both opinions explicitly confined their application of a greatly diluted rule of reason to companies approaching pure monopolies—accounting for something like 90 per cent in the first, "probably 85%" in the second, of the national supplies of a physically distinct product. Moreover, even in these extreme cases, the courts paid at least lip service to the necessity for sustaining a charge of monopolizing, rather than of mere enjoyment of a monopoly. "It does not follow because 'Alcoa' had such a monopoly, that it 'monopolized' the ingot market . . . monopoly may have been thrust upon it." In both cases, besides, there was abundant evidence of *conduct* on the part of the defendants indicating plainly an intent to make aluminum and shoe machinery their respective preserves. Except for the squeeze on fabricators, Judge Hand minimized this evidence in the *Alcoa* case. But Judge Wyzanski, while placing a very narrow interpretation on the "intent to monopolize" requisite for Section 2 conviction, plainly predicated his condemnation of United Shoe on his finding that the company had not attained and maintained its "overwhelming strength" solely by virtue of its "ability, economies of scale, research, natural advantages, and adaptation to inevitable economic laws." Rather, its "own business policies," its *actions*, while not inherently predatory or immoral, had "erected" substantial "barriers to competition." "[These] are contracts, arrangements, and policies which . . . further the dominance of a particular firm. In this sense, they are unnatural barriers; they unnecessarily exclude actual and potential competition; they restrict a free market."

In the other leading cases, it is even more clear that the offense of monopolizing consisted not in the mere enjoyment of monopoly power, let alone "the displacement of inferior by superior business methods," but in an unreasonable course of conduct, involving a consistent effort to obtain or maintain market control by methods other than those of normal competition. In the famous *American Tobacco, Paramount,* and *Griffith* cases, in which the Supreme Court held it sufficient for condemnation under Section 2, the monopolizing section, to show the existence of a power to exclude competitors, it added the proviso that the power had to be accompanied by an intent to use it. In all three, the existence of both the power and the requisite intent was found in a course of conduct—a history of the actual unreasonable use of monopoly leverage to exclude competitors from the market.

Several commentators have read the Supreme Court's decision in the *Tobacco* case as holding that "monopolizing" might consist in the mere joint power to raise prices and not merely in the power to exclude. Had the Court said this, the legality of all oligopolistic markets would truly have been jeopardized. But the issue before the Supreme Court was simply this: is actual exclusion of competitors necessary to establish a Section 2 violation? The Court said it was not; the Government had to prove only that the companies had conspired to obtain and maintain the power to exclude and had demonstrated an intent to use that power.

Monopoly in Law and Its Rationale · The economic rationale of the law rests on two assumptions. The first is that the will to "get ahead," to outdo others—in short to compete—is so strong and so widespread that it needs only to be channelized by negative prohibitions. The second is that cost functions and optimum business size are such, in most industries, that out of fair rivalry the numbers of sellers and buyers emerging will not be so small as seriously to weaken the force of competition in the market. These assumptions have often been questioned but seldom refuted on the basis of concrete examinations of the structural pattern and performance of specific industries. From these assumptions it follows that the law need only prevent the deliberate impairment, misdirection, or suppression of competition to protect both the public interest and the legitimate interests of business competitors.

The common law rules dealing with restraints of trade and unfair competitive practices were concerned less with protecting the consumer than with protecting businessmen from one another. The antitrust laws sought both ends, finding no incompatibility between them. The recent critics of our antitrust policy argue, essentially, that the enforcement agencies have confused the two and in consequence weakened the force of competition. Unfortunately, as we shall argue below, the distinction between preserving competitors and preserving competition is by no means so clear or so easily drawn as is implied both by the rationale of the antitrust laws and by the contentions of those economists who have been criticizing antitrust enforcement agencies for failing to draw it.

The Market Structure Test of Monopoly · (1) ITS NATURE. Economists have developed two fairly distinct tests of monopoly. One looks to market structure for evidences of those characteristics from which, according to the theory of the firm, undesirable results follow. The other criterion applies the maxim "by their fruits ye shall know them." It may begin by identifying structural impurities, but its primary emphasis is on the economic record, that is, market performance; only if the results are "bad" is the monopoly power deemed excessive.[1]

Of these two concepts, it was the former which alone underlay Professor Mason's well-known contrast of "monopoly in law and economics." Following Chamberlin, he observed that to the economist "monopoly" describes a market situation in which an individual seller has the power to influence price. Such exploitative monopoly power may arise without collusion or exclusion, the traditional legal evidences of monopoly. Conversely, illegal actions may fail to create the exploitative power which alone signifies monopoly to the economist. Though Mason judiciously made no such recommendation, one possible implication of the contrast he drew was that the focus of the "antiquated and inadequate" law should be altered to conform to the theory of imperfect competition, and of oligopoly in particular.

Other economists have drawn this implication and have urged that antitrust policy ought to be directed not only against single sellers, but also against oligopoly or market power *per se*. Professor Arthur Burns' monumental proof of the "decline of competition," which is really only a thorough demonstration of the absence of pure competition, concludes that direct public regulation is required to do the job which competition no longer does; on the other hand, Professor Eugene Rostow, finding similar tendencies in industrial structure and market behavior, argues that the laws should attack monopoly power *per se*, and has found in recent antitrust decisions evidence of such a trend. Professor J. K. Galbraith has clearly declared that the antitrust laws are defective because they cannot reach non-collusive oligopoly, and Professor M. A. Adelman has stated that "until and unless we decide that the real problem is market control and how much and what kind we ought to permit, the situation will remain confused." Regardless of their differences, implicitly or explicitly

---

1. The two tests are not mutually exclusive; it is seldom suggested that either be applied without consideration of the other. Both assume that a radically imperfect market structure will sooner or later produce a defective performance. However, it is clearly one thing to apply judgments to a market situation *per se* and quite another to attempt to evaluate the results, judging the structure mainly in terms of those findings.

the foregoing writers have adopted the first concept of monopoly distinguished above and have stressed the necessity of a structural transformation of markets—on the ground, as Professor George J. Stigler has put it, that "an industry which does not have a competitive structure will not have competitive behavior."

(2) ITS DIFFICULTIES. It is ironic that many economists, trained in the Chamberlinian tradition, now chide the Department of Justice and the courts for having learned their lessons too well. It is the author's thesis that the courts have not followed the lead of the theory of monopolistic competition as far as some critics (or friends) of recent decisions would have us believe, that they have been wise not to do so, and that the antitrust laws will continue to play an effective role in preserving workable competition only if the courts resist some of the policy implications of the new economic criticism as well as they have resisted the old.

The concept of workable competition strongly suggests the expediency of the traditional approach to antitrust problems in preference to applying a market structure test. If monopoly elements inevitably pervade the economy and are in some measure essential to a good performance, it would clearly be quixotic to attack monopoly power *per se*. If the courts were really prepared now to outlaw "the power to raise prices," as some enthusiastically read the recent *American Tobacco* decision, few sellers would be exempt; the economy would have to be "purified" right out of the twentieth century. Yet there exists no generally accepted economic yardstick appropriate for incorporation into law with which objectively to measure monopoly power or determine what degree is compatible with workable competition.

The scrutiny of the law might be directed at the sources of monopoly power, rather than toward the power itself. But these causal factors, similarly, are neither measurable nor, taken individually, unequivocal in their implications concerning the workability of competition. Whether their influence is, on balance, beneficent or harmful depends on a host of conditioning circumstances which defy incorporation into legal prohibitions: every market structure is in large measure *sui generis*.

Product differentiation, for example, is often a means of competition that serves the public, providing minimum assurances of quality and catering to a real consumer desire for product improvement or variation. Difficulty of entry, when not deliberately devised or imposed, or the concentration of patents scarcely provide a sufficient basis for antitrust action against firms whose monopoly power they may enhance. Similarly, there are serious dangers in setting upper limits to business size or market shares *ex ante*. They include: the difficulty of defining products and markets in a way that will be generally acceptable and will stay put; the risk of preventing unmeasurable economies of scale, including the economies of experience, technical skill, and research; the possible damping effect on business enterprise of such upper limits; the possible compatibility of oligopoly and forthright rivalry, particularly in innovation; the tendencies of giant business units constantly to change their product "mixes" and thereby to intensify interproduct and interindustry competition.

It does not follow that the market structure concept of monopoly has nothing to contribute to effective antitrust policy. It may supply guidance for legal remedies when a business has habitually indulged in practices which violate the law, by suggesting for removal market elements which may have fostered the illicit conduct. And the avoidance or offsetting of industrial concentration may very well assume a central position in guiding other Government policies which bear on business performance. It suggests the need for measures beyond the antitrust laws to curb and counteract the forces which help to generate monopoly power: revising the tax laws, organizing technical research and assisting private, cooperative research organizations, providing credit facilities for new ventures, defining quality standards and enforcing grade labeling, underwriting full employment, ensuring sustained, adequate supplies and fair distribution of scarce raw materials, assisting private parties to resolve patent infringement controversies, and so on. Such measures are, of course, not at all incompatible with the traditional focus of antitrust policy. On the contrary, as Professor Fellner suggests, they would further implement the traditional conception of unfair competition by attacking positively what the law already attacks negatively— competitive disadvantages not attributable to inefficiency.

The Market Performance Test · (1) ITS NATURE. Should antitrust scrutiny, then, be focused mainly on market performance? In 1949, Mason suggested an appraisal of an industry's performance as one possible way of deciding, at law, whether it was workably competitive. Both concepts, market performance and workable competition, are essentially pragmatic. How much competition, how many sellers, how standardized a product, how free an entry, how little collusion are required for workability? Enough, it is averred, to give the consumer a real range of choice, to ensure efficiency, to hold profits to reasonable levels, to yield technological progress and a passing on of its gains in lower prices while avoiding cut-throat competition. The law . . . should evaluate the economic results in the light of the available alternative market structure and attack the structure only when the foregoing tests warrant it. In legal terms, [it is suggested] that the rule of reason be revivified, given an essentially economic content, and applied in all antitrust proceedings. The legality or illegality of all business structures and practices would then turn on their impact on the workability of competition, as judged in turn largely by economic results.

(2) ITS DIFFICULTIES. Apart from devising judicial, administrative, or legislative remedies, a problem in connection with which comparative market performance under the condemned and the projected organizations is an inescapable consideration, the usefulness or validity of this criterion as the basic, self-sufficient guide to public policy is as much open to question as is that of market structure.

First, it must be recognized that market performance is not necessarily a sign either of competition or monopoly. It is a "way of looking at competition," in Mason's words, only in the sense that it looks for the results which idealized competition is supposed by static theory to achieve. And if the results are "good," the market which produced them becomes, *ipso facto*, "workably competitive." Such an approach has an obvious attraction. Ignoring the irrelevant forms, dismissing the complexities of traditional legal inquiries, it judges situations in terms of what really counts: their results. It accords with the plausible aphorism that there can be too much competition as well as too little. It recognizes the commonplace axiom that competition is, after all, not an end in itself. As for the aphorism, it is correct, though the cure for "too much competition" is not self-regulation of industry, but attacks on the circumstances which make it "too much"—consumer ignorance, the business cycle, the immobility of labor, and so forth. As for the axiom, while the general American bias in favor of competition is indeed rationalized largely by an expectation that in the long run it will produce the best economic results, it is also true that fair competition is an "end in itself." For it is indissolubly linked with the noneconomic values of free enterprise —equality of opportunity, the channeling of the profit motive into socially constructive channels, and the diffusion of economic power.

To put the matter bluntly, the market performance test looks at the wrong end of the process. The essential task of public policy in a free enterprise system should be to preserve the framework of a fair field and no favors, letting the results take care of themselves. Obviously, if the results go too far astray the legislative process may have to be invoked to re-examine and reconstitute the institutional framework, either in particular phases or in its entirety. Obviously, too, where it appears that it is some antitrust proscription which is responsible for the poor performance, that proscription should be revised. But the most arresting aspect of much of the current criticism of antitrust policy is the paucity of concrete economic evidence adduced to demonstrate that the kinds of market structure and behavior consistent with the antitrust laws fall short in their performance in ways which only a relaxation of those statutes will remedy.

Yet on the basis of this sketchy evidence of public necessity, the proponents of a market performance test for antitrust would dilute if not eradicate the suspicion with which the law now regards the practices of collusion, coercion, and exclusion. They would permit businessmen to do these things provided they can at some future date, when and if called upon to do so, demonstrate in any of a great number of possible ways that the practices produced "good" economic results. In view of the weak punitive provisions of the antitrust laws, which most of these critics would further dilute by shutting the door to treble damage suits where the violations were not "wilful," it is difficult to doubt that the adoption of such a rule of reason would be regarded by the business world as an invitation to "reasonable cartelization" of the economy.

Most advocates of a "workable competition" test in antitrust law would deny that they would have the law look only to results. For example, the Business Advisory Council of the Department of

Commerce states that "the government, instead of attempting the impossible task of deciding where Bigness is more or less efficient, should rely upon the powerful action of Effective Competition. . . ." One interpretation of this statement might be that its authors would not have the determination of antitrust violations depend on an appraisal of the end results—for example, on the efficiency with which the defendants have operated. However, the Council goes on immediately to list some eleven separate tests that it would have the courts and administrative agencies apply before they can condemn any specific practices. The list is a grab bag almost all the components of which have this one thing in common: they are tests of market performance or results.

The insistence of economists on economic tests might be understandable if objective standards capable of commanding general acceptance had in fact been developed. Certainly the second deficiency of the market performance test as a substantive basis for antitrust is its vagueness and uncertainty. The grounds on which the courts have for over fifty years refused to evaluate the reasonableness of prices collusively fixed still command respect today. The adoption of vague tests of "public welfare" could only weaken the legal safeguards of the competitive system, by providing antitrust defendants with an unlimited supply of legal loopholes. Economic results are to be used as a basis for acquittal only: no critic has yet suggested that a poor performance provides a sufficient basis for prosecution. If "efficiency," "progressiveness," and "usefulness for national defense" are to acquit a company or industry, the Government should presumably condone most instances of cartelization or monopolizing in the fields of electronics, chemicals, petroleum, and chain store distribution, regardless of whether the specific restraints had anything to do with the good over-all performance. If it is to be left to the courts or administrative commissions to determine whether, in the absence of the restraints, progress might or might not have been even more rapid, prices and profits even more reasonable, grave difficulties will be encountered because of the elusiveness of this test. The burden surely rests on the critics of the antitrust laws to demonstrate that those predatory or collusive actions which the law attacks are indeed requisite to a good performance. This is something they have for the most part failed to do.

The Alternatives in a Free Enterprise System · Only two general methods of regulating private business appear practicable. One is to establish fairly definite standards in statutory law, leaving businessmen free within those limits to pursue their own interest. So far as this writer can see, such standards can only be standards of *conduct*. In this case, legal uncertainties will arise only at the boundaries, though these boundaries may admittedly be vexatiously elusive. It is difficult to envisage equally clear criteria of acceptable and unacceptable economic performance. Poor results may issue through no conscious actions or fault of the businessmen concerned. A progressive and efficient company may yet violate the law in ways which contribute little or not at all to its good performance or which may have kept the record of its industry from being even better.

The only effective alternative is to leave the maintaining of competition to an administrative commission, vested with broad and pervasive powers of investigation, reorganization, and regulation, industry by industry. Such a commission would have to decide, in each case, whether particular prices or profits had been too high or too low, capacity too great or little, progress in reducing costs, improving quality, and introducing new products too rapid or too slow; and it would have to be empowered, on the basis of such decisions, to fashion such alterations in business structure as might appear appropriate. It is questionable whether any group is competent to make such decisions, whether such delegation of responsibility would be politically acceptable, and whether such a change would make for greater clarity and dependability of businessmen's expectations than the antitrust laws as they now stand.

PROBLEMS CREATED BY BUSINESS INTEGRATION

If the law is sound in condemning actions rather than market power or inadequate performance, the problem of defining the actions which it should prohibit remains. The most vexatious problems arise in applying the traditional legal prohibitions to big, integrated business units. It has been recent antitrust developments in this area that have prompted the most vehement criticisms and represent our primary concern. Here we encounter the familiar dilemma of the "double standard," the ambivalence of the law in dealing with restrictive agreements on the one hand and proprietary concentrations of market power on the other. If the "economic" tests be rejected, the double standard is inevitable. The only circumstances in which antitrust proceedings against big business units or their organizers are warranted is when they overstep the rules of a free enterprise system: rules prohibiting monopolizing, either by collusion or by exclusion.

All types of business integration have in common the encompassing of a variety of operations—different products, different markets, different productive and distributive functions—under a single financial control. In addition a business may seek the advantages of integration by bargaining rather than financial consolidation. Some of the most significant and controversial developments in the antitrust field have been in the treatment of practices by which businesses have obtained preferential access to independently produced supplies and to independently operated market outlets. The Department of Justice and FTC have been attacking big, integrated business units for obtaining or exerting "unfair" competitive advantages over their nonintegrated competitors, whether by persuasion or coercion of independent suppliers and distributors or by virtue of their integrated operations.

The basic antitrust dilemma in this area, which makes it impossible for public policy ever to adopt simple, objective, mechanically applicable, and universally acceptable criteria, arises from the fact that business size and integration almost inevitably confer certain "unfair" competitive advantages and give rise to corresponding possibilities of the extension of monopoly. The only necessary condition is the existence of substantial imperfections of competition in some of the fields in which an integrated company operates. The very fact that a company sells in a number of markets or performs a number of functions, in some of which it is subjected to weaker competitive pressures than in others, gives it a leverage and a staying power in its more highly competitive operations which have nothing to do with its relative efficiency there. The more favorable access to scarce raw materials which a vertically integrated company may enjoy is merely one variant of the general case, springing from imperfections of competition in the supply of these materials. Similarly, the advantage enjoyed by a company with an accepted brand when it undertakes the sale of some new product may be entirely strategic, resting simply on consumer ignorance. And the elimination of competitors from a market opportunity which inevitably results from the absorption of a customer by a supplier confers a strategic advantage on the integrating firm, entirely apart from any resultant saving in cost, to the extent that market outlets for nonintegrated suppliers are appreciably restricted in consequence.

If all competitors were equally able to integrate, no unfairness or danger of an extension of monopoly would enter. But inequity may be introduced by mere inequality in the ability of these companies to attract capital—an inequality which tends to be cumulative. It would not follow, from the fact that only similarly integrated companies might be able to compete with the dominant firms in aluminum, motion picture production and exhibition, and petroleum refining, that integration is the more efficient way of doing business in the social sense. The nonintegrated aluminum fabricator, motion picture exhibitor, or oil marketer might suffer only the strategic disadvantage of less adequate access to supplies or markets. Thus, integration that links areas in which competition is already seriously defective to other areas accomplishes by financial consolidation something very much like what is accomplished by the tie-ins prohibited in Section 3 of the Clayton Act. In the same way, the mere fact of its importance as a customer or supplier offers to a large firm a corresponding opportunity for competitive advantages unrelated to efficiency, in access to supplies or markets, whether or not it actively seeks them.

The problem of public policy created by these strategic advantages cannot be exorcised merely by demonstrating the absurdity of any attempt to attack all of them, and of outlawing integration *per se*. In strict logic, one may maintain that the root cause of inequity and possible monopoly power is the imperfection of competition in the less workably competitive fields in which the integrated firm operates rather than the integration which ties this operation to others. It does not follow, as some have suggested, that corrective government intervention may therefore properly be directed only against the offending stratum. Where the imperfection is not practically remediable (if, for example, it springs from a patent monopoly, inexpansibility of supply of some basic material, product differentiation, or the limited size of a market) there may be no practical alternative to attacking instead the financial tie-in which permits one firm to carry the advantages over into other fields.

Moreover, given pre-existing competitive imperfections, integration may itself permit an extension or magnification of total monopoly power. True, if the separate components of a vertical integration had before joining been exploiting to the maximum any monopoly power they may have enjoyed, the mere combining of seller and buyer might not permit them to do any more. However, even here, the merging of interests might permit the further suppression of competition in one of the strata, a more selective exploitation of the less elastic demands for a monopolized raw material, and a mutual reinforcement of monopoly power by making more difficult competitive entry at both levels.

This competitive leverage inherent in integration may appear in a number of possible forms and be exercised in a number of possible ways, though most of these practices may be employed by any wealthy competitor, integrated or not. The integrated firm may deliberately "manipulate its margins" so as to exert pressure on nonintegrated rivals greater than they can cope with, even though their efficiency in the one field in which they alone operate may be superior to that of the integrated unit. Indeed, the margins of the integrated firm will be "manipulated" whether it wills it or not, under the impact of varying competitive pressures in its diverse fields of operation. The more profitable operations thus inevitably "subsidize" those in the more competitive fields. The "subsidy" permits a competitive "squeeze," the most dramatic instances of which arise out of vertical integration.

The perplexing problem is that in their manifestations and exercise the competitive advantages stemming from gains in efficiency attributable to integration are in practice inseparable from the merely strategic advantages. For most of the former arise from the fuller utilization of a firm's capacity—whether measured by its physical plant, managerial talents, technological skills, or the ideas issuing from its research laboratories. The costs of the combined operations are always in some measure joint and their prices and margins therefore subject to variation according to competitive conditions in their respective markets. Thus an integrated firm must, if it is to compete vigorously, charge little more than incremental costs in certain fields, and in this way again, in effect, "subsidize" its competitive operations there by allocating an otherwise disproportionate part of the overhead to other operations. It is impossible, therefore, for a large, integrated firm to exploit its socially acceptable advantages or even to meet competition, without at the same time exploiting those advantages which are purely strategic. Conversely, it may avoid violating the basic proscriptions of the antitrust laws only by a policy of conservatism and inertia which runs counter to another purpose of the law. A policy of eliminating the strategic advantages of integration would seriously undermine the vigor of competition itself, since a prime source of competition in modern capitalism is provided by the ability and desire of burgeoning giants to press aggressively into new markets—cutting across accepted channels of distribution, following the logic of their interests and technology vertically, horizontally, and circularly.

Integration, moreover, performs a competitive function even where its advantages are entirely strategic. . . . The easiest curb on monopoly power and the most effective cure for poor performance, the one most consistent with free enterprise, is freedom of entry. And this manifestly includes the right of an existing business to extend its operations into any area its managers see fit to enter—in short, to integrate.

The same dilemma confronts public policy in dealing with business practices. We want all firms, large and small, to bargain vigorously for supplies, to try to beat down the price. We want them to put pressure on their distributors to improve the latter's competitive performance, using the threat of contract termination if necessary. We want them to be able to make mutually binding, long-term contractual commitments, where these permit a more rational planning of operations over time and provide mutual benefits in terms of cost and service. We want all firms to be free to reduce their margins to meet or undercut a competitor's price, if their interests as competitors rather than as would-be monopolists so dictate. Price discrimination may be the only possible form of effective price rivalry in imperfect markets. Yet the threat remains that such activities may, in some circumstances, violate the essential rules of the free enterprise game, may drive out of business smaller competitors whose only deficiency is a strategic one, and may enhance or preserve monopoly power.

THE RULE OF REASON

The Strategic Role of "Intent" in the Rule of Reason · The basic
and ineradicable difficulty in distinguishing between competitive
and anticompetitive practices by integrated companies made inevitable the development of some kind of a rule of reason in antitrust jurisprudence. The rule has taken two forms. First, at least
between 1911 and the *Alcoa* decision in 1945, the courts generally
took the position that large firms, whatever their market control,
were to be judged primarily by this criterion: did the circumstances of their formation and the characteristic pattern of their
market behavior evince an intent to monopolize? Second, the
prohibitions of the Clayton Act were qualified by the cost-saving
and good-faith defenses and by the necessity for demonstrating
a tendency substantially to impair competition.

In applying the rule of reason to "monopolizing" cases under
the Sherman Act, courts have laid heavy stress on the intent
underlying the actions in question. As we have already indicated,
the economic criticism of the antitrust policy springs largely from
a dissatisfaction with such an allegedly subjective criterion. It is
pointed out that it is often extremely difficult to apply, since the
evidence is often equivocal. More important, the "new critics"
would probably agree among themselves that intent is an irrelevant consideration in economic rule making. They feel that the
antitrust laws should be framed in terms of objective standards,
rather than what some of them take to be moral judgments, in
terms of consequences rather than psychological motivation. The
only relevant test, whether of integration or of competitive tactics,
they would hold, is the persistence or suppression of competition
as an effective force in the market. And their measure of the competitiveness of a market is economic performance.

Unfortunately, the "objective" standard—the vitality of market
competition—is disturbingly elusive. Among economists urging
its adoption are those who feel that the rule of reason of 1911 represented a departure from that test and those who feel it embodied
just such a test, those who feel it was precisely by such a standard
that U.S. Steel was exonerated in 1920 and 1948, and those who
felt, with the Supreme Court minorities, that application of such
an objective standard would have compelled a decree of dissolu-

tion. The same range of opinion, using the same test, may be documented with respect to any number of other cases.

The fact is that economics offers no objective measure of the vitality of competition, in all its aspects, or any way of balancing its possible attenuation in certain respects or in certain markets against its intensification in other markets or in other respects. Economic analysis has devised no tests of the efficiency or inefficiency of integration; the determination must be left to the market, not to the Government. Nor does the "objective" standard proposed by the economist-critics of our antitrust policy meet the argument which gave rise to the Clayton and Federal Trade Commission Acts, that it may be desirable to forbid certain unfair actions before they have had an opportunity to do appreciable damage. Nor, finally, does such a standard satisfy the need for rules of fair business dealing, entirely apart from any observable impact of unfair or inherently exclusionary tactics on market structure or performance. No one can say in what imponderable ways the unfair elimination of a single competitor weakens the vitality of competition among the survivors.

Thus we return to the traditional conception. The function of antitrust legislation can be only to see to it that no one attempts to stifle or pervert the process of competition by collusion, by unreasonable financial agglomeration, or by exclusion. Illegality must inhere in the act, not in the result, and the test of intent is only a means of defining the act. In the words of Chief Justice White, in the *Standard Oil* decision, the antitrust laws condemn "all *contracts* or *acts* . . . unreasonably restrictive of competitive conditions, *either* from the nature . . . of the contract or act, *or* where the surrounding circumstances were such as . . . to give rise to the inference or presumption that they had been entered into or done with the intent to do wrong to the general public *and* to limit the right of individuals, thus restraining the free flow of commerce. . . ." The quest for an explanatory intent does not involve psychoanalysis. The question is not: "Why did A *really* do what he did?" but simply: "What was A really doing? Was he competing—or suppressing competition?" "To what kind of activities may one most reasonably attribute the formation and growth of Company B—to technological imperatives, vigorous competition, and 'satisfied customers,' or to anticompetitive manipulations?" The attempt is simply to provide a logical ordering and interpretation of the objective record in order to ascertain whether the course of action shown is one condemned by law. Intent must be inferred primarily from the overt acts actually committed, interpreted in the light of the surrounding circumstances.

Most individual business acts—merging, agreeing, or competing —provide on their face, at best, no more than equivocal evidence of their underlying character or aim. Accordingly, it would be the height of folly either to sanction or to proscribe them *per se.* "Suppressing competition" cannot be defined as clearly as "sneezing." It can only be inferred from a complex series of actions and consequences. A state medical association expels some doctors for "a breach of medical ethics." A publishing company which owns a morning and an evening newspaper refuses to accept advertisements in either one separately. A number of cement manufacturers quote identical delivered prices. A chain store reduces its margins in a particular locality at a particular time. A pipeline company owned by an oil refiner establishes minimum tenders. A man standing in front of a bank which is being robbed whistles loudly when a policeman comes into view. How does one decide when to exonerate, when to condemn these acts or courses of conduct? The logical test, it might appear, would be an evaluation of their objective consequences. But, as we have argued, in the first place the consequences are often impossible to trace. To take only one example, how can one tell whether a competing newspaper might have been born had it not had to contend with a large competitor charging advertisers a unit rate? Secondly, there are no scientific standards for drawing the line between desirable and undesirable consequences, even where they are traceable. Finally, it may be desirable in certain circumstances to prohibit such actions, regardless of whether there are demonstrable, or even probable, evil economic consequences. It is not ridiculous for the Government to argue, of certain actions, that "survival of competitors does not exonerate the defendants. For a case to fall within the Sherman Act, it is not necessary for the defendants to have succeeded in what they intended to do."

The inescapable conclusion is that, from a practical standpoint, the criterion of intent alone "fills the bill" for a sensible antitrust policy in such cases. Why did the loiterer whistle? Why was the doctor dismissed? Why did one firm buy out another? The point is not to ascertain whether the business units in question were driven by some sort of collective neurosis but simply to ascertain *what* they were doing. Was the loiterer helping to rob the bank? Were the cement companies systematically suppressing competition? Were the chain stores or the refiners exerting their leverage to squeeze out competitors?

Thus a host of actions, themselves individually unexceptionable, may form together a consistent pattern, explicable and condemnable solely on the basis of the general policy which they seem to mirror. Only if it is a fact that the man's whistle was part of a broader plan can his participation in the robbery legitimately be inferred. Only as part of a price-fixing conspiracy may an individual act of price reporting or freight absorption be objectionable. As Justice Holmes said a half century ago, "The plan may make the parts unlawful." A recent decision states, in the same vein:

> While it must be admitted that not all of these acts are prohibited, nevertheless, we must view them in the broad panorama of other acts and their association with each other to note, not only the effect—but to pierce the veil for evidence of intent. . . .
>
> It is clear then that the intent . . . to dominate this industry by monopoly is obvious and that the result of the . . . conspiracy was to restrict competitors which latter is illegal under the Sherman Act.

The quest for a unifying and underlying intent is in most of these cases inescapable, even though the statute seems to say, simply and objectively, "these things you may not do."

Supplementary Economic Criteria · It does not follow that an intent to suppress competition is or should be either a sufficient or a necessary basis for condemnation. Intent unaccompanied by overt action cannot be made the basis of judicial action. It must be accompanied, first, by the power to restrain or exclude, and, second, by some evidence that the power has been or, barring interference, will be exercised. But no "systematic economic assessment" of market power is required. As always the primary evidence is the actions of the defendants. As Judge Taft put it 55 years ago: "The most cogent evidence that they had this power is the fact, everywhere apparent in the record, that they exercised it." Objective consequences or lack of them are surely relevant, as well, in determining whether actions were reasonable or unreasonable. Indeed, where, in certain cases, the evidence of power and

its exercise is clear, and where the consequences are both sufficiently manifest and plainly objectionable, it has not and should
not have been necessary to demonstrate a "specific" illegal intent.

But where the external evidence both of actions and results is
equivocal—and we have argued it is inevitably so in most cases
of business integration—an investigation of intent is and always
has been essential. As Chief Justice Hughes observed: "Good intentions will not save a plan otherwise objectionable, but knowledge of actual intent is an aid in the interpretation of facts and
prediction of consequence." Or as Justice Lurton stated, more
positively: "Whether a particular act, contract or agreement was
a reasonable and normal method in furtherance of trade and
commerce may, in doubtful cases, turn upon the intent to be inferred from the extent of the control thereby secured over the
commerce affected, as well as by the method which was used."

Thus economic considerations are by no means irrelevant in
the rule of reason. Market power and economic consequences
must be considered. But they are not decisive. Mere unexercised
power to exclude, the mere exclusion of competitors which occurs
when a supplier consolidates with a customer, the mere power to
influence price all remain and should remain free from condemnation. And the relevant consequences to be appraised are not
the effects of the defendants' actions on economic performance,
but those implied in the traditional legal criteria of monopolizing:
the mutual suppression of rivalry or the unfair exclusion or
threatened exclusion of competitors.

There is no disposition here to minimize the difficulties in im-
puting the intent that renders the acquisition or exercise of market power and the exclusion unreasonable. But no equally acceptable alternative presents itself. The difficulties inhere in the
situation. Only to the extent that we are prepared to outlaw
specific practices or situations *per se* can a consideration of intent
be dispensed with. Since, on balance, it would be clearly destructive of competition itself to apply any such blanket condemnation
to business integration, inquiry must be made in each case to
determine whether power has been unreasonably attained or used.
Central to such an investigation must be an inquiry into the underlying intent. Where investigation discloses unreasonably collusive
or unfairly exclusive tactics, those acts cannot, consistently with
a free enterprise system, be condoned because of the absence of

clear evidence that they have actually diminished the force of competition in the market or contributed to a poor economic performance, narrowly construed. This is the only "workable" rule of antitrust policy.

Concentration and Antitrust Policy

CARL KAYSEN

Carl Kaysen is Director of the Institute for Advanced Study. The following paper is taken from his testimony before the Senate Subcommittee on Antitrust and Monopoly in 1965.

DR. KAYSEN: Concentration in the large, taken alone, without reference to concentration in particular markets, has no direct significance for antitrust policy insofar as that policy reflects concern with monopoly and competition. Of course, antitrust policy may be directed toward other goals, or other public policies may be focused specifically on the question of the overall size distribution of business, and for such purposes an examination of the level and trends of overall concentration may be useful.

Concentration measures for particular markets have more direct bearing on antitrust policies. The immediate purpose of the computations cited above at the time they were made was to give some broad indication of the size and importance of markets in the economy where the more significant and difficult problems of antitrust policy might arise. In my judgment, that purpose is still important.

The kinds of antitrust problems which I characterize as the "more significant and difficult" are those involving monopolization, mergers, business practices such as requirements contracts, exclusive dealing arrangements, certain kinds of patent pools, which cannot in general be judged as "competitive" or "anti-competitive" in effect without consideration of the market context in which they appear.

Further, market concentration measures can provide a useful guide to the antitrust enforcement agencies in allocating their efforts. Other things being equal, more concentrated markets deserve more attention than less concentrated ones, in terms both of initial investigatory effort, and enforcement activity where ostensible violations of the law appear. Other things are not equal: markets differ in size and economic importance; enforcement agencies must consider the complaints of businessmen who consider themselves injured by allegedly illegal practices of suppliers, customers or rivals; some cases and situations are more important from the viewpoint of legal precedent than others. So market structure is one factor among many, but it remains one worth examining when enforcement agencies form judgments about what to do.

In the determination of specific cases, appropriate concentration figures, in general, are one kind of evidence relevant to the determination of the issues. The appropriate concentration figures will usually be defined in relation to markets the boundaries of which are more carefully drawn in terms of products and geography than those defined by groupings of census products and industries and used for broad descriptive purposes. Particularly in cases involving the issues of illegal monopolization, or attempts to monopolize under the Sherman Act, the evidence on concentration becomes one among many kinds which must be evaluated for an overall picture of the structure and functioning of the market which they provide.

In merger cases, where enforcement activity is essentially preventive, concentration measurements may appropriately play a larger role. The recent Supreme Court decisions in horizontal merger cases, in which acquired and acquiring firms operate in the same market, have moved fairly far toward establishing a presumption of illegality for horizontal mergers involving firms with market shares totaling 20 percent or more. In properly defined markets, such a rule appears to me entirely appropriate on economic grounds, if the presumption of illegality is rebuttable by evidence that the merger involves substantial economies of scale not achievable by other means, or that the acquired firm was in failing condition.

A somewhat similar rule, applying a rebuttable presumption of illegality for vertical mergers in which a firm with a market share of 20 percent or more acquires a substantial customer or supplier could also be justified on economic grounds.

In both cases, the justification rests on the argument that forbidding expansion of particular firms by the kind of mergers proscribed—while it would block the plans of those firms and deprive them of what would otherwise be profitable opportunities—would not deny the economy substantial advantages, and would preserve market structures more conducive to competition. Where economic signals called for expansion, and growth by merger was blocked, growth by new investment would take place instead, although, of course, not necessarily in the same firms. This, in general, would result in greater expansions of total capacity in the relevant market, and wider distribution of its ownership, which are both conducive to more effective competition.

No similarly simple formulation of a rule for conglomerate mergers in terms of concentration levels can be made. Indeed, for truly conglomerate mergers, single market concentration figures have no particular significance. The rationale for decisions in such situations must go beyond concentration figures and include at least such questions as the nature of entry barriers in the various markets involved, and how they would be affected by the merger, and the importance of the acquiring firm as a potential competitor in the markets in which the acquired firm operates. . . .

DR. BLAIR: Professor Kaysen, following the same line of discussion, the question, is it not, is the point in the legal proceeding at which the examination of the particular facts in individual market areas takes place? As I understand the book that you and Professor Turner wrote [1]—an excellent contribution to knowledge and understanding—the heart of your argument is that the economic profession has now developed enough knowledge from empirical inquiry and theoretical reasoning to establish certain rebuttable presumptions, based fundamentally on market shares. Upon a showing that the market share is in excess of certain levels, which you set forth in the book, there would be a presumption of illegality which could only be overborne by a showing on the part of the defendant company that it met certain standards, which you set forth in the book.

For example, in talking not about future accretions to concentration through merger but about existing concentration, you suggest a statute directed against "unreasonable market power."

1. Carl Kaysen and Donald F. Turner, *Anti-Trust Policy*, Cambridge, Mass.: Harvard University Press, 1959.

Market power shall be conclusively presumed where for 5 years or more one company has accounted for 50 percent or more of annual sales in the market or four or fewer companies have accounted for 80 percent of such sales.

The context of my question is, in essence, whether your response should not go to the question of the point in the legal proceedings at which the examination of the facts in the particular case would take place.

DR. KAYSEN: This is a somewhat complicated question, and I beg your indulgence in the way I answer it. I think one has to first ask what is the situation now in respect to present practice under present law. Under present law, present practice is not described by the section that Mr. Blair read from this volume on antitrust policy which Professor Turner and I wrote a few years ago.

At present, market share is only one kind of evidence. And it does not have a special role that other evidence does not have.

Now then, the next question one can go to is what argument is there for modifying, changing the present law? Now, the context in which the proposal that Mr. Blair quoted was placed in this volume was a discussion of possible alternatives to or amendments to or expansions of the Sherman Act. And let me say that we were writing in an academic and speculative fashion. We were not trying to draft a statute in a legislative process.

We sketched a number of possible alternatives. All these possible alternatives were based on a conclusion about the present law; that a situation like that of the automobile industry, or the steel industry, or the flat glass industry, in which firms have a considerable degree of market power as an economist would define market power, is not reachable under the Sherman Act as presently interpreted. Then the question is: Is it desirable to do anything about that kind of market power? We have a rather long discussion in the book and give reasons for believing that it is. I think reasonable men can differ on this proposition.

If the question of desirability is answered affirmatively, the next question is then: What can be done? And here we suggest two alternatives.

One is simply to redefine the standard of liability in terms not of monopolization, intent to monopolize, conspiracy to monopolize—the words of the present law, with whatever interpretation the cases law have given to them—but rather explicitly in terms of market power, in the sense of markets that are less competitive than the facts of economies of scale, transport costs, the geography of demand, the nature of consumer preferences dictate.

Now it is perfectly clear, just to expand on this a little, that if we look at an industry like the steel industry, there are a few firms, and I do not have the numbers freshly in mind, something like 10 or a dozen which account for a very large share of the output. From a technical point of view, it would be impossible, inconsistent with economic efficiency, to have 200 firms in the steel industry. The scale of production is so large that the 200 firms would have to be inefficiently small firms. On the other hand, from the technical point of view—and I want to make it clear that I am using this industry for illustrative purposes and not trying to express an opinion about the goodness or badness of its conduct or its legality—that from a technical point of view it would be perfectly possible to have 30 or 40 firms, in my judgment, rather than the dozen sharing that amount of capacity.

Then one possible standard of law would be to say where a determination can be made, on an examination of all the relevant facts, that markets are less competitive than they need be, then there might be a change. This doesn't mean only concentration, it means looking at the facts on prices and costs, output and capacity, and the like.

The second alternative is the alternative described in the proposed statutory language or rather rough statutory language that Mr. Blair quoted. If the proposal embodied in the first alternative appears impracticable because the administrative problems of adjudication, of trying these cases and making determinations would be very great, and, also, because the proceedings would be protracted, and the incentive effects of having protracted proceedings might be undesirable.

Businessmen might feel that the notion that lengthy proceedings are going to go on in industry after industry over a great many years is discouraging and even threatening. Then one could say if this remedy is to be tried at all, it ought to be done in a more surgical fashion, with a simpler administrative procedure on the basis of a rebuttable presumption. That is the context in which this proposal was placed.

Comments on Standards for Antitrust Policy

EDWARD S. MASON

The following article is taken from the preface contributed by Professor Mason, of Harvard University, to Antitrust Policy *by Carl Kaysen and Donald Turner.*

IT IS unnecessary here to reassess public opinion and Congressional intentions, circa 1890, in order to assert with some confidence that the Sherman law was aimed at two targets: "unreasonable" market power (a situation), and "unfair"—exclusionary, restrictive, oppressive—practices (a type of conduct). Opinions differed then—as they differ now—on which was the main target and on the reciprocal relationship between power and practices. But neither target has, for long, been out of sight. One can, of course, quote Senator Hoar to the effect that oppressive practices were the wrong to be remedied, while monopoly achieved without benefit of such practice was unobjectionable. Equally valid and prestigeful testimony, however, supports the view that the principal evils to be remedied were those huge agglomerations of capital, the trusts.

Justice Holmes, in his much quoted dissent in the *Northern Securities* case, aptly observed that, "The Act says nothing about competition." [1] Neither does it mention monopoly. The operational words are "restraint" and "monopolizing." But it was the emphasis given by the Court in previous cases to another word in the statute, "every," that led eventually to the enunciation of the "rule of reason." To many, the rule of reason represented an abandonment of the attack on monopoly in favor of a much attenuated rule relating to conduct. Good trusts were distinguished from bad trusts. But, of course, the questions of size and market power were always relevant since conduct on the part of a small com-

1. Northern Securities Co. v. United States, 193 U.S. 197 (1904).

petitor does not, necessarily, have the same significance as similar conduct by a large one.

The Court, in 1920, somewhat gratuitously, found that "size is no offense." And indeed, during the ensuing twelve years of Republican administration, which embraced our second merger movement, size was not much of an offense. But by 1932 Justice Cardozo was proclaiming that "size carries with it an opportunity for abuse that is not to be ignored when the opportunity is proved to have been utilized in the past." [2] And from then on, a long series of decisions, including *Tobacco, Alcoa,* and *United Shoe,* has laid increasing emphasis on market power. Monopoly (or market power) "without more" is still no offense under the antitrust laws, but the "more" is being attenuated into what mathematicians might call the second order of smalls.

There is a school of thought that, while holding the limitation of monopoly to be the chief objective of antitrust policy, believes that all undesirable market situations can, in fact, be reached by a rule on restrictive conduct. The contention is that the history of every large firm will, on examination, reveal practices that can legitimately be made the basis of an antitrust suit. If one is willing to become an antitrust archaeologist, this may well be true. But if the undesirability lies primarily in the situation, i.e., the market power structure, rather than in the conduct, this procedure somewhat resembles an attack on kidnaping by prosecuting kidnapers for income tax violation. And when, as in *United Shoe,* the conduct complained of is that which is not "economically inevitable," extensive reliance on a rule of conduct appears somewhat misplaced. Moreover, while a careful study of the ancient history of existing firms may reveal derelictions on which a charge can be based, this may not hold true in the future.

There is another school of thought that favors subsuming both the market situation of a firm and its conduct under a rule of "intent." [3] According to its leading practitioner, "The distinction between 'market control' and 'restriction of competition' is not only elusive, it is nonexistent." Neither "control" nor "restriction,"

2. United States v. Swift and Co., 286 U.S. 106 (1932).

3. See Myron W. Watkins, review of "Economic Concentration and the Monopoly Problem" by Edward S. Mason, *American Economic Review* (September 1957), pp. 747–753; and Alfred E. Kahn, "Standards for Antitrust Policy," [*supra,* p. 159 ff].

moreover, provides an adequate test of violation. "It is inadequate because it focuses the issue on the pattern of market structure, the possession of market power, and ignores the animus lying behind the development of that structural pattern. Intent provides an appropriate *primary* criterion of compliance with or violation of the law, because of the nature of the antitrust law itself. The Sherman Act prescribes a rule of conduct. It does not condemn monopoly; it prohibits monopolizing." [4] In further elaboration of the meaning of "intent" it is asserted that "intent, in law, is always an inference drawn from *conduct*. Personal motives are irrelevant. It is the pattern of conduct in a specific set of circumstances that reveals the intent, according to common experience, on which turns the issue of whether an offense has been committed." [5]

But, when we turn to the "specific set of circumstances" in which a specified type of conduct may or may not evidence an "intent to monopolize," the market position of the firm inevitably looms large. Unless we are to prohibit these specified types of conduct as illegal per se, they must be judged with reference to some situation. Let us quote from another advocate of the primacy of intent. "A state medical association expels some doctors for 'a breach of medical ethics.' A publishing company which owns a morning and an evening newspaper refuses to accept advertisements in either one separately. A number of cement manufacturers quote identical delivered prices. A chain store reduces its margins in a particular locality at a particular time. A pipe line company owned by an oil refiner establishes minimum tenders. A man standing in front of a bank which is being robbed whistles loudly when a policeman comes into view. How does one decide when to exonerate, when to condemn these . . . courses of conduct?" [6]

The primary answer to be given to these questions, I submit, is that the conduct is to be condemned when the actor is shown to have the power or the capabilities to make his conduct effective. If the rule of "intent" means merely that the legal significance of action is to be judged largely with reference to the market power of the actor, I have no fault to find with it, though I do

4. Watkins, *op. cit.*, p. 749.
5. *Ibid.*, p. 751.
6. Kahn, [*op. cit., supra,* p. 161].

not think that subsuming, and confusing, both elements under the term "intent" gets us very far forward.[7] But that "intent to monopolize," inferred exclusively from conduct, either is, or should be, the law I would strongly deny.

After all, is it necessary at this late date to argue that mergers, agreements, and various types of business practices have a significance with respect to the maintenance of competiton that depends largely on the market position of the merging, agreeing, or practicing firms? The attention paid in recent cases to defining the relevant market and assessing the position of firms in this market is sufficient indication that the courts, at least, are aware of this dependence.

An evaluation of market power, or control, or monopoly, as an essential element in the assessment of the competitive significance of business conduct, obviously presents economic analysis with a set of problems it is not very well equipped to handle. We shall have more to say on this later. But whatever the difficulty, it is a set of problems that cannot be avoided. It has not, in fact, ever been avoided in cases involving large firms, though the emphasis on conduct was much stronger thirty years ago than it is today. It cannot be avoided in the selection of cases by the Antitrust Division and the Federal Trade Commission unless the Division and the Commission abdicate their positive role in the enforcement of antitrust in favor of a mere follow-up of the complaints that flow in from business quarters. An assessment of the relation between power and practices is unavoidable in remedy proceedings. The choice between an injunction or a "cease and desist" order as against some form of divestiture depends on the

7. This discussion reminds me of the differences between the alleged practices of American and British military intelligence officers during World War II. The Americans extolled the merits of their formulation of the central problem, defined as an evaluation of enemy "capabilities," as against an alleged British evaluation of enemy "intentions." According to the American officers, an evaluation of intentions leads toward a subjective assessment of "desires" and away from a hard core and objective assessment of what the enemy can do. I do not know, in fact, whether the choice of "intentions" led the British in this direction, but there is no reason why it should have. A proper assessment of intentions includes both capabilities and interests. A reasonable man does not "intend" what he manifestly cannot do. Nor does he use his capabilities in the pursuit of aims in which he has no interests. Obviously, an evaluation of both capabilities and interests (whether or not exhibited by previous conduct) is necessary to a sensible evaluation of intentions.

anticipated consequences for competition of a prohibition of particular practices. And this, in turn, depends largely on the power of the relevant firms or the structure of the market. If the power is large, injunction may be without effect.

Finally, an assessment of market power is of the essence of merger policy. How else can the line be drawn between permitted and prohibited mergers other than by assessing the probable consequences of a proposed or an accomplished merger on the "level" or "vigor" of competition, i.e., by assessing the change in the distribution of market power?

While the problem of market power cannot be—and has not been—avoided in the administration of the antitrust laws, it would admittedly be a long step to advocate a market power standard "without more" as a test of violation, in addition to the present "market power plus conduct" standard. . . . The Sherman Law is a criminal as well as a civil statute, and as Justice Holmes has said, "The words cannot be read one way in a suit which is to end in fine and imprisonment and another way in one which seeks an injunction." [8] In fact, they have been increasingly so read, which is perhaps one of the difficulties with the attenuated "conduct" standard used in recent antitrust cases. In any case, a criminal statute is obviously inappropriate when the wrong to be remedied is a situation rather than a type of conduct.

There remains, however, the large question of whether current tools of analysis are adequate to make an acceptable distinction between permissible and nonpermissible situations of market power. Returning to our earlier discussion of the task of evaluating any branch of economic policy, we are here concerned with the state of knowledge concerning relationships among the variables to be manipulated and the ends to be attained. [At this point,] it may be useful to attempt to clear away certain obvious misconceptions.

The espousal of a standard aimed at the avoidance of "unreasonable" market power or the preservation of a minimum "level of competition" is most decidedly not an argument for the acceptance of tests of business performance. Business performance, as the term is currently used, is a normative concept; performance is either "good" or "bad." Goodness and badness obviously have to be judged with reference to their approach to—or departure from

8. His dissent in the Northern Securities Case, 193 U.S. 197 (1904).

—some ideal type, and in the search for the ideal, one of two standards or both are customarily brought forward. The first is a performance consistent with the existence of pure competition, or of some variant that may take account of a "real" desire on the part of buyers for some degree of product differentiation. The second is "progressiveness," "dynamism," or some rate of innovation.

The first ideal type of performance has the merit of being more or less clearly defined and is backed by a respectable body of analysis having to do with the behavior of prices and quantities of goods and resources under conditions of static equilibrium. Unfortunately, the situations and types of conduct we have to deal with are not static. But the second ideal type of performance cannot even be defined. There is no known way of ascertaining whether the progressiveness of firms or the rate of innovation in a particular industry constitutes good or bad performance in a given situation. This inability, however, has not prevented many admirers of the "new" or "dynamic" competition from advocating performance tests of antitrust violation, with heavy weight given to evidences of "progressive" behavior. As I have suggested elsewhere, a proposal to rely on such tests is an invitation to nonenforcement.

The fact that we cannot directly measure the goodness or badness of business performance, however, does not mean that we are uninterested in performance. The ultimate justification of an anti-monopoly policy rests heavily on the belief that the maintenance of competition has an important contribution to make to efficiency in resource use and to continuous product and process improvement. Efficiency and progressiveness enforced by the market, rather than dispensed as largess by publicly minded custodians of private power, have been the traditional objectives. Unless it can be assumed that antitrust has some significant effect of this sort on the functioning of the economy, it is little more than a device for policing business morality. But it does not follow that an analysis of these effects can provide us with acceptable tests of antitrust violation.

The other main misconception is that market power or the plane of competition can be inferred directly and exclusively from data relating to the structure of the market. As the phrase is currently used, market structure refers to those permanent, or slowly changing, competitive limitations of which a firm must take account in formulating its own policies. The most important of these limitations are the number and size distribution of buyers and sellers in the market, the conditions of entry of new firms, and the extent of product differentiation, including geographical dispersion.

Despite Stigler's observation that "an industry which does not have a competitive structure will not have competitive behavior," [9] a study of structure is not enough. This is so for two reasons. Many if not most of the markets with which antitrust is concerned do not approach very closely the only two models, pure competition and pure monopoly, that permit us to infer with assurance—at least under equilibrium conditions—behavior from structure. Secondly, if we include, as elements of market structure, data on growth trends and susceptibility to cyclical variations, as we frequently must if we are to explain the behavior of firms, we are fairly far removed from the universe of static market models.

If we reject both performance and structure-without-more as inadequate, where are we to find evidence of market power? The answer given by [Kaysen and Turner] is essentially that it is to be found in the combined study of market structure and business behavior. The critical problem—and the chief difficulty confronting anyone who wishes to reassess antitrust policy—is presented by oligopoly. A large fraction of manufacturing output in the United States is produced in industries in which three or four or five firms account for sixty percent or more of the total. And if the industry data are "adjusted" to take account of market realities, a serious degree of concentration still remains. The exclusive application of structural standards—at least on certain definitions—might condemn all such markets. On the other hand, the application of performance standards might excuse all. To those who believe . . . that there is a substantial monopoly problem in the oligopolistic structure of American industry, but that not all highly concentrated markets fall under the ban, there is presented the problem of separating the sheep from the goats.

9. George J. Stigler, "The Case Against Big Business," [*supra.* p. 12].

A New "Worst" in Antitrust

FORTUNE

The following editorial appeared in the April 1966 issue of Fortune. *It recommends a basic reappraisal and modification of antitrust law.*

NOW WE HAVE a new disaster on the antitrust front. The Federal Trade Commission has issued a ruling in the National Tea Co. case that banishes any lingering doubt that antitrust policy has gone hogwild. The FTC's ruling invokes the language of certain Supreme Court decisions of recent years. These decisions, in turn, flow from that branch of antitrust policy that distrusts markets, resists change, and measures competition solely by the number of competitors. The majority opinion in the National Tea case carries this reactionary philosophy to such lengths as to make plain the need for the kind of basic reappraisal of antitrust law advocated [by] *Fortune*—i.e., an act of Congress that preserves the safeguards against restraints of trade but permits all the honest mergers the market will bear. [More specifically, Congress should amend the antitrust statutes to make it clear that the national policy is to foster competition by punishing restraints of trade, including conspiracies to fix prices, limit production, allocate markets, and suppress innovation; but that it is not the national policy to prefer any particular size, shape, or number of firms to any other size, shape, or number; and that mergers—horizontal, vertical, or conglomerate—are entirely legal unless they spring from a manifest attempt to restrain trade.] Only congressional action will stop the tendency to freeze the economy into shapes that may become more inefficient and inappropriate in the decades ahead.

Prior to 1945, National Tea was a regional chain of groceries operating in eight states. In that year it got a new management and soon made a decision, fraught with business risk, to transform itself from a regional to a national chain. Between 1945 and 1958 its sales increased from $107 million a year to $794 million.

According to the FTC's figures, $250 million of this increase was directly attributable to the acquisition of twenty-six firms operating 485 retail stores in 188 cities of sixteen states. In becoming the fifth-largest food retailer in the U.S., National Tea did not gobble up its competitors; nearly all of its mergers represented the geographical extension of National into local markets where it had not previously operated.

The FTC's findings make no serious attempt to show that this expansion was accompanied by unfair or "predatory" practices on the part of National, or that consumers or suppliers were disadvantaged in any specific way, or that the quality of competition in retail food—locally or nationally—was made less lively by the merger activities of the company. Instead, the FTC builds its case upon a superficial count of changes in the number of *units* in retail food during the principal period of National's merger activity. The FTC says that National's early acquisitions triggered a merger movement throughout the industry. It recites with horror what it calls an "almost incredible" record of change: between 1948 and 1958 the total number of U.S. grocery stores declined by 100,000 or nearly 30 percent; the number of chains with eleven or more stores dropped from 210 to 180; the twenty largest chains of 1958 had 30.1 percent of the U.S. retail food business, although these twenty companies had had only 21.1 percent in 1948.

All this so-called "analysis" in the FTC's argument is neither necessary nor meaningful. Any child alive in the 1950's could see that a restructuring of food retailing was then going on. The business was adjusting itself, through market mechanisms that included merger, to vast and profound changes in the American way of life. There is not a word in the FTC majority opinion that relates changes in the number of stores and chains to the proliferation of suburbs, the construction of shopping centers, and the final triumph of the supermarket—an innovation in retailing that has since spread across the Western world. The most important single cause of these changes was the automobile revolution—for which National Tea Co. can hardly be held responsible and which not even the FTC can stop.

The FTC majority, however, true to a tradition deeply embedded in the reactionary side of antitrust regards the changes in the structure of food retailing as an upsetting of the "balance." Use of this word implies that there had been some eternally right number and size of retail food establishments, some Pythagorean harmony, that was violated by the changes in the ratios of business done by large, medium, and small concerns. That which change disturbed was not a "balance"; it was just the way things used to be.

The FTC's majority opinion, written by Chairman Paul Rand Dixon, proudly states the axiom on which the National Tea ruling rests: "Competition is likely to be greatest where there are many sellers, none of which has any significant market share." Chairman Dixon did not think this up himself. He is quoting from the Supreme Court of the United States in the Philadelphia National Bank decision of 1963. The Court, in turn, is echoing one line of economic opinion that casts in pseudo-scientific language a nostalgic popular prejudice in favor of the society of small farmers and shopkeepers that preceded the transition to the twentieth-century economy. The principle enunciated by the Supreme Court and lovingly repeated by Chairman Dixon is both clear and familiar; it merely happens to be untrue.

Nowhere is its falsity more obvious than in food retailing. Plenty of living American men and women remember an era when virtually all groceries were sold through very small stores none of which had "any significant market share." Was this era the high point of competition in food retailing? Many little towns had, in fact, only one place where a given kind of food could be bought. In a typical city neighborhood, defined by the range of a housewife's willingness to lug groceries home on foot, there might be three or four relaxed "competitors." If she did not like the price or quality offered by them, she could take her black-string market bag, board a trolley car, and try her luck among the relaxed "competitors" of some other neighborhood.

Competition in the retail food business today is more intense than it has ever been—if it is measured by any standard other than that of numbers of units and market shares. National Tea, that bloated colossus with less than 2 percent of the nation's retail food business, was in 1958 losing money in 141 cities. The FTC admits that the retail food business is "dynamic" and that entry into the field is not difficult.

Nevertheless, it found that twenty-four of National's twenty-six mergers had been illegal because they were part of a general trend toward less competition in the retail food business. Amazingly, the FTC did not, however, order National to divest itself of its acquisitions. *It prescribed a much worse remedy.* National was forbidden to acquire any other company for a period of ten years, without the prior approval of Big Brother, the FTC. The FTC's language is so broad that this order is being widely interpreted as forbidding mergers, without express FTC consent, throughout the whole retail food business. If the Supreme Court upholds the FTC decision (and why should the Court deny its own offspring?) thousands of independent proprietors and small chains will lose a valuable right to sell out to concerns already in the food business. More important, the U.S. economy will lose an important part of the flexibility it will need to meet the next wave of social and economic change.

A lone voice, Commissioner Philip Elman filed a brilliant dissent in the National Tea case—brilliant, that is, compared to the majority opinion. Elman points with scorn and indignation to the failure of the commission to find a single local market where competition has been really lessened by the presence of National Tea.

Yet the temptation to make Commissioner Elman the hero of this episode must be firmly resisted. What *he* wants is a set of elaborate economic studies by the FTC of the market structures of various industries. On the basis of such studies, the FTC would develop "rules" or "guideposts" telling each industry what kinds of mergers, if any, would be tolerated by government policy.

Elman's position is responsive to the demands of those businessmen who keep saying that all they want is a clear and certain antitrust policy, regardless of what it is. This attitude can lead to more trouble than the present near chaos. Elman's proposal for guidelines and rules is based on the assumption that the government—with the help of business, consumers, and economists—can determine, from time to time, the "right" future structure of a given industry.

Such a system would substitute an especially insidious and irresponsible kind of government planning for the action of the market in determining, through the rewards and punishments of business risk, the evolutionary path of U.S. business. Would any "study" carried out by a government agency in the 1940's have resulted in a rule that would have encouraged the retail food business to adjust, as effectively as it did, to the drastic social and economic changes of the Fifties? Could any study, undertaken now, foresee and translate into a merger "rule" the kind of market structure that will be appropriate for the U.S. food business of 1975?

As Elman points out, there are signs that since 1958 the trend toward concentration in the biggest supermarket chains has slowed markedly. Customers appear to be shifting toward smaller chains of "convenience" stores. But who can say, as a matter of law, where and in what way and at what pace this new trend—if it is a trend—should proceed? In the decades of accelerating innovation ahead of us there are so many variables that the structure of business cannot be scientifically determined and centrally planned. Let the market, groping its way through the decisions of competing corporations, find the future.

The Antitrust Chief Replies

DONALD F. TURNER

*Donald F. Turner is Assistant Attorney General in charge of the
Antitrust Division of the Department of Justice. Before accepting
this post, he was Professor of Law at Harvard University. The
following article was written in reply to* Fortune's *proposed modification of the antitrust laws (contained in the previous selection).*

I WILL NOT GO SO FAR as to say that [*Fortune's*] analysis is non-
sense, or that [its] proposal would be folly. I doubt that any one
of us knows or could know enough about the facts to warrant
conclusions so strong. However, I have no hesitancy in saying not
only that no affirmative case has been made out for the proposition
which *Fortune* suggests, but also that the best economic information and thinking available to us indicates that a strong antimerger policy, at least insofar as horizontal-type mergers are
concerned, is almost certainly right.

There is no doubt that some conceived and still conceive of the
Sherman Act and Section 7 of the Clayton Act as weapons
against bigness per se, as protectors of small business come what
may, and as protectors of what were and are thought to be great
social values. But so long as such sentiments are not allowed to
override judgments based on competitive concepts, it seems to me
that the presence of such diverse motives is totally irrelevant to
the question whether the law, as economic policy, is silly or wise.

The principal purpose of antimerger law is to forestall the creation of, or an increase in, market power. Its purpose is to preserve
competitively structured markets insofar as natural forces will
permit. I need only briefly restate the traditional reasons which
are mustered in support of such a policy. If we can avoid the
creation of undue market power, by and large we expect to
achieve better market performance—better in terms of lower
prices, higher quality products, and innovations both in product
and in technology. We also expect to minimize the misallocation
of resources that results from monopoly or oligopoly pricing.

Consequently, if there is validity in this traditional economic reasoning, an antimerger law clearly makes sense, even based almost entirely as in Philadelphia Bank, on structural considerations. For there is obviously a polar distance between our present law on horizontal mergers and a law, as proposed by *Fortune,* that would make mergers lawful "unless they spring from a manifest attempt to restrain trade."

If there is validity in the traditional competitive analysis, a tough antimerger law is not going to do any significant harm to the economy, even though, as I have argued repeatedly elsewhere, it must be based on general rules that are bound to stop some mergers that in fact are innocuous or even somewhat beneficial. For a tough rule on horizontal mergers does not stop the economy from achieving the principal objects with which the antitrust critics are concerned. If we exercise reasonable restraint in formulating rules on other kinds of mergers, a tough rule on horizontal mergers simply shuts off some merger alternatives, not all. It may indeed in some instances prevent the merger which would most readily accommodate efficiency gains; but there seems to be little doubt that in many cases superiority of the substantial horizontal merger in this respect will be at best marginal and there may be no superiority at all.

Moreover, even if the general body of merger prohibitions went well beyond its present scope, the avenue of internal growth remains open and this is the avenue by which many if not most firms have achieved whatever economies there are in large size. There seems to be little reason to believe that any significant economies will long go unrealized because this or that merger has been prohibited. Again, this is not to say that there will never be a case in which growth through merger is more advantageous to the economy than internal growth or expansion. There undoubtedly will be some such cases, but if we are right in being concerned about undue concentration in markets, it is more than a fair guess that the gains from a strong antimerger policy will far outweigh the losses.

The economic purpose of an antimerger policy is precisely the same as the purpose behind the antitrust prohibitions on such anticompetitive agreements as price fixing. The purpose is to prevent, wherever natural economic forces do not compel it, development of the concentrated market structure that produces the same adverse effects on performance as those produced by price fixing and similar agreements.

THE EFFECTS OF CONCENTRATION

I now turn to the question whether our traditional analysis, which looks with disfavor upon concentrated market structures, is no longer valid—or at least no longer sufficiently valid to make a strong antimerger policy worthwhile. The most important assertions [by] *Fortune* seem to be these: (1) That concentration in the production of a particular product is of little or no significance because of interproduct competition; (2) that traditional analysis "tends to ignore the element around which competition in fact increasingly centers—managerial brains"; and (3) that in creating larger-size companies mergers usually produce greater efficiencies, most importantly in research and development.[1]

As for interproduct competition, it no doubt does impose ceilings on the power of the manufacturers of a particular product to raise prices. If the products are close enough substitutes and the costs of production are comparable, the ceiling may be as tight or nearly as tight as would be imposed by additional sellers of precisely the same product. But what conclusions can be drawn from this? There is of course the well-recognized fact that antimerger law and antimonopoly law will often involve some rather difficult problems of market definition, and that these problems should be approached in a rational way.

But it seems to me preposterous to suggest that we should cease to be concerned about concentration in the production of a particular product simply because the existence of other products narrows the range of price exploitation that otherwise would obtain. Though, to quote *Fortune*, "beer competes with . . . candy," a monopoly or an oligopoly in the beer industry would still have power to raise price well above competitive levels before any significant number of customers would decide to quench their thirst with Hershey bars. And the fact that aluminum wire competes with copper wire and that many copper and aluminum products compete with steel products simply does not mean that concentration in any one of these industries has no impact on the

1. [These arguments were presented in *Fortune*, March, 1966.—*Editor.*]

price of its products or has no impact on other aspects of competitive performance. Therefore, it does not mean that antitrust concern with concentration has lost its *raison d'être*.

Indeed, it would not be entirely facetious for me to suggest that those who praise the virtues of interproduct competition do not really take themselves all that seriously. Even the editors of *Fortune* continue to praise the virtue of making price-fixing agreements unlawful. Yet price-fixing agreements among producers of the same product would be a matter of no consequence if interproduct competition denied producers the power to raise prices.

That significant increase in concentration in the production of particular products will normally lead to less competition is strongly supported by empirical evidence. A study by Professor Joe S. Bain on the relation of profit rates to industry concentration in forty industries defined more or less along traditional product lines shows a significant correlation between higher than average profits and high concentration. Another more recent study shows that among industries with medium entry barriers (again defined along traditional product lines), the industry that is more highly concentrated shows higher profits. A recent thorough study of the banking industry also shows that concentration of banks in a local market goes hand in hand with higher interest rates—a direct correlation between concentration and a higher price for the product sold, in this case, money.

Were it correct, as many assert, that increased concentration does not lead to diminished competition, either because of interproduct competition or for any other reason, it remains for them to explain why it is that even among industries with stationary demand and constant output, those that are highly concentrated set prices significantly higher than costs plus normal profit. To repeat, what evidence we have tends to support the commonplace conclusion that significantly increased concentration means diminished competition and the extraction of monopoly profits from the consumer.

ECONOMIES OF SCALE

Let me now turn to the contention that traditional analysis "tends to ignore the element around which competition in fact increasingly centers—managerial brains." I can only say that the contention if true (and I don't believe it is) seems to me to be largely irrelevant to the appropriateness of antimerger policy unless management is so scarce a resource that it can only be utilized to full advantage by permitting levels of concentration well beyond what other economies of scale would dictate. I know of no evidence that management is that scarce a resource. But even if we suppose that first-class management is so scarce that we should encourage a greater concentration of business assets than we now have, it seems clear that valid competitive considerations would still dictate directing such further concentration toward conglomerate forms rather than permitting underutilized management to fulfill itself by substantial horizontal mergers.

I should like to turn now to the question of whether economies of scale generally are so significant that an abandonment or substantial curtailment of antimerger policy is in order. Let me summarize some of the evidence. One statistical study, which was carried out some years ago, concerned the relationship between corporate size and profit rate among manufacturing corporations. The primary finding of this study is that average profit rates increased as firm size grew to approximately the $5-million total-asset mark, but that once this level had been reached profit rates were constant or even tended slightly downward. In short, among corporations with assets exceeding $5 million, profit rates are not crucially dependent on firm size. If it were true that better managers tended to concentrate in larger firms, or that economies of scale were continuous, then profits should increase with size throughout the whole of the distribution. The statistics, however, simply do not bear this out.

THE LIMITS OF THE ARGUMENT

In a study whose results appear to be typical, Professor Bain set out to measure statistically the extent of scale economies within twenty of the leading manufacturing industries. By this, I mean he attempted to measure the minimum size of plant which was sufficiently large to realize all of the engineering and technical savings which are associated with mass production. Having done this, he examined whether concentration was greater or less than appeared to be required for optimal efficiency. His conclusion was this:

"Referring to the first four firms in each of our industries, it appears that concentration by the large firms is in every case but one greater than required by singleplant economies, and in more than half of the cases very substantially greater." This finding indicates that an active merger policy intended to limit increases in market concentration is unlikely to result in lower efficiency, that an antimerger policy and efficiency are not in conflict.

Bain's study deals with economies of scale within fixed technologies, and the critics of antitrust merger policy quite properly suggest that we need also to concern ourselves with the relationships between competition and technological innovations. By no means the first to do so, *Fortune* refers admiringly to the writings of Professor J. A. Schumpeter, who advanced the view that some combination of large firm size and monopoly is required if firms are to invest substantial funds for innovation. While Schumpeter's writings are strong and lucid, and there is a good deal of implicit appeal to the arguments which he makes, we still need to ask ourselves whether this approach has empirical as well as theoretical justification, and if so just what the limits of the argument are.

We have had several studies designed to test the validity and dimensions of the proposition that both the amount of research and the efficiency of research are correlated with size of firm. I believe it is accurate to say, on the basis of these studies, that once we get a firm large enough to do significant research at all there are no evident economies of scale, either in research per size of firm or in research productivity for any given amount spent. It is indeed true that larger firms are much more likely to have research laboratories than small firms. Nevertheless, among firms which do have research organizations, small firms tend to spend *proportionately* as much as their larger counterparts, and in some instances they spend more.

RESEARCH AND INNOVATION

Another most interesting study showed that between 1899 and 1937 the industries in which labor productivity increased most sharply were those characterized by declining concentration. Not only was this true, but industries of low concentration showed better performance than those with high concentration. Since we frequently presume that research and innovation are directed toward lowering costs, leading thereby to higher levels of output per manhour, those studies suggest that increasing concentration has not led to more innovation but rather that the opposite may have been the case, and that "it is the competition of new rivals within an industry, not the competition of new industries, that is associated with rapid technological progress."

The last question which deserves comment is whether large firms and large research laboratories are necessary for *efficient* research activity. The argument here is that even if smaller firms spend proportionately as much as or more than their large rivals on research and development, smaller laboratories are inherently less efficient than their larger counterparts and turn out relatively less in the way of innovations. There is no overwhelming evidence on the point because of the difficulties involved in measuring output of research laboratories. Here again there are undoubtedly situations in which research of any kind requires expensive facilities which firms below some minimum size could not afford. However, two studies suggest that in general there is little reason to suppose any persistent economies in large size. Indeed, they suggest the contrary.

The proposition that the factual premise for an antimerger policy has disappeared rests on little more than sheer assertion; the weight of the evidence we have indicates that there is about as much justification today for an antimerger policy directed against substantial horizontal mergers as there ever has been. In this connection I cannot but point out again that antimerger law, even if stretched well beyond its present bounds, leaves open most alternatives whereby any advantages of large size may be legitimately obtained. All in all, the costs of being too lenient on mergers still appear to be higher than the costs of being too strict.

PART FOUR Competition: Its Relation to Some Major Macroeconomic and Social Problems in the United States

Monopoly Power: Cause of Inflation at Less Than Full Employment

ABBA LERNER

Abba Lerner is Professor of Economics at the City University of New York. The following paper is taken from his testimony before the Joint Economic Committee of Congress.

THE UNDERSTANDING of the nature of inflation and of its appropriate treatment, cure, and prevention has been badly served by the concentration of economic theory on the analysis of perfect competition. Economists have had good reason for this concentration, primarily because the study of perfect competition has brought out the ways in which the competitive capitalist or profit-and-loss system can bring about the most efficient production and distribution of what the consumer wants. But perfect competition has been useful more as a norm by which the efficiency of the economy can be gauged than as an accurate description of its actual operation.

In a perfectly competitive economy, nobody would have any power over any price—or any wage, which is the price of labor. All prices would be determined only by supply and demand on the market. Whenever there was an excess of supply over demand the price would fall; whenever there was an excess of demand over supply, the price would rise, and conversely a price could rise only when there was an excess demand and could fall only if there was an excess supply.

Inflation, or rising prices in general, could occur only if there was a general excess of demand or of spending, and the natural cure would be simply to cut out the excess demands by restrictive monetary or fiscal measures. Price stability would be restored as soon as demand was no longer excessive. People would then no longer be trying to buy more than the economy is able to provide. But as long as prices were not falling, we would know that there is still sufficient overall demand for what the economy is able to produce.

In a perfectly competitive economy every supplier of anything would be able to sell as much as he wanted to at the market price without any effort, and he would not be able to sell any at all at any higher price. There would be no need for or any possibility of applying the art of selling. With all prices determined by the equation of supply and demand on the market, buyers and sellers would be able to decide only on how much to buy or to sell at this market price. Nobody would ever be free to decide on one price rather than another. There could therefore be no administered prices.

That we are not living in a perfectly competitive economy is thus evident at every turn, and in most other branches of economics this is well taken care of. Economists deal with imperfect competition, monopoly, oligopoly, price leadership, marketing, collective bargaining, and a host of problems that have no place in the perfectly competitive economy. But in dealing with the problem of the stability of the general price level, economists have tended to assume that we are indeed in a perfectly competitive economy in which all prices are market determined so that a rising or falling price level is a clear indication of excessive or deficient demand. It followed that adjusting the level of demand in the degree necessary to stop such movements would bring about just the right level of demand and cure or prevent both depression and inflation.

Pre-Keynesian economists went one step further and argued that no policy at all was necessary as long as the quantity of money was held relatively stable. Any tendency for prices in general to rise or to fall would cure itself. Rising prices would reduce the real value of the money stock as each dollar lost value.

This would induce a decrease in demand as people cut their spending in attempts to restore the real value of the money stock. Since rising prices—in a perfectly competitive economy—could only be caused by excess demand, this would remove the cause and cure the inflation. Conversely depression would cure itself because the falling prices, which—in a perfectly competitive economy—necessarily result from depression, would increase the real value of the money stock. This would induce more spending and remove the insufficiency of demand which constitutes the depression.

Since Keynes, most economists have considered this automatic cure for depression to be impractical because prices and wages refuse to fall in response to small and temporary deficiencies of demand. Instead of suffering from long and severe depressions and undermining our long-term rate of growth, while waiting for wages and prices to fall so as to raise the value of the money stock and thereby increase demand, it is possible and more practical to increase demand painlessly by expansionary monetary or fiscal measures. But this still leaves intact the identification of deflation with deficient demand or depression and of inflation with excess demand, just as they must be in the perfectly competitive economy.

The Keynesian revolution merely says that the deflation of prices by depression is too little and too late. But the tardiness of wages and prices to fall in response to depression is only a result of their being determined by administrative decisions by businesses, by unions, or by combinations of these, instead of by the equation of supply and demand in perfect markets. The administrative decisions may not only display a reluctance to reduce prices and wages when there is excess supply, they may also display a propensity to raise wages and prices. The Keynesian analysis considered only the first possibility. What I want to stress now is that the administration which is responsible for that is also responsible for making wages and prices rise even though there is deficient demand.

And just as it may take a long and severe depression to overcome the reluctance to reduce wages and prices, so it may take considerable depression even to overcome the propensity to raise them. This is, in fact, the case, and this constitutes the essence of our problem. The level of demand that divides prosperity from depression is not the same as that which divides inflation from deflation. We need something like 2 percent unemployment to allow for necessary movements from job to job in a changing economy but it seems to take about 7 percent unemployment, which means serious depression, to stop wages from rising faster than is compatible with price level stability. When unemployment is between these two figures, we suffer from depression and from inflation at the same time. Attempts to cure the inflation by restricting demand have the effect of aggravating the depression. Attempts to cure the depression by increasing demand have the effect of aggravating the inflation.

In this dilemma we seem strangely to be more concerned about the inflation than about the depression, and have been treating the inflation by restricting demand just as if it were a symptom of excess demand, as it would be in a perfectly competitive economy. But when inflation is found in conjunction with depression—i.e., with more than 2 percent unemployment—it is not due to excess demand; to buyers trying to buy more goods than the economy is able to provide. It is due to sellers of products, or of labor, or both, administratively raising prices and/or wages even while demand is deficient, the induced depression not being sufficiently severe to stop them. It is not a buyers' inflation, but a sellers' inflation, and our frustrations come from treating the latter with the proper [remedy] for the former; namely, restriction of demand.

There are a number of continuing changes in our economy that for some time have been strengthening the tendency of prices to rise even in the face of depression and which seem likely to continue to strengthen this tendency; confidence that the Government will increase demand whenever necessary to prevent severe depressions, continuing experience of rising prices and expectation of more of the same, continuing experience of increasing real income and expectation of still more from much advertised automation, atomic energy, et cetera, increasing political experience by trade unions and business lobbies, increasingly effective informal and often tacit agreement by businessmen to act in unison, the growing consensus that increased efficiency in a particular firm or industry calls for proportionage wage increases, and even the raising of markups by businessmen who are made to feel, by the induced depression itself, that they cannot count on so much prosperity and must charge more so as to break even at a lower output.

When the nature of sellers' inflation is recognized, treatment may take one of three forms: The first is to address appeals to business and to labor to exercise restraint in order to save the economy from the evils of inflation—or from the evils of the depression that will result if the authorities resorted to monetary or fiscal restriction. Such appeals are not likely to be very successful as each price administrator will tend to feel that someone else ought to respond first. A suggested refinement of this hortatory treatment is to have studies made and publicized of the expected inflationary effects of projected or threatened wage or price increases. This would be a useful thing to do, but still would leave each price administrator with the excuse, in many cases quite sound, that the efficiency of the economy calls for other prices to be reduced rather than for his price to be held down.

The second form of treatment consists of measures like a more active antimonopoly program, removing restrictions on foreign competition, outlawing the extortions called fair trading, revamping those public utility commissions that have been using regulation to establish monopolies to regulate, extending antimonopoly measures to include labor, and other devices for increasing the competitiveness of the economy as a whole. Such measures are well worthwhile in their own right, but are likely to be of only temporary effectiveness against sellers' inflation. The price reductions that this will bring about will serve to offset other price and wage increases, but when these price decreases have been fully carried out, the other wage and price increases will continue, for it is certain that even all the reforms together will not establish the perfectly competitive economy, and the reductions may well be swamped by further improvements in the arts of large-scale organization and tacit agreement that are responsible for the administered prices and wages that caused sellers' inflation in the first place.

The third form is unlikely to be adopted until the first two have been tried and found inadequate. This consists of the revolutionary idea of combating sellers' inflation by curbing the inflationary activity of sellers. It calls for regulating the most important administered prices—but only prices, not outputs or services as in the case of public utilities—so that they are made to behave the way competitive prices do. The less important administered prices will then follow suit as they do now. The regulation would prevent an administered price from being raised if output was less than, say, 80 percent of capacity, and would call for a reduction of price if output was less than, say, 70 percent of capacity. Prices would then rise only when capacity was well utilized and would fall when there was much excess capacity, just as they do in a competitive market. Capacity would then be used rather than wasted.

Important administrative wages would be subject to slightly different regulations. Unlike the general price level, which we want to keep stable, average wages must rise with increasing average productivity and with any reductions in the rate of markup which might result from the successful maintenance of price level stability with full employment. But particular wages, like particular prices, must be able to move in response to changes in particular markets. The regulation would take the form of starting with a normal rate of wage increase, say, 1 percent every 4 months, and provide for a larger wage increase, say, 2 percent, where labor was more than twice as scarce, as measured in some established way by the unemployment and vacancy figures. Correspondingly there would be no increase where, by the same index, labor was only half as scarce as on the average.

With the most important administered prices and wages thus made to behave like competitive prices, and the less important administered prices and wages generally following suit, inflation would become coincident with excess demand and deflation with depression and deficient demand. Monetary and fiscal policy would then really be able to prevent both inflation and depression by increasing or decreasing demand, according as the price level is rising or falling. It is not to be expected that the regulation will quickly become popular enough for application, but it would be most advisable for the details of its operation to be studied and for its compatibility with all essential freedoms to be investigated, so that it could be put into effect when the other approaches have failed, or have been exhausted. It is also possible that the knowledge that this approach was being seriously considered and worked at would make the other approaches somewhat more effective.

Monopoly Power and Inflation: A Somewhat Different View

WILLIAM J. FELLNER

William J. Fellner was Professor of Economics at Yale University before becoming a member of the President's Council of Economic Advisers in 1973. The following paper is taken from his testimony before the Joint Economic Committee of Congress.

GENERAL ECONOMIC analysis is becoming increasingly oriented to the investigation of paths of growth rather than of static equilibrium conditions. This has important implications also with respect to the analysis of market power.

Earlier it was usual to base the main economic objection to the concentration of market power on the proposition that such concentration distorts the allocation of resources to specific uses. In the lines of activity where appreciable market power exists, producers find it profitable to use fewer resources than would be justified by the relationship of costs to consumer preferences. This stays a valid proposition, but its significance is somewhat reduced if we look at an economy from a dynamic point of view and make it our business to appraise the results obtainable along a path of growth. Whatever the degree of malallocation of resources may be at any given level of general activity, changes in resource input in various lines of activity do respond properly to changes in costs and in consumer demand, except if, unexpectedly, the degree of concentration of market power were to show a rising tendency. It remains true that the monopolist produces relatively too little and the competitive producer relatively too much, but this is not the aspect of the problem which at present would deserve the primary emphasis.

As for the speed at which an economy is moving along a growth path, the proposition has been advanced in economic theory that firms possessing market power retard the introduction of improved methods. I will not go into this matter in detail, but

I will say here that the assumptions on which this particular proposition rests are very restrictive. For this reason the argument is inconclusive.

PROBLEMS NOW IN THE FOREGROUND

The main reason why high market power creates difficulties at present is that powerful unions and corporations are apt to engage in inflationary wage and price raising action at levels of activity which are not yet so high as to be associated with excess demand. The dangers of such inflation—cost push inflation—are very considerable.

In a highly competitive noninflationary economy prices would have to decrease gradually in the industries where the productivity of physical inputs is rising at a higher rate than it does on the average in the various sectors of the economy; in the industries with slower than average productivity increases prices would be rising; and the average price level would remain stable. As for wage rates, if the relationship between the occupational preferences of the labor force and the availability of various occupations stayed the same, and if the relationship between the distribution of skills and the demand for various skills also stayed stable, wages would be rising across the board roughly in proportion to the average increase in labor productivity over the economy as a whole. Changes in wage differentials would reflect changes in the distribution of the tastes and skills of the labor force relative to the distribution which is needed.

In a fully competitive economy monetary and fiscal policy could create the aggregate monetary demand which is required for near-capacity production at a stable general price level, and the economic system would actually tend to use up this demand for near-capacity production with no price inflation. But where there exist important sectors with unions and corporations possessing high market power, part of the effective demand needed for full use without inflation will be used up for wage and price increases at an underemployment level of output. The monetary-fiscal authority then becomes faced with a choice between accepting enough underemployment to break the inflationary pattern or accepting inflation. This kind of inflation, if not curbed, is likely to show an accelerating tendency and, sooner or later, to cause grave disturbances.

In what follows I shall have mainly these difficulties in mind, although these are not the only ones which the concentration of market power creates for a growth oriented policy. For example, the insistence of unions on not overworking the labor force during work hours may shade over into productivity slowing practices by which the demand for specific varieties of labor is artificially increased. This, too, may retard the growth process noticeably.

REMEDIAL POSSIBILITIES

There exist several types of policy by which market power could be reduced to more easily manageable proportions.

The cleanest solution would be to reduce the size of unions and of corporations sufficiently to assure that in each major industry there should be a fair number of independent bargaining pairs (each pair consisting of a firm and a union). Broadened antitrust legislation would have to be enforced against collusion between these pairs of bargaining units. After such a reform we could set ourselves the objective of approximating full employment, without fearing that the monetary demand will be used up for feeding an inflationary process. This is because each bargaining pair would be under appreciable competitive pressure from the others. Furthermore, at the high levels of employment which we are envisaging here, there would be no danger of a flattening of the uptrend in real wages. There is no reason to expect that the trend in labor's share in the national income would be changed.

An alternative method of dealing with the problem would be to suspend (outlaw) collective bargaining for wages for any period in which the aggregate unemployment rate in the economy is lower than a stated percentage (but not for periods in which there is more than, say, 4 percent unemployment). Monetary and fiscal policy could then be aiming at practically full employment. The idea underlying this suggestion is that the general trend in real wage rates takes care of itself in the labor market whenever the level of employment is high enough. In these periods collective bargaining for wages has mainly the effect of causing inflation, not of raising real wage rates. The highly organized sections of the labor force obtain wage-differentials in their own favor, but the catching-up process starts soon in the other sectors, and the inflationary process gets rolling.

Of these two methods the first—the reduction of the size of units possessing excessive market power—is perhaps more satisfactory in terms of fundamental principles. But both suggestions seem logical, even though appreciable political difficulties stand in the way of both. Still, I think we have been giving solutions of this sort too little attention. We have been overlooking the fact that bypassing suggestions of this character leads into other difficulties which are also likely to prove substantial. What are the other possibilities?

One of the other possibilities is to leave the institutional setting unchanged and to use monetary-fiscal restraints as soon as the degree of resource-utilization reaches the point where cost-push inflation becomes a serious threat. In essence this is the policy which we have been using, perhaps half-heartedly. It is a policy of compromise with the Devil. The desirability of this particular compromise depends in part on how high the degree of employment is which proves compatible with a reasonably stable price level. Very much depends also on what the long run growth rate is which proves compatible with the degree of employment at which the present methods of wagesetting lead to no appreciable inflation.

This compromise may turn out tolerably well, if for example at a 95 to 96 percent level of employment the economy should be growing rather smoothly, without much change in the price level, at an average yearly rate determined by population growth plus an appreciable increase in labor productivity. But the compromise is inevitably a risky one, because the degree of employment at which inflation ceases to be a serious problem may turn out to be lower than I have assumed in my illustration, and because at a reduced degree of utilization the long run growth rate may also prove to be intolerably low. Only experience can show whether, given the present institutional arrangements in the labor market, it will be possible to get a reasonable degree of utilization and acceptable growth rates without much inflation.

If the answer to this question should come out unfavorably, and if we shall not dare to enforce more competition in the wage-setting procedure, then we shall probably be moving toward direct administrative wage and price controls. This, to me, seems the least desirable alternative, because it would render the allocation of resources thoroughly arbitrary. Furthermore, there would take place a very great concentration of power in the hands of the executive branch of the Government. I will add that I see no essential difference between direct controls and so-called friendly agreements concluded by the Government, the representatives of labor, and those of industry—with the Big Stick behind the scenes. In summary, I would like to list the remedial possibilities as I see them. We may reduce the size of the bargaining units in the labor market through what essentially is an extension of "antimonopoly action"; secondly, we may suspend collective bargaining for wages, for periods in which the overall unemployment rate is lower than a stated figure—here if I may add again a sentence to the effect, instead of expressing this in terms of the overall rate of unemployment falling below a stated figure we could express it in terms of unemployment of long duration, let us say more than 15 weeks' duration. Thirdly, we may aim for the maximum degree of employment and the maximum growth rate which are compatible with no appreciable inflation (especially with no accelerating inflation), given the present wage-setting procedures; fourthly, we may use direct administrative wage and price controls. I find the last of these alternatives exceedingly undesirable. On my interpretation, we are now engaged in an experiment moving along the lines of the third of these four alternatives. It is too early to tell whether the results will come out favorably. In the event that the results of this experiment should not prove reasonably satisfactory, I would like to urge giving the first two possibilities very serious attention.

The Need for More Competition in
Defense Procurement

JOINT ECONOMIC COMMITTEE

The following article is taken from a report issued by the Joint Economic Committee of Congress in 1969. This report was a very widely read, influential, and controversial document.

1. ECONOMIC INEFFICIENCY AND WASTE

THE EXTENSIVE and pervasive economic inefficiency and waste that occurs in the military procurement program has been well documented by the investigations of this subcommittee, by other committees of the House and Senate, and by the General Accounting Office. The absence of effective inventory controls and effective management practices over Government-owned property is well known. In the past, literally billions of dollars have been wasted on weapons systems that have had to be canceled because they did not work. Other systems have performed far below contract specifications. For example, one study referred to in the hearings shows that of a sample of 13 major Air Force and Navy aircraft and missile programs initiated since 1955 at a total cost of $40 billion, less than 40 percent produced systems with acceptable electronic performance. Two of the programs were canceled after total program costs of $2 billion were paid. Two programs costing $10 billion were phased out after 3 years for low reliability. Five programs costing $13 billion give poor performance; that is, their electronics reliability is less than 75 percent of initial specifications.

Actual costs of expensive programs frequently overrun estimated costs by several hundred percent. Assistant Secretary of the Air Force Robert H. Charles testified that "The procurement of our major weapons systems has in the past been characterized by enormous cost overruns—several hundred percent—and by technical performance that did not come up to promise." The greatest amount of cost overruns occur in negotiated, as opposed to competitive, contracts. Even where overruns do not occur, there is evidence that prices are being negotiated at too high a level from the beginning. Most procurement dollars are spent in the environment of negotiation. It is precisely in this area that the Department of Defense (DOD) has the heaviest responsibility for obtaining the best military equipment and supplies at the least possible price. In the judgment of the subcommittee, the DOD has not adequately fulfilled this responsibility.

2. A SUBSIDY TO CONTRACTORS

The major portion of procurement costs are in the costs of research and development, material, labor, and overhead for which contractors are reimbursed. In theory, competition requires contractors to be efficient in order to minimize costs and maximize profits, and inefficient contractors should not be able to underbid their more efficient competitors. Competition is a method of cost control. However, as we have said, most defense contracts are awarded through negotiation, not competition. A number of mechanisms, such as the cost and other price data submissions required by the Truth-in-Negotiations Act, and incentive contracting, have been designed to act as cost controls for negotiated contracts, in lieu of competition. In the judgment of the subcommittee, these mechanisms have not constituted an effective system of controls over the costs of procurement.

The result of the absence of effective cost controls, coupled with a number of policies and practices discussed in this report, has resulted in a vast subsidy for the defense industry, particularly the larger contractors. These practices include loose handling of Government-owned property, interest-free financing of contractors, absence of comprehensive profits reports and studies, lack of uniform accounting standards, reverse incentives, and a special patent policy lucrative to the contractor. All of these things tend to benefit the contractor at the public's expense.

3. AN INFLATED DEFENSE BUDGET

The total effect of unnecessary cost overruns, of hidden profits in "fat" contracts, of inefficiency and waste, and of the absence of cost controls is to create a bloated defense budget. Admiral Rickover testified that $2 billion of excessive costs results from the absence of uniform accounting standards alone. There is evidence that literally billions of dollars are being wasted in defense spending each year.

It is the judgment of the subcommittee that the defense budget has been bloated and inflated far beyond what an economy minded and efficient Department of Defense could and should attain.

4. LOW COMPETITION AND HIGH CONCENTRATION

Defense buying practices are reducing competition for Government contracts and increasing economic concentration within the defense industry. Formally advertised competitive military contract dollar awards dropped from 13.4 percent in fiscal year 1967 to 11.5 percent in fiscal year 1968. Single source procurement increased to 57.9 percent. These figures constitute a record low for competition and a record high for single source procurement over the past 5 years. Negotiated procurement in which more than one source was solicited comprised 30.6 percent of total contract awards, also a record low over the past 5 years.

The DOD maintains that there is a substantial degree of competition in negotiated procurement where more than one source of supply was solicited. However, too often in these cases technical performance rather than price has been the basis for contract awards. Competition must involve dollar cost as well as nonprice elements such as technical performance and date of delivery. Activity involving only one nonprice element usually cannot be considered competition, nor does it contribute beneficially to the public interest in defense procurement.

It is widely acknowledged that *true* competition significantly reduces the costs of procurement. Some experts believe that in the absence of effective competition, procurement costs are 25 percent to 50 percent higher than what they would be under competitive conditions. However, instead of competition, it is becoming increasingly clear that the "buy-in, get well later" method is commonly employed by contract rivals. Under this approach, a contractor may bid a lower price, higher performance, and earlier delivery than his rivals, knowing Pentagon officials will accept increased costs, less than promised performance, and late delivery. Inadequate management controls at the highest levels of Government have contributed to the development of these practices. The prevalence of these practices goes far in explaining why the estimated costs of individual contracts almost always increased and the performance of the weapon procured was often less than promised. Weapons procured in this manner, in the absence of true competition, have been characterized by high costs, poor performance, and late delivery of the end product.

DOD procurement is highly concentrated. A relatively small number of contractors receive most of the dollar value of defense contract awards. In fiscal year 1968, the 100 largest defense contractors were awarded 67.4 percent of total defense contracts, the highest percentage since 1965. To get on the list of the top 100 in fiscal year 1968 required $50 million in awards, up from $46 million in fiscal year 1967. These large contractors generally have assets of $250 million or more. Small firms (as defined by the Small Business Administration) received only 18.4 percent of defense prime contracts in fiscal year 1968, down from 20.3 percent in fiscal year 1967 and 21.4 percent in fiscal year 1966.

The larger, dominant defense firms tend to hold entrenched positions. Eighty-four of the top 100 firms appeared on both the fiscal year 1968 and fiscal year 1967 lists. Eighteen of the top 25 in 1967 were in the top 25 in 1968. The same five companies received prime contract awards of more than $1 billion each in fiscal 1968 as in fiscal year 1967. There is other evidence of entrenchment and concentration in the defense industry, such as the tendency of divisions of certain large contractors to obtain major contracts from one service, for example, the Air Force, while divisions of the same or other large contractors consistently obtain major awards from the other services. In some specific areas of military procurement the Government does business not only with sole-source suppliers, but with absolute monopolies. The nature of the purchases and the limited quantities may not be adequate to justify more than one producer. For this reason, the Federal Government must improve its capability to control procurement costs in the absence of competition. . . .

5. PATENT POLICY

The Government's patent policy similarly tends to reduce competition and increase the concentration of economic power. Briefly, the Government permits contractors to obtain exclusive patent rights, free of charge, on inventions produced in the performance of Government contracts. The Defense Department normally retains only a nonexclusive royalty-free license for itself. The contractor, in other words, obtains a monopoly which he can exploit for his own private gain in the commercial market for inventions paid for by public moneys. This "fringe benefit" of doing business under Government contracts does not get reported as part of the contractor's profits. In effect, the public pays twice. Once through the Government contract; again in the marketing of the private monopoly.

It should be noted that the contractor's own patent policy differs from that of the Department of Defense. When contractors award contracts to independent research institutes, the contractors, not the research institutes, retain the patent rights. Further, the employees of contractors generally must agree that the contractor gets the patent rights to any inventions developed during their employment.

Admiral Rickover and Professor Weidenbaum agreed that permitting contractors to obtain patent rights from Government contracts reduces competition in defense industries because the "ins" get a competitive advantage over the "outs." Rickover stated that one-half of the patents acquired by contractors as a result of Government-financed research and development work are owned by 20 large corporations, ". . . the very same companies that receive the lion's share of contracts."

In contrast to general Government policy, the Atomic Energy Commission and the National Aeronautics and Space Administration are required by law to take Government title to inventions developed under Government contracts, subject to waiver of rights by the Government. The Government's policy amounts to a special privilege to contractors at the expense of taxpayers.

Market Structure and Racial Discrimination

EDWIN MANSFIELD

Edwin Mansfield is Professor of Economics at the Wharton School, University of Pennsylvania. This short piece was written expressly for this volume.

ONE OF THE most important social problems plaguing the United States at the present time is racial discrimination. Is there any evidence that industries dominated by a few firms are less inclined to hire blacks than are industries composed of a large number of small firms? Certainly, it is not clear from economic theory that any such relationship should exist. Gary Becker's data for the pre-war South suggest that there may have been some tendency for discrimination to have been greater where monopoly power was great than where it was small. But his data are relatively old and pertain only to the South.[1]

This article summarizes briefly the principal conclusions of a study carried out by William G. Shepherd of the University of Michigan, the primary objective of the study being to explore the relationship between the extent to which an industry employed blacks in white-collar jobs in 1966 and the concentration ratio in the industry.[2] The data pertain to eight major metropolitan areas (Atlanta, Chicago, Cleveland, Kansas City, Los Angeles, New York, San Francisco, and Washington) and to 46 two-digit manufacturing and service industry groups.

The empirical results are as follows. First, there seems to be an inverse correlation between the *average* black share of white-collar employment in an industry and the industry's concentration ratio. In other words, industries dominated by a few large firms tend to give a smaller percentage of white-collar jobs to blacks than do less concentrated industries. More specifically,

---

1. Gary Becker, *The Economics of Discrimination*, University of Chicago, 1957.
2. William G. Shepherd, "Market Power and Racial Discrimination in White-Collar Employment," *Antitrust Bulletin*, 1969, pp. 141–159.

an increase in the concentration ratio of 20 percentage points seems to be associated with a 30 to 40 percent drop in the black share of white-collar employment.

Second, there seems to be an inverse correlation between the *highest* black share of white-collar employment by a firm in an industry and the industry's concentration ratio. In other words, in industries dominated by a few large firms, the highest black share of white-collar employment is lower than in industries that are less concentrated. Data regarding the highest black share of white-collar employment are of interest because they indicate how far at least some firms have been able to go in increasing the black share.

Third, there seems to be an inverse correlation between the average black share of employment *of officials, managers, and professionals* in an industry and the industry's concentration ratio. In other words, in industries dominated by a few large firms, the average black share of employment in these higher positions is lower than in industries that are less concentrated. Data regarding the black share of employment in these higher positions are important because the data concerning all white-collar employment tend to be dominated by the large number of clerical jobs, often occupied by black women.

The data are rough in many respects, and these correlations must be interpreted with caution. Nonetheless, the results are of interest, since they seem to bear out the hypothesis that market power is directly related to discrimination in white-collar employment. As Shepherd puts it, "Generally speaking, it is in competitive firms and non-profit agencies that employment tends to be relatively non-discriminatory, not in firms with market power."[3]

3. *Ibid.*, p. 155.

Protecting the Environment: A Case Study of Market Failure

COUNCIL OF ECONOMIC ADVISERS

The following paper is taken from the 1971 Annual Report of the Council of Economic Advisers.

As THE ECONOMY grows, more waste of various types is produced. This does not cause major problems as long as the population is widely dispersed and the environment is not overloaded. As the population is increasingly concentrated in urban areas, however, the assimilative capacity of the environment in these areas tends to be exceeded. It then becomes more and more important that these limited environmental resources be used to the best advantage.

While it might be tempting to say that no one should be allowed to do any polluting, such a ban would require the cessation of virtually all economic activity. Since society places a value both on material goods and on clean air and water, arrangements must be devised that permit the value we place on each to determine our choices. Additional industrial development, increased use of pesticides on farms, and a growing volume of municipal sewage mean dirtier water downstream and fewer opportunities for recreation. On the other hand, stricter rules for pollution control generally mean either higher taxes or higher prices for goods. What we seek, therefore, is a set of rules for use of the environment which balances the advantages of each activity against its costs in other activities forgone. We want to eliminate pollution only when the physical and aesthetic discomfort it creates and its damage to people and things are more costly than the value of the good things—the abundance of industrial or farm products and efficient transportation—whose production has caused the pollution. . . .

Problems similar to those arising from pollution have frequently been handled by granting private title to limited resources. Agricultural and forest land were once common property with poorly defined usage rights. As demands on these resources grew, their use by one party inflicted damage on others. The adjudication of conflicting claims to these resources by granting private title to them served the important social purpose of providing an incentive for these resources to be used more efficiently.

Air and water resources are harder to divide into meaningful private parcels than land. If each landowner had title to clean air around his property, a factory in New York that would emit air pollutants might have to deal with 8 million "property owners," making it difficult to operate any factories at all.

Because private property arrangements cannot be applied generally to our aid and water resources, environmental problems connected with their use have to be solved within a framework of common property. The procedures and rules that we develop for resources regarded as common property must encourage their efficient use, just as would be true if they were private property.

A set of rules for the efficient use of air and water should not only permit no more fouling of air and water than we wish to tolerate, but it should also ensure that the tolerated degree of pollution occurs for the most productive reasons. The rules should also encourage the use of resources to limit the damage done by the pollution that is allowed. Finally, the rules and procedures should not themselves entail a higher cost of administration and enforcement than the cost of having no rules.

As our society has become increasingly aware of the conflicting claims on air and water, specific rules have been developed for the use of these resources that recognize their limited nature. As early as 1899 a Federal law was passed regulating the disposal of waste in rivers and harbors. However, only with recent legal opinions and legislation has it become clear that the law could be used to reduce pollution, and the President has recently issued an Executive Order to use the law in this way.

Two problems must be faced in setting up rules for use of the environment. First, it must be decided how much pollution, if any, will be tolerated and under what circumstances changes in this amount will be permitted. Toward this end, the Federal Government has established the Environmental Protection Agency. This Agency, together with State and local authorities, develops standards for ambient air and water quality. These standards are statements of environmental quality goals considered desirable for particular areas or for the Nation as a whole. Since past arrangements, which imposed no cost on those who polluted the environment, led to excessive pollution, these air and water quality goals have uniformly sought reduction of pollution. Once such goals are developed, the next problem is to devise a system of rules for attaining them. Particular polluters must be led to change their actions so that, in fact, less pollution is produced. The Federal Government and other authorities have also been active in devising rules to implement attainment of environmental goals.

Foremost among the new rules has been the setting of Government standards applicable to particular pollution sources. Under this system, the Government requires that each source reduce its emissions of pollutants by an amount sufficient to keep the total of all emissions within the environmental quality standard. All sources are ordinarily required to reduce emissions by the same percentage. While such Government standards have been applied most extensively to automobiles, similar standards are now being developed and implemented for other pollution sources.

This system of Government standards provides one mechanism for attaining environmental goals that recognizes the increasing scarcity of environmental resources. If this system is to generate efficient results, the goal must, of course, be appropriate. That is, the control of emissions that is required at each source must produce a high enough quality of air and water so that further improvements is not worth the costs of further control. If Government standards are to achieve the best use of environmental resources, there must also be substantial uniformity of the cost of control among pollution sources. Where these costs differ, the same environmental quality could be attained more cheaply by having the source with low control costs undertake more control than the source with high costs; but this would not occur if uniform standards were applied to all sources. The standards might, of course, be made nonuniform to account for differences in control cost, but only at considerable administrative cost because the Government agency setting the standards would need detailed knowledge about many different pollution-causing activities. It is also difficult politically to set variable standards. Many, including of course the owner, would think it unfair to penalize a plant with low control costs for its efficiency in pollution control by imposing an especially tough standard on such a plant.

Differences in control cost were perhaps an unimportant problem when attention focused on automobile exhausts. While there are some differences among types of cars in the cost of controlling exhaust emissions, the common technology of the internal combustion engine limited these differences and seemed to justify the application of common standards to all cars. In other cases a pollutant may prove so damaging that a common standard, namely, an outright ban on all discharges, would also be called for even if there are differences in control costs. However, as attention focuses on industrial and agricultural pollutants that are not to be eliminated completely, differences in control costs will prove to be more of a problem. Particular pollutants are emitted from sources with diverse processes, sizes, and ages; and large differences in the cost of control can be expected. For example, sulphur oxides, which are one of the most damaging pollutants of the air, are emitted by electric powerplants, steel mills, nonferrous metal smelters, and home-heating systems. The differences in the size of these sources and the diversity of their processes make it almost certain that a given reduction of sulphur oxides cannot be accomplished at the same cost at each source. It is already known that there are economies of scale in sulphur oxide abatement, so that, for example, a given degree of control could be attained less expensively at one large powerplant than in many home-heating systems.

One way that differences in control costs could be taken into account would be to set "prices" for the use of the air and water. If each potential polluter were faced with a price for each unit of pollutant he discharged, he would have to compare this with the costs of pollution control in his particular circumstance. If control costs were relatively low, he would engage in extensive control to avoid paying the price being charged for polluting. If control costs were high, less control would be undertaken. Since sources with low control costs would carry out more than average control and those with high control costs less than average, a given level of environmental quality could be attained with expenditure of less productive resources than if all sources had to meet a common standard. At the same time, discovery of new techniques to control pollution would be encouraged, because every reduction in pollution would lower the payments for the right to emit pollutants. Of course, a price system, like a system of standards must be employed in a way that is consistent with environmental goals. The right to use air and water must be priced high enough so that the abatement encouraged improves the quality of the environment enough to justify the abatement expenses, while further improvement would not be worth additional expenditures.

There are three methods by which prices may be established for use of air and water: subsidies for control of pollution, charges for emissions of pollution (also called effluent fees), and sales of transferable environmental usage rights.

In the case of pollution abatement subsidies, the "price" paid by the polluter is the subsidy he forgoes. The more he fouls the air and water, the less he receives in subsidies. This approach can attain the efficiency inherent in a price system, but it entails substantial administrative as well as fiscal costs. In order to keep its subsidy payments down, the Government agency will have to incur the expense of ascertaining the level of pollution that would have occurred without any pollution control. As new products and processes are developed, this administrative task would grow more expensive, because in their case no record of past pollution would be available.

Alternatively charges could be levied on pollution. A charge on emissions of harmful substances would limit the amount of emissions indirectly. The higher the charge, the more a polluter would be willing to spend to avoid contaminating the environment (and thereby avoiding the charge). Another alternative would be an environmental usage certificate system. It would limit the amount of pollutants directly, but allow the price for pollution to be set indirectly. Under this system, as under a system of pollution standards, a Government agency would set a specific limit on the total amount of pollutants that could be emitted. It would then issue certificates which would each give the holder the right to emit some part of the total amount. Such certificates could be sold by the Government agency at auction and could be resold by owners. The Government auction and private resale market would thus establish a price on use of the environment. The more pollution a user engaged in, the more certificates he would have to buy. Groups especially concerned about the environment, such as conservation groups, would have a direct method of affecting the environment. They could themselves buy and hold some of the certificates, thus directly reducing the amount of emissions permitted and increasing the cost of pollution.

In general, any choice between emission charges and usage certificates should depend on which is easier to determine: the right price for pollution or the right quantity. If the amount of damage done by a pollutant can be measured easily and it appears that each unit of pollutant does roughly the same damage, an emission charge would be called for. If the damage per unit of pollutant may rise substantially with higher total emissions, a usage certificate system would be in order. Both the charge and the certificate approach would, like a system of standards, reduce the total amount of air and water pollution. However, by introducing a price mechanism, charges or certificates would allow the limited amount of tolerable pollution to be allocated efficiently when differences in the cost of control are present. Such efficiency would reduce the resource cost of pollution control and would therefore enable us to afford cleaner air and water than we could if common standards were imposed in the face of differences in control costs.

Pollution charges and certificates have not yet been widely used in this country, though some municipalities have levied charges on industrial sewage discharge. A system of water pollution charges has been used in the Ruhr basin for some time, and new proposals for pollution charges have been advanced in this country. This Administration has already proposed a tax on lead additives in gasoline which reduce the effectiveness of certain devices used to control auto exhaust emissions. This tax should encourage drivers to switch to unleaded or low-lead gasoline, refiners to produce such gasoline, and carmakers to equip their cars with the low-cost catalytic filters which work only with unleaded gasoline.

Railway Freight Transportation: A Case Study of Competition and Government Regulation

COUNCIL OF ECONOMIC ADVISERS

This paper is taken from the 1971 Annual Report of the Council of Economic Advisers.

WHEN THE Interstate Commerce Commission (ICC) was established in 1887, the railroads had a near monopoly of freight transportation. Public demand for control of this monopoly was one of the factors leading to the creation of the Commission. Another source of pressure for railroad regulation, however, may also have played a role in the development of ICC regulation. While railroads as a group had a near monopoly of freight traffic, there were often several railroads along the same traffic routes. The absence of antitrust laws made it attractive for rival railroads to collude among themselves in setting rates. As is frequently the case, such private cartels tended to break down when some members secretly reduced rates to lure business away from others. The railroads themselves supported the establishment of a Government agency that would end the instability of these private rate cartels. The powers given to the ICC in 1887 and subsequently may therefore not have been designed primarily to promote competition among railroads.

The ICC now regulates all rail traffic, 39 percent of truck traffic, and 10 percent of inland water traffic. The regulation is comprehensive, covering rates, types of service offered, and the ability of firms to enter and leave the industry or particular markets. While groups outside the transportation industry do influence the exercise of the Commission's powers, the main thrust of regulation has been to ameliorate the effects of competition among the carriers and to mediate competitive disputes among them.

Early attempts by railroads to eliminate rate competition under regulation were not completely successful. Early in the 20th century, therefore, and with the support of the railroads, the ICC was given power to approve minimum rates—rates below which a particular railroad could not go. The railroads used this power to institutionalize the value-of-service rate structure whereby goods of higher value were charged the highest freight rates even if it cost no more to carry them. Private costs to shippers were thus allowed to diverge from the social costs of transportation. This rate structure was most profitable to the railroads at the time, but its institutionalization under minimum rate regulation eventually became a source of their present problems.

The value-of-service rate structure helped expose the rails to competition from trucks. Because rates did not correspond to costs there were substantial differences in the profitability of carrying different goods. New trucking companies saw the prospect of capturing some of the profitable high-rate traffic from the railroads. With the spread of the highway network, the then unregulated truckers undercut rates on the high-rate traffic and diverted some of it from the rails.

This reduced the profitability of the railroads and they argued for suppression of the truck competition. In 1935, ICC regulation was extended to cover much of intercity trucking (and barge traffic in 1940). In order to resolve the competitive dispute between rails and trucks, the existing rate competition was suppressed. The value-of-service rate structure was carried over from rails to trucks. At the same time, minimum rate regulation was applied to all common carrier motor carriers, so that existing rate competition between trucking firms was reduced. All carriers were left to compete on nonprice grounds, such as speed and the quality and frequency of service.

As the highway network grew, however, trucks continued to attract high-valued freight from the rails. Much of this was manufactured goods, where superior service offered by trucks frequently gave them an advantage. Thus the railroads' share of the freight market continued to fall. From 1939 to 1969, their share of intercity freight traffic fell from 62 to 41 percent, while the truckers' share rose from 10 to 21 percent. At the same time, the railroads became more heavily dependent on low-valued, low-rate traffic.

INEFFICIENCIES DUE TO REGULATION

This shift of traffic from railroads to trucks did not always come about because trucking costs were below those of the rails. Part of it occurred because the value-of-service rate structure was unrelated to the costs of transportation. Even on long-haul traffic, where rail costs are much below truck costs, a shipper would frequently choose to ship by truck if trucks offered better service. By preventing carriers from fully reflecting cost advantages in their rates, regulation maintained high-cost transportation. In some rate cases where a low-cost carrier sought to exercise its advantage by offering a lower rate, the ICC prevented this so that the high-cost carrier would not be damaged financially, even though the public interest would have been better served by lower rates. More recently there has been some increase in competition between modes of transportation, but the ability of carriers to set minimum rates in concert continues to suppress competition among railroads and among motor carriers.

The application of the value-of-service rate structure to all modes also contributed to the problems of rural depopulation and metropolitan congestion which were mentioned earlier. Under the value-of-service rate structure, rates on finished goods tend to be higher than those on raw materials. These higher rates on finished goods give manufacturers an incentive to locate close to or in the metropolitan areas where their major consumer markets are found, rather than in the areas where raw materials are produced.

The preservation of value-of-service rates also induces excessive reliance on unregulated private or contract carriage. Wherever regulated rates are held above costs, some shippers have an incentive to buy or rent their own vehicles, usually trucks. This may save money for the shipper even if the cost of operating these vehicles is above the cost to the regulated carriers, as it might be because under present regulations these trucks must often return empty to the shipper's location. These added costs represent wasted economic resources.

Transport regulation extends beyond rates. Under existing legislation, a firm that seeks to enter the industry or a particular market must first obtain a certificate from the ICC. This has protected existing carriers from competition because new carriers have not been permitted to enter freely even if they could meet safety and reliability standards. This restriction of entry has inhibited the formation of new trucking firms, though trucking is the most rapidly growing form of regulated surface freight transportation. Further, a certificate to enter a market often contains numerous service restrictions designed to protect established carriers. There are, for example, restrictions on the commodities which may be carried and the number of towns between two points which may be served. In the absence of these restrictions, the same service could be performed equally well by fewer trucks.

This restriction of competition has had in the long run an increasingly adverse effect on many of the intended beneficiaries, especially the railroads. With rate competition among carriers minimized, carriers sometimes strive to gain customers by having the most equipment available and offering the most frequent service. This is one reason why the transportation industry as a whole has had more capacity than the total traffic requires; another reason is to be found in the obstacles to abandonment of unprofitable service. The costs of carrying this excess capacity have in turn tended to dissipate some of the financial gains to carriers that resulted from suppression of rate competition.

AN ALTERNATIVE TO REGULATION

The development of the transportation industry under regulation suggests that the public as well as large sections of the industry would be well served by relying more on the forces of competition. The rationale for regulation found in the railroads' monopoly position in the 19th century has become increasingly obsolete. Transportation could be a viably competitive industry today since most shippers already have a choice among modes, and with fewer entry restrictions they would have more choice among carriers. By frustrating this potential for competition, regulation appears to have promoted high freight rates and numerous inefficiencies, and in the long run to have weakened firms financially. This raises the question of whether the introduction of competition in transportation may require fundamental institutional reform. Legislative attempts to promote competition under the present regulatory system have had only limited success. This is illustrated by experience with the Transportation Act of 1958, which sought to increase competition among trucks, rails, and barges within the present regulatory framework. While such intermodal competition has increased somewhat, it has often not been permitted when the financial viability of some carrier was threatened.

If it appears that the full benefits of competition can not be attained within the framework of the existing regulatory process, substantial deregulation of surface freight transportation may have to be considered. This approach would involve the removal of regulatory obstacles to competition so that free market forces would ultimately be allowed to establish prices and allocate resources in the same way that they do in other industries. In view of the magnitude of the changes that would be brought about by such deregulation, it would probably be advisable to introduce competition gradually. Carriers, for example, might initially be given freedom to set rates within a narrow band above and below the present regulated levels, and this band could widen over time. Freedom to enter markets could be initiated by removal of the service restrictions on existing ICC truck certificates and of the restrictions on intermodal ownership by existing carriers. At some future point, restrictions on entry by new firms could be lifted. Restrictions against carriers' leaving unprofitable markets could also be lessened gradually by, for example, permitting them to abandon without ICC approval a fixed percentage of service each year for several years. As regulatory restraints on competition in transportation are removed, it would appear appropriate that transportation firms become subject to the antitrust laws, from which they are now substantially exempt. In particular, it would be necessary to guard against predatory pricing, intended to establish a monopoly, and against monopolistic pricing, of which there are instances even under present arrangements.

Deregulation would, of course, produce profound changes extending beyond the transportation industry itself. With restrictions on competition removed, transport rates would be likely to fall; and since high-cost carriers would no longer be protected from competition the rate structure would change. Rates based on the costs of efficient carriers would tend to replace the current value-of-service rate structure. Under a cost-based rate structure, commodity distinctions would tend to disappear, and rates would be based primarily on such factors as the size and weight of shipment.

Deregulation and a shift to cost-based rates would also lead to a better use of transport resources. For many long-haul shipments, rail costs are below truck costs, while the reverse is true for short-haul shipments. Once carriers are permitted to compete and take advantage of these cost differences, some long-haul shipments would shift from trucks to the rails and some short-haul shipments would shift the other way. More generally, since traffic would flow to carriers with the lowest costs, the total resource cost of transportation would be reduced.

Many shipments that now move by rail over branch lines to main lines would instead originate by truck, transferring to the rails at the main line. To reduce the costs of such transfer, many of these multimodal freight shipments would be sealed in containers which could be interchanged among modes. In this way, both those shippers located close to the main line and those farther away could take advantage of the flexibility and short-haul cost advantage of trucks as well as the long-haul cost advantage of rails. At the same time, much of the cost to the rails of maintaining excess track and underutilized equipment on these lines would be removed.

Many shippers in small towns oppose railroad abandonments of branch lines today, because they fear that under present regulation lower-cost truck service would not be substituted. However, if carriers were free to compete on rates as well as to enter and leave markets as they saw fit, the abandonment of high-cost rail branch lines would create a new market for trucks. Competition among trucks would frequently result in lower freight rates for branch-line shippers than they now face. Such shippers would also greatly benefit by the savings from the multimodal long-haul shipments that increased competition in transportation would stimulate. Regulation is sometimes justified as protecting shippers in nonmetropolitan areas from loss of service. It is argued that without the service requirements imposed by regulation not only railroads but trucks as well would abandon nonmetropolitan areas for the more populous markets. It appears, on the contrary, that regulation prevents many nonmetropolitan shippers from realizing the benefits of competition.

Suggested Further Readings

Adams, Walter, and Horace Gray, *Monopoly in America: The Government as Promoter* (Macmillan, 1955).

Adelman, Morris, "The A. and P. Case: A Study in Applied Economic Theory," *Quarterly Journal of Economics*, May 1949.

———, "The Measurement of Industrial Concentration," *Review of Economics and Statistics*, November 1951.

Alchian, A., "Uncertainty, Evolution, and Economic Theory," *Journal of Political Economy*, June 1950.

Bain, Joe, *Barriers to New Competition: Their Character and Consequences in Manufacturing Industries* (Harvard, 1956).

———, *Industrial Organization* (Wiley, 1959).

Berle, A. A., *Power without Property: A New Development in American Political Economy* (Harcourt, Brace, 1959).

——— and G. C. Means, *The Modern Corporation and Private Property* (Macmillan, 1932).

Burns, A. R., *The Decline of Competition* (McGraw-Hill, 1936).

Chamberlin, E. H., *Monopoly and Competition and their Regulation* (Macmillan, 1954).

———, *The Theory of Monopolistic Competition* (Harvard, 1933).

Clark, J. M., "Toward a Concept of Workable Competition," *American Economic Review*, June 1940.

Dewey, Donald, *Monopoly in Economics and Law* (Rand McNally, 1959).

Edwards, C. D. *Maintaining Competition: Requisites of a Governmental Policy* (McGraw-Hill, 1949).

Fellner, William, "The Influence of Market Structure on Technological Progress," *Quarterly Journal of Economics*, November 1951.

Galbraith, J. K., *American Capitalism* (Houghton Mifflin, 1952).

———, *The New Industrial State* (Houghton Mifflin, 1967).

Harberger, A. C., "Monopoly and Resource Allocation," *American Economic Review*, May 1954.

Heflebower, R. B., "Toward a Theory of Industrial Markets and Prices," *American Economic Review*, May 1954.

Jewkes, John, David Sawers, and Richard Stillerman, *The Sources of Invention* (St. Martin's Press and Macmillan, 1958).

Kaysen, Carl, "Basing Point Pricing and Public Policy," *Quarterly Journal of Economics*, August 1949.

——— and D. Turner, *Anti-Trust Policy* (Harvard, 1959).

Levi, Edward, "The Anti-Trust Laws and Monopoly," *University of Chicago Law Journal*, 1947.

———, "Economic Consequences of Some Recent Antitrust Decisions," *American Economic Review*, May 1949.

————, "The Sherman Act and the Enforcement of Competition," *American Economic Review*, May 1948.

Lewis, Ben, *Price and Production Controls in British Industry* (Chicago, 1937).

Lilienthal, David, *Big Business: A New Era* (Harper, 1953).

McGee, John, "Predatory Price Cutting: The Standard Oil (N.J.) Case," *Journal of Law and Economics*, October 1958.

Mckie, James, "The Decline of Monopoly in the Metal Container Industry," *American Economic Review*, May 1955.

Machlup, Fritz, *The Political Economy of Monopoly* (Johns Hopkins, 1952).

Mansfield, Edwin, *The Economics of Technological Change* (Norton, 1968).

————, "Size of Firm, Market Structure, and Innovation," *Journal of Political Economy*, December 1963.

Markham, J. W., "An Alternative Approach to the Concept of Workable Competition," *American Economic Review*, June 1950.

————, "The Nature and Significance of Price Leadership," *American Economic Review*, December 1951.

Mason, E. S., "The Current Status of the Monopoly Problem in the United States," *Harvard Law Review*, June 1949.

————, "Monopoly in Law and Economics," *Yale Law Journal*, November 1937.

National Bureau of Economic Research, *Business Concentration and Price Policy* (Princeton, 1955).

Nelson, Richard, Merton Peck, and Edward Kalachek, *Technology, Economic Growth and Public Policy* (Brookings Institution, 1967).

Nutter, G. W., *The Extent of Enterprise Monopoly in the United States, 1899–1939* (Chicago, 1951).

Oppenheim, S. C., "Federal Antitrust Legislation: Guideposts to a Revised National Anti-Trust Policy," *Michigan Law Review*, June 1952.

Schumpeter, Joseph, *Capitalism, Socialism, and Democracy* (Harper, 1942).

Stigler, George, "Monopoly and Oligopoly by Merger," *American Economic Review*, May 1950.

————, "The Statistics of Monopoly and Merger," *Journal of Political Economy*, February 1956.

Stocking, G. W., and W. F. Mueller, "The Cellophane Case and the New Competition," *American Economic Review*, March 1955.

———— and M. W. Watkins, *Monopoly and Free Enterprise* (Twentieth Century Fund, 1951).

Thorelli, H. B., *The Federal Antitrust Policy* (Johns Hopkins, 1955).

U.S. Attorney General's National Committee to Study the Antitrust Laws Report (U.S. Government Printing Office, 1955).

U.S. Temporary National Economic Committee, Monograph 38, *A Study of the Construction and Enforcement of the Federal Anti-Trust Laws*, by Milton Handler (U.S. Government Printing Office, 1941).

Whitney, Simon, *Antitrust Policies* (Twentieth Century Fund, 1958).

Wilcox, Clair, *Public Policies Toward Business* (Irwin, 1960).